CROWDOCRACY

"I predict Crowdocracy will come to be seen as a landmark book; not for totally getting it right, but for being the first to get enough of it right to help launch a movement for fundamental democratic renewal. Our global polls show citizen trust in established democracies at an all-time low. A tipping point is nigh and this book will help shift the balance much as a crystal lowered into a supersaturated solution transforms liquid into form."

Doug Miller, President, GlobeScan Foundation

"It is increasingly apparent that democracies struggle to cope with today's challenges. Democracy as a system asks too much of too few, and not enough of everyone else. I have no doubt we are entering a phase of exploration for what could come next. I'm excited by Crowdocracy's promise: it is conceptually solid and is based on concrete practices that have proven their worth in real life setting. Let experimentation begin!"

Frederic Laloux, author of Reinventing Organizations

CROWDOCRACY
The End of Politics

ALAN WATKINS &
IMAN STRATENUS

First published in Great Britain in 2016
by Urbane Publications Ltd
Suite 3, Brown Europe House, 33/34 Gleamingwood Drive,
Chatham, Kent ME5 8RZ

A CIP catalogue record for this book is available
from the British Library.

ISBN 978-1-910692-15-8
EPUB 978-1-910692-16-5
MOBI 978-1-910692-17-2

Design and Typeset by The Invisible Man
Cover design by Julie Martin

Printed and bound by
CPI Group (UK) Ltd, Croydon, CR0 4YY

urbanepublications.com

The publisher supports the Forest Stewardship Council® (FSC®),
the leading international forest-certification organisation. This book
is made from acid-free paper from an FSC®-certified provider. FSC
is the only forest-certification scheme supported by the leading
environmental organisations, including Greenpeace.

Contents

Contents

Crowdocracy

Acknowledgements

Alan Watkins

First and foremost I would like to acknowledge you the reader for being brave enough to pick this book up or hopefully purchase it. The power of any idea is nothing without an audience, someone to read what we have written, listen to the audiobook and talk about it with others. There are no authors without readers. As Satish Kumar has said, 'You are, therefore I am.' [1]

The idea of the *Wicked and Wise* book series began in 2014 when I was sitting watching the BBC News. As I witnessed yet another story of pain and suffering that are most news channels' stock in trade, the tide of negativity got to me. Many of the problems reported have been going on for years. I wondered if the news anchors themselves ever got bored with telling the same basic story, year in, year out. It got me thinking what can anyone do about this monotonous diet of tragedy? The awfulness is only ever interrupted by some

---

[1] Kumar, S. (2002) *You Are Therefore I Am*, Devon: Green Books.

celebrity nonsense or a story about a bizarrely skilled pet. So you may share my exasperation.

At the heart of each book in the *Wicked & Wise* series is the idea that we are stuck and we need to break through on a whole range of wicked issues, for all our sakes. The fact that this second book in the series addresses decision making and the governance of complex systems is providential. If we can change the quality of decision making in complex systems and in the political arena in particular we may just start to shift many other wicked problems in the process.

Writing this book would never have been achieved if many people had not supported the process in explicit and subtle ways. I would, of course, like to thank my co-author Iman Stratenus for showing up at just the right time to enable this second book in the series and our wonderful collaboration to start. It has been a real pleasure to work with Iman, move at such speed with so little ego impairing our debates and the process. I think we have produced a brilliant book, which may not only provoke some serious debate but also offers many thought provoking ideas even if you reject the central premise. I am deeply proud of this book and the quality standard we have set – which I have to now maintain!

I would like to acknowledge our editor Karen McCreadie. Karen has again been absolutely invaluable in marshalling all the arguments, prompting Iman and me all the way through, finding obscure references and constantly challenging us to do better. Thank you also to Matthew at Urbane Publishing. We could not continue this series without his unwavering support, commitment and enthusiasm. Without him this book would not be in your hands. I am truly excited at what we may be able to achieve with this series if we can get these books in enough of the right hands. I would also like to thank my 'brother' and mentor Ken Wilber. His ongoing support for this project sustained us, not to mention his willingness to write the foreword and support what we are trying to achieve with the series.

Carol, my co-director deserves special mention. After recovering from the shock that I wanted to write three books this year (this is the third) she stepped up to the plate and managed all the necessary details. My very dear colleagues at Complete Coherence all deserve a mention as they have all picked up things in many subtle ways that have helped Iman, me and the business to keep going. So thanks to Louise, Rebecca, Nathalie, Leanne, Maryam, Denise, Alan, Katie, Nick, Chris, Pip, Rachel, Grainne, Gestur, Russel, Peter, Zander, Orowa, Ceri, Jamie and Helen. But perhaps the person who is most responsible for enabling me to write this book is my beautiful wife Sarah. She has again taken up most of the slack while I was writing late at night, early in the morning and even during any ten minutes period of not driving our car that I can sneak in. I could not have done any of this without her loving care, hard work, relentless support and preparedness to share my vision. We genuinely live our lives in the belief that if we all lean into the wicked challenges we face and unlock our innate wisdom we can all live much happier and healthier lives.

Alan Watkins
Romsey, England, November 2015

Iman Stratenus

I had my epiphany into the wisdom of the crowd in China. I was the leader of a company with well over 3000 people spread across the vast country. We had to make a major transformation to get the company back on track. Challenged by the situation (out of my depth really), my intuition guided me to trust the people inside the company. Long story short (I have captured my version of it in a book called *In China, We Trust*), they accepted my trust and largely guided themselves out of the troubles and into a prolonged period of success and joy. This changed my view of life and the role of the leader fundamentally. One wise man I met on this journey was Alan Watkins.

When I was young, I thought I would end up in politics and – full disclosure – I tried to get in, in 2002. My party did not win that election. When I left my country (the Netherlands) soon after, the ambition waned. A few years later, I had a conversation with Israel Berman who advised me that politics was not for people who wanted to make a difference: 'In politics, people are only interested in making you fail. You won't find what you are looking for.' I am still grateful for that advice.

It took a few years before the concept of changing the entire system of democracy dawned on me. While I could see both the need for a transformation and the outline of a new system with increasing clarity, it felt in many ways too daunting and bold. When Alan was apparently thinking along the same lines, it was time to start exploring it together. On a sunny afternoon we sat overlooking the Thames and the Houses of Parliament and we mapped out what has become this book. We joked that we were redesigning the purpose of those impressive buildings into an Internet café.

We wrote this book as a mini crowd: Alan, Karen McCreadie and myself. It was without exaggeration one of the best collaborative experiences of my life. We shared, listened, challenged and moved it along, in an experience of flow for much of the time.

I owe gratitude to my teacher Julio Olalla for helping me find my voice and encouraging me in writing this book. He taught me wisdom is a love affair with questions and to embrace life always as a beginner. How liberating these lessons have been.

Thank you, Margaret Wheatley, for your continued inspiration and invitation to being a 'Warrior for the Human Spirit'. I humbly accept.

Other people who have been very helpful to us: Stephen Kull, Doug Miller, Frederic Laloux, Rohinton Medhora, Lord Stone, and of course Ken Wilber. Many, many thanks. Thank you Matthew Smith at Urbane Publications, for believing in this bold subject and for supporting us along the way.

I am blessed to be living on a hill overlooking the ocean in Portugal and having some wonderful people around me, who are always there to support me. Thank you Folef van Nispen, Henriëtte Meijers, and Patricia Trigo da Silva for being here and being who you are.

I am blessed also to live my life as a member of a small crowd, with Quirine and our children, Julie, Coco, Benine, Hugo and Sophie. All of us contribute to the love, joy and wisdom of our crowd. My children have been very interested in the process of writing this book and have supported me every step of the way, as has Quirine. You are all the brightest stars in my universe.

One of my children asked me one morning if I could dedicate this book to them. I am only happy to fulfil this request. So, here you go: I dedicate this book to you, my children and your generation, in the hope that you will find inspiration in it to let the wisdom of future crowds emerge, and follow meaningful, peaceful, fair and sustainable paths in harmony with all that is.

Iman Stratenus
Sintra, Portugal, November 2015

Foreword

For most people, the following book will be incredibly intriguing, illuminating, perplexing, puzzling, and truly informative – in short, simultaneously deeply educational and surprisingly confusing. It concerns a little-known – but quite substantially researched – fact about knowledge and its acquisition. The simplest way to put it is that credible research consistently shows that groups of smart people and not so smart people get the answers right to all sorts of problems more often than groups of just smart people alone. Put crudely, smart and run-of-the-mill is smarter than smart alone. And right there is the first truly puzzling part: by adding not-so-smart people to groups, you get better answers than groups composed solely of experts. At first glance, this doesn't make sense, does it? But in many areas (not all areas, but a huge number) there is a staggering amount of research that consistently demonstrates this. And people studying this phenomenon are quite convinced that groups of smart people and not-so-smart people are wiser than groups of smart people alone. There is some mysterious factor – we'll look into what that could be in a moment –where having a diverse group ends up giving better answers than having a narrow, even if expert, group.

And this applies to all sorts of different areas and disciplines and examples and problems. One of the earliest and most famous concerns Charles Darwin's distinguished cousin, Francis Galton. Galton attended (in 1906) the annual West of England Fat Stock and Poultry Exhibition. One of the displays involved guessing the weight of a fat ox. Eight hundred people entered the contest and gave their guess as to the ox's weight. Many of these were expert butchers and farmers – but many were average individuals who had no idea what the ox should weigh. What Galton found was that if the not-so-smart crowd was a single person, it would have guessed 1,197 pounds. The actual weight was 1,198. And not a single expert got the correct weight, nor were they even close to what the overall crowd guessed. The diverse crowd was 'smarter' than the narrow experts.

Consistently when market predictions are made, groups of normal, non-market-educated people do significantly better than professional market analysts. In business, when more of the major decisions of the company are turned over to teams of ordinary (non-management) employees, the company is almost always more profitable, with less staff turnover, fewer sick days, and higher staff happiness. It's essentially the Wikipedia phenomenon. When the creation and maintenance of a professional product is turned over to literally anybody in the entire country, expert or not, the result is better. This phenomenon actually put professional encyclopedias out of business. Iceland turned the writing of its new constitution over to every citizen in the country, and the new constitution was composed in much the same way Wikipedia is, with results that many experts acknowledged were better than what they could have come up with. There are leading-edge companies where teams of ordinary employees make all major decisions about the company, including salary, hiring and firing policies, major machinery purchases, marketing, product creation, and fundamental management in general. Such companies were highlighted in LaLoux's astonishing book, *Reinventing Organizations* (for which I was glad to write a Foreword), and they are some of the most wildly successful, highly respected, and incredibly profitable companies in the world. We are seeing similar 'smart crowd' organisations being created in education, politics, medicine, judicial systems, community governance, as well as various online digital services.

The theme of this book is simple: although democracy, as Winston Churchill put it, is 'the worst form of government except for all the others that have been tried', even this is becoming thin, and democracy is more and more frequently running up against problems that it just does not handle very well at all. In fact, in many cases it actually exacerbates the problem. Democracy is starting evolutionarily to run up against its successor, a successor that will, like all the major previous stages in evolution, 'transcend yet include' its predecessor. That is, the next form of more highly evolved governance systems will transcend and include democracy, taking its viable and true aspects (and 'including' them) and jettisoning its out-dated and less than workable components (thus 'transcending' them – hence 'transcend and include'). The authors of this book believe that the next form of evolutionarily higher governance is indeed 'crowdocracy', the application of this principle of smart collective intelligence (the 'smart crowd') to the structure of governance itself. In a sense, this is the best of democracy, because it takes democracy even more seriously and literally than its half-hearted predecessors, and actually gives to the people the full capacity to govern themselves. The entire population is given the reins of government, given complete control of the legislative branch, and through items ranging from carefully structured town meetings to sophisticated online web portals, giving every person in the country a chance to propose, craft, debate, participate in, and finally vote on every legislative product and service of the government itself – truly a government 'of the people, by the people, and for the people' – and for the first time in history. This is why crowdocracy is the best of democracy – or the next highest form of democracy, or the next evolutionary step beyond democracy, however one wishes to word it.

So crowdocracy 'includes' the best of democracy, but it also 'transcends' the weaknesses in present-day democracy. There are, of course, hundreds of books written on the deficiencies of democracy as presently practised. Many of those have merit; many don't. But I'll simply say that no variations of democracy today – including social democracy, sociocracy, and holacracy – actually and fully give the total control of the governing system to the entire population. But notice a fascinating fact: what you see in history is a slow, inexorable, undeniable growth in the number of people who are treated as real individuals and thus given a direct and actual hand in their own governance. From a tribe with only a single chief, to a monarchy with a king and queen, to an aristocracy of landed gentry and a feudal system of slowly distributed wealth, to early democracies (all built on slavery – one out of every three people in Athens were slaves), to democracies that included freed slaves, and then included women, to early attempts at sociocracy and a theoretical flattening of hierarchies to include even more individuals (but a flattening that was never fully achieved), to social democracy (still operating with representative electives or bodies that actually had most of the power). But in each and every one of those cases, we see the number of humans allowed to participate in their own governance grow and grow and grow – evolution drives toward the recognition of more and more people as true individuals with real rights and responsibilities and leadership capacities. The next step is clearly a form of governance in which every qualified citizen is genuinely given a direct voice in all aspects of the governing system – and that is crowdocracy – including and preserving the best of democracy, while transcending, negating, and going beyond its obvious weaknesses. This would be Wikipedia turned loose on government.

As for 'transcending' the weaknesses of democracy, certainly the way it is run today, we only have to look at who really holds power in the US. The authors of this book report the findings of Professors Gilens of Princeton and Page of Northwestern. For the last twenty years they have been looking at data to answer the question, 'Does the government represent the people?' What they found was that, 'The preferences of the average American appear to have only a miniscule, near-zero, statistically non-significant impact upon public policy.' The research shows that there is hardly any correlation between the opinions of the vast majority of the people – on any given subject. The authors state: 'There was about a 30 per cent chance that any proposition would become law, whether the public agreed with it or not. However, for the richest 10 per cent of Americans, the outlook was quite different. Seventy per cent of laws were passed if the wealthy were in favour of a law while zero per cent of laws were passed when the wealthy were against that law. So, the richest 10 per cent of the US can effectively veto legislation, whereas the opinion of the other 90 per cent have no influence whatsoever. Clearly what the majority want has little to do with how politicians make decisions.'

Crowdocracy would put an end to that, since the total population itself introduces, shapes and votes on legislation.

As I indicated, this is probably the first time you have heard of 'smart groups' (as counterintuitive as they are), and it's probably raising more questions than it's answering. The following book is designed to address each of these issues in a simple and introductory fashion, getting the conversation going in a wide scale manner, and, in effect, mobilising the crowd itself to decide on the issue of crowdocracy. They do a terrific, often brilliant, job of this, as I think you'll easily agree.

I'd like to spend the rest of my time addressing some of the specific issues that will come up as you read this, and that have a strong role to play in the idea itself. Because the first thing you learn about crowdocracy (or perhaps I should say the 'second thing', the first being 'smart and not-so-smart' is smarter than 'smart alone'), is that there are still several qualifications that need to be met for the smart crowd to actually kick in successfully.

Take, for example, an item that the authors themselves mention, in various ways, in numerous contexts – and that is the necessity for some component of the crowd to be able to engage in high-level integration capacities. In fact, in several places they point out that without being able integrate the various suggestions coming from all the different members of the crowd, the result can easily degenerate into 'mob rule', the 'herd mentality', and even 'lynch mobs'. The idea of the 'smart crowd' is driven, in part, by the notion that a greater degree of diversity will be smarter than a narrower degree of diversity, no matter how 'expert' the narrower degree is. The point is that having people across a larger span of development, race, education, gender, creed, cultural background, familial relations, and various contexts in general, means the larger the pool from which solutions can be chosen, and the more likely that good, accurate, and true solutions will be offered while the negative 'solutions' will cancel each other out, leaving only the better ones. But these 'better ones' can themselves span a huge range, and the point is to be able to bring them together into coherent, integrated, suggested solutions – or else you just get more fragmentation, brokenness, isolation.

Now the capacity to form high-level integrations is itself a developmental emergent – that is, it comes into being only at some of the very highest levels of growth and development. Lower levels just can't do it. And yet the developmental range of individuals that will go into making up the best 'smart crowds' is one of the questions that research so far hasn't determined – just how much of these highest levels of integrative capacity are needed to make an otherwise diverse crowd actually 'smart'? What is known is that taking everybody from just a given range is not a good idea. As an extreme case just to indicate what's involved, we wouldn't want our crowd composed of a wide range of individuals (race, sex, culture, beliefs, education) who were all under 7 years old. There's not enough development in the mix to be able to give serious and well-conceived solutions – most of the issues wouldn't even be understood. In this regard, the authors themselves say that, looking at the large scale, crowdocracy probably will not (or even could not) get started in tribal to autocratic times (which translates in individual developmental stages to archaic, magic, and early mythic stages). The whole idea about pointing to crowdocracy as an evolutionary leap forward – a truly higher evolutionary stage – is that all of the previous stages have to be in place to at least some degree – so that they can, indeed, be 'included'. (This is one of the major problems plaguing Marxism – as an allegedly higher stage of social evolution, it was supposed to occur only in societies at a late capitalistic stage, but it appeared almost entirely in societies at an agrarian, pre-capitalistic stage: something was very wrong here, as its subsequent history demonstrated.)

Similarly, do we really want open-heart surgery performed by a medically uneducated, but otherwise diverse, crowd?

So one of the questions yet to be addressed with crowdocracy is just what developmental span is necessary in order for it to really work. As noted, the authors repeatedly emphasise the necessity for high-level integrative powers – and they take one full branch of government, the judiciary, and refer to them also as 'the guardians'. This branch would be responsible for overseeing all aspects of the crowdocracy process, making sure it followed the crowd-created constitution and also providing the mandatory integrative power and help. They state that 'all guardians would need to go through training to ensure they are sufficiently developed to enable them to skillfully integrate multiple perspectives'; and that they would 'need to learn how to integrate opposing views'. The tricky point here is that developmental psychologists are rather unanimous that the highest levels of such integrative power occur only in around 5–10 per cent of the population; individuals at lower levels simply cannot integrate complex and opposing views. This in itself puts a real limit on just how much of 'the people' can fully participate in crowdocracy.

But this is simply part of the running questions that the authors themselves point out need to be studied. After all, the claim of crowdocracy is that it is the sheer diversity of the crowd that engages 'emergent intelligence' and hence the 'smart crowd'. So, they correctly ask, 'If diversity is so critical then we have to consider what sort of diversity matters. Is it age? Political orientation? Geographic diversity including city dwellers and rural communities? Does diversity of morality of ethics matter? Do we need to ensure we have a spectrum of value systems? Do we need people who operate from different levels of ego maturity? Does diversity of spiritual and religious practice matter?' Among numerous other questions. But these are indicative of just what questions we really do need to know before large-scale, serious crowdocracy can be safely put into place. As of today, we don't know the answers to those questions, and yet the future of crowdocracy crucially depends on them.

Speaking of which, the authors discuss various ways of introducing crowdocracy, from 'starting big' to 'starting small'. Perhaps from what I've said thus far, 'starting small' might seem the best and wisest choice. There are all sorts of areas – many of them discussed by the authors with wisdom and insight – where crowdocratic 'experiments' that 'start small' could be easily introduced right now. As there presumably begins to occur significant successes from these experiments, the population would become more and more accustomed to the idea itself, and more willing to try it themselves – perhaps in their local community governance, education systems, or judiciary.

But given the already-documented successes of 'smart groups', how are we to account for this seemingly counterintuitive phenomenon (at least in the areas where it has been demonstrated to work)? It's so counterintuitive, what could be supporting it?

There's a saying in Integral Theory that 'everybody's right'. This comes directly from developmental studies themselves, where the lower stages of development all insist that their truth and values are the only real truth and values that exist, and all the others are silly, goofy, or just plain wrong. But at the very higher and highest stages of development, these higher stages begin to believe that all of the earlier, lower stages actually have some degree of truth. They are all 'true but partial'. And this is exactly what crowdocracy seems to verify. If, instead of taking just experts from the highest levels, we include individuals from all levels of development, then we have access to a very large sum total of 'true but partial' truths, and that sum total is what gives rise to 'emergent intelligence' and 'smart groups', and in ways that just the higher stages themselves cannot do.

In certain narrow tasks – yes, such as heart surgery – you want a fully trained expert from the highest levels of development to be in charge. But in so many other areas – covering the broad scale of issues and concerns that face the entire spectrum of human problems and human development – you want people who remain close to those 'lower levels' who will be more in touch with their corresponding issues, contours, textures, and facts. Except for the already-acknowledged areas of real specialisation, like heart surgery or quantum mechanics, most of the problems and deep issues that face human beings stem from an incredibly wide range of developmental issues, often embracing many different levels at once – and if you consistently select only those operating from the highest level (no matter how much sense that initially seems to make), you are not going to get a really full-spectrum solution to any of those problems.

Crowdocracy is based on this fundamental Integral principle that 'everybody is right' (or 'true but partial'), and it is simply a putting into action of that principle in as many places as possible when we want truly 'full-spectrum' solutions to our problems – particularly our 'wicked problems' – where one of the reasons they are 'wicked' is that not a wide enough range of developmental and Integral diversity has been taken into account to produce real solutions.

Given the growing recognition of the remarkable nature of 'smart crowds', it appears that what we might be facing is a transition period where there is 1) more intense research into exactly the types of diversity that are required for 'smart crowds' to work with both general issues as well more specialised types for more specialised services; 2) 'starting small' with 'experiments' in crowdocracy, especially in those areas that we have answers in more detail for issue #1 (just given); and 3) a gradual expansion, across more and more disciplines, of those areas that prove amenable to crowdocracy. There's a wide range of possible outcomes, stretching across a broad spectrum from a truly widespread application of crowdocracy in virtually most of the decision-making bodies in the whole of society, to a relatively few number of smaller applications in just a few areas where it becomes simply another tool or method for gaining knowledge in specific areas. What seems apparent, from what we already know, is that the application of this smart crowd principle will increasingly be applied to more and more areas across the societal board, and will end up being a truly evolutionary advancement in culture and consciousness driven by the evolutionary imperative of more and more recognised individuals having more and more say and actual participation in their own affairs.

If you want to get really metaphysical about it, a virtually unanimous tenet of the world's great Wisdom Traditions is that every human being has, not only a relative, conventional, finite Self, but an real, true, ultimate, and infinite Self (which is universally said to be one with God or Spirit). And evolution is, in one of its deepest aspects, the unfolding of more and more individuals as God-realised, as being a genuine manifestation of Spirit here on earth. With each stage of evolution, more and more individuals are accorded the dignity and integrity of being realised as a true manifestation of God – and this is directly manifested in the numbers of individuals that, at each stage of governance, are allowed to have a hand in the actual running of that governing process. This evolutionary unfolding is accompanied by greater and greater degrees of education, of higher ethical capacities, higher capacities for love, care, and compassion; and higher and wider degrees of consciousness and awareness – as their ultimate Spiritual nature comes more to the fore via evolutionary unfolding. Every home is not only a person's castle, it is a person's temple. Again, this is exactly what we see when we look at the successively evolving forms of governance over the ages, with each one including more and more individuals in the makeup of its active structure. With crowdocracy, this spiritual dignity is finally conferred upon essentially each and every individual – on all of them, no exceptions – and the human being is allowed to express some of their highest potentials by being given the right and the responsibility to craft the very nature of society and its rules that will govern them all. If there is an Omega point – or more likely, an ever-increasing series of them – then this universal bequeathing of truly self-governing, self-organising capacities on each and every human being, bar none, certainly marks at least one Omega point in our ongoing, creative, divinising, awakening, ever-enlightening evolution.

Ken Wilber
Denver, Colorado USA, Jan 2016

Preface

This book is about the power of ideas not the idea of power.

It is the second in the *Wicked & Wise* series dedicated to looking at the world's toughest problems and how we might bring greater wisdom to bear in solving them. The first book in the series, co-authored by Alan Watkins and Ken Wilber explained what makes a problem 'wicked'. If we stand any chance of solving these complex issues we must first appreciate that a wicked problem:

1. Is multi-dimensional
2. Has multiple stakeholders
3. Has multiple causes
4. Has multiple symptoms
5. Has multiple solutions, and
6. Is constantly evolving

If you would like to understand these characteristics in more detail then feel free to read Chapter 9 first although it is not necessary. These factors go directly to the heart of wicked problems and explain why they are so intractable and the first book offered an 'integrally coherent' approach that could, if applied, help us make real progress.[1] This second book in the series looks specifically at the wicked problem of government and governance.

More than anything this book is an exploration...

We live in times of great challenge. Humanity now dominates the global ecosystems. Our doing or wrongdoing will determine the fate of our own species, and most other species on this planet. We believe that we have the moral obligation to deal wisely with this power, for the sake of all future generations. Our concern is that we may not be living up to this responsibility.

This book is not written from the belief that we 'know all the answers'. Rather, we approach life from the viewpoint of curiosity: wanting to ask the right questions and explore the possible solutions.

The question we pose is: what system *could* we create that enables us to govern our communities, organisations and nations fairly and more wisely?

In seeking to answer this question ourselves we have outlined a system of governance that we believe could work better than the model we currently use. We suggest that democracy may be past its sell-by-date and that a new model is emerging, one that represents an evolutionary step forward from democracy and taps into the collective intelligence of the crowd. This evolution is called 'crowdocracy'. Governance of a nation is both a wicked problem in itself and crucial to solving many of the other wicked problems we face. Crowdocracy may therefore, be the wise solution for national governance and

---

[1] Watkins, A. and Wilber, K. (2015) *Wicked & Wise: How to Solve the World's Toughest Problems*, London: Urbane Publications.

also the framework in which the crowd can solve many other wicked problems. As such it is perhaps doubly important and this is the reason we have chosen this topic as the focus for the second book in the series.

At the same time, we pose the same question to you. We do not claim to present the whole map, or even the only map. We are genuinely hoping to explore the variations and alternatives with you.

We do not claim we are the first people to come up with the ideas laid out in the pages ahead. We build on the great work of others before us and where possible we have tried to credit them. In the information age and given the laws of quantum physics, undoubtedly these ideas have not only sprung up in our minds, but have emerged in the minds of others too. As Aristotle so rightly pointed out, 'It is not once nor twice but times without number that the same ideas make their appearance in the world.'[2]

Our intention is to explore our collective human intelligence. We therefore invite you to join us on this exploration and build on the ideas we present in this book.

---

[2] Aristotle (350 BC) *On The Heavens*, Manual of Greek Mathematics

Crowdocracy

Chapter 1:

Introducing
Crowdocracy

When aliens first landed on earth, as depicted in Alex
Graham's *New Yorker* cartoon in 1953, they demanded,
'Take me to your leader'. But who is actually in charge?
Who governs Britain, the USA, Greece, Syria or any
nation for that matter? Who would the bug-eyed creatures
be taken to if they showed up today? The US President,
the Head of the United Nations, the G7 leaders? Are
politicians actually in charge? Are presidents? Are prime
ministers? Maybe big business actually runs the world?[1]
Or is there some secret illuminati or 'Superclass'[2] of
unelected power brokers who are calling the shots?

It matters who is in charge.

Most nations on earth believe that in order to solve the
complicated or even wicked issues they face, responsibility must
be delegated to a few democratically elected representatives in
government.

---

[1] Vitali, S., Glattfelder, J.B. and Battiston, S. (2011) *The network of global
    corporate control*, PLos One 6(10): Epub 2011 Oct 26, www.ncbi.nlm.nih.
    gov/pubmed/?term=The+network+of+global+corporate+control

[2] Rothkoft, D. (2009) *Superclass: The Global Power Elite and the World
    They Are Making*, Abacus.

But is democracy the best way to make the big calls? Has democracy, in fact, had its day? The evidence suggests that the 'high tide' mark for democracy was fifteen years ago in 2000. We are now seeing a range of new ways of making decisions starting to emerge around the world. The new models are an evolutionary step forward that transcend and include the best aspects of democracy and all the previous forms of governance. These new systems signal the beginning of a sea change, a shift in the balance of power away from the rule by the elite minority to rule by all of us. The ultimate version of this movement is called crowdocracy.

Crowdocracy is a linguistic blend of 'crowd' and 'democracy'. It builds on the philosophy of direct democracy and many recent experiments such as citizen assemblies and crowdsourcing legislation as well as many other emergent decision-making models that seek to put the power directly in the hands of the people.

We believe democracy is no longer good enough and is ready for its next major leap forward and we will explain why in more detail in Chapter 2. Many people have become disillusioned with their democratically chosen leaders. Chinese political scientist and venture capitalist, Eric Li, suggests that many of us experience the 'continuous cycle of elect and regret' that is now commonplace in the democratic process.

We agree. Democracy, in its current format, is no longer capable of dealing with the challenges of our time. It is impossible to look at the world as it currently is with all our 'wicked' or extremely complex and challenging problems and conclude that we are getting it right. We may be getting it right for some of us but certainly not for all of us. For a long time, the power has been in the hands of a small elite minority who decide our destiny. It used to be a royal elite, for some it is now more likely to be a religious elite telling us how we must interpret this or that holy book. However, for most of us it is a political elite drawn from the upper echelons of society together with a subtler financial elite pulling the strings from behind the scenes. We are rendered powerless; our voice is silenced by whatever form of elitism is working through a political system that gives us virtually no say while appearing to allow us to participate. As French philosopher Paul Valéry suggested, 'Politics is the art of preventing people from becoming involved in affairs which concern them.'[3] In Chapter 3 we will explain the evolution of decision making so we can appreciate how we got here.

We urgently need something better than democracy. So, the question is do we need to find wiser, more balanced, more experienced representatives to govern us? Or do we challenge the very notion of representation and all take charge? What if we all had a say in everything?

Until recently that option was impossible to even consider. Representation is not just a choice born out of philosophical principle; it is also a pragmatic choice. We simply could not all be involved in everything. But today we can. Technology has made it possible for very large groups of people to interact and collaborate with each other, anywhere, anytime.

But even so, is such an approach really a good idea? Would we collectively create better, wiser, fairer policy if we were all involved in the creation of that policy? Studies into the wisdom of crowds, which we will explore fully in Chapter 4, suggest that may be the case. Under the right circumstances and with the right checks and balances, 'diversity trumps ability' – all of us are much wiser than any individual or small group representing us could ever be. This may appear counterintuitive because we have been conditioned to rely on experts when we are unsure of the answer. But, the size, number and complexity of the challenges we now face mean it is simply impossible for any small group of representatives, regardless of how smart they may be, to know enough to successfully address all that we need to

---

[3] Valéry, P. (1943) Tel Quel

solve. Thankfully they don't need to: when we come together we can ignite a collective wisdom where each of us brings a slightly different perspective and each of us contributes a part of the solution. This group intelligence is an 'emergent' phenomenon – meaning that the crowd is more than the sum of its parts. It is more than simply a function of the individual citizen's intelligence in whatever form that may take but rather this collective intelligence can't actually be found in the individuals themselves – it exists only in the whole crowd.[4] This collective wisdom is already a well-known phenomenon in the natural world. Perhaps it is time that humans apply the power of this collective intelligence to the design of government and governance.

That said, it is already happening...Thousands of people around the world are already engaged in deliberative or direct democracy movements, citizen assemblies and a whole range of other inclusive participatory movements. Even governments and mainstream political systems are experimenting. For example, Iceland has sought to include its entire population in drafting a new constitution; Finland allows its citizens to propose new legislation; a political movement in Argentina only votes according to what the members of the movement want. The crowd is raising its voice online: Change.org now has more than 125 million participants drafting and signing petitions aimed at influencing those who govern. Outside the domain of politics, crowds are collaborating to create a shared knowledge base (Wikipedia), shared computer operating systems (Linux) and shared crowdfunding platforms (Kickstarter). We will explore a number of these initiatives in more detail in Chapter 5.

We believe the next evolutionary stage in national governance is one in which we all get involved in everything. This is not only preferable it is increasingly necessary. For a start it's naïve to think another group of experts or even randomly chosen individuals will govern better than we all could, if we were to govern ourselves

---

[4] Landemore, H. (2013) *Democratic Reason: Politics, collective intelligence and the rule of the many*, New Jersey: Princeton University Press.

collectively. Plus, as said, technology is already enabling people to get involved in increasingly significant numbers as evidenced by the crowd engagement on sites such as Charge.org. Whilst inspiring, these crowds are subject to direction, and possibly manipulation, by unseen forces that bring the crowd's attention to certain causes over others. Without a robust system with fail-safes and a crowd sourced constitutional ideology there is effectively nothing to stop a noisy crowd being influenced for and against decisions in much the same way as powerful vested interests exert influence right now. Whilst all of us must and should get involved in finding solutions, it has to be done within a robust framework that can withstand the manoeuvrings, manipulations and machinations of undue influence from all quarters. We believe crowdocracy could be that framework.

Our vision is that one day we can all contribute our ideas of how much tax we should pay, how the collected taxes should be spent, which roads must be built and even if we should go to war or not. The process would be much more thoughtful and structured than how we currently vote to choose our country's most talented singer. But properly structured and managed, we could all decide whether we welcome immigrants or not, and how best to support those people once they arrive. This participation would also increase the legitimacy of governance, because people tend to believe in and support what they have a hand in creating.

So how would this look and feel? Imagine the scene: one day in the not so distant future, you are asked to cast your online vote on a proposal, brought forward by your fellow citizens, to support the new Energy Act, which has the ambitious goal of fully transitioning out of fossil fuels. The proposal contains an integrated approach meaning opinion and ideas came from a wide range of people and those often disparate views were integrated and consolidated into a genuinely shared outcome that would probably never have been possible before the introduction of crowdocracy. The Energy Act – which was created with the involvement of a few thousand people – contains a massive investment in clean fuels, requirements for producers to create energy efficient products, a huge bail out for fossil fuel companies (mostly because of the implications on the collective pension funds that are still very dependent on oil and gas investments) and a host of other elements that, taken collectively, will finally get our society on course to being zero-carbon.

It amazes you that this entire proposal, presented in a detailed 200 page text document, a 25-minute summary video and a one page infographic has been endorsed by the media, NGOs and even businesses, many of which used to hold strongly opposing views. For example, environmentalists and capitalists worked together to co-create a series of solutions that now has a massive chance of being passed into law. Of course, there are dissenters, who also present their case on 'The Crowd' – the online platform built to orchestrate crowdocracy – but it seems they have a hard time making a case against the integrated proposal that has been put forward.

While you are fascinated and inspired by this potentially historic event of a crowdocratically endorsed and legislated Energy Act, your next-door neighbour is even more active than you on The Crowd. He is not so much involved in the public governance domains, but in the domain of football. Since the corruption scandals nearly brought down the governing body of global football, FIFA has now become crowdocratic as well. It is now no longer run by bureaucrats who make all the decisions. The world's largest crowd – all members of football clubs globally – collectively decide on the rules of the game, the rules of how the game is organised and – to the delight of millions – where the next World Cup is hosted. Every four years there is an eruption of creativity, when thousands of proposals are put forward based on the love of the beautiful game and the spectacle rather than which potential host nation has the deepest pockets. After a few rounds of initial voting, ten proposals make it to the final round. Contrary to what most people predicted when crowdocracy was launched, it is not the major populations that get their way;

Brazilians and Chinese have shown to be just as likely to endorse a creative version of a World Cup – such as the one that was held on 10 different islands in the Caribbean – as the populations of these tiny nations themselves. Football players across the world have also shown what they care about most: having fun playing and watching their sport.

This might seem like the pie-in-the-sky ramblings of a couple of dreamers but versions of this vision have already happened and *are* happening in different parts of the world – right now.

We are not radicals; we believe in evolution not revolution. We believe in the democratic principle that the power to decide should rest with the people – all the people. A society can, in our view, only be fairly and wisely governed if all the people have a say. Democracy has brought freedom and prosperity to millions of people. The fact that we can publish a book challenging the status quo is a testament to democracy's ability to accept dissent but it is time for change.

We have a historic opportunity to transform ourselves from cynical and suspicious spectators of our current political system to engaged participants and actors in the governance of our communities and society at large. It will require lots of people to engage in the process to collectively create a mechanism whereby we can all participate and then have the maturity to let go of what has been created for the benefit of all.

In this book, we suggest what a first draft of crowdocracy could look like, to inspire our collective thinking. We outline how the legislative arm of government, where policy is proposed and passed by politicians, would be handed over to the crowd, collaborating in an online platform. The executive arm of government would focus on exactly what its name suggests: executing that policy. The judiciary arm of government would expand its current scope of judging what is enacted to also become the guardians of the crowdocratic process. In Chapters 6, 7, and 8 we outline how this could work, the various transition models that could move us closer to that vision, the challenges we will face and the possible implications of crowdocracy for the future across all areas of society.

Essentially, crowdocracy describes a vision where the problems (local, national and international) are placed fully in the hands of the people. We are in charge, we decide what happens, it is our choice that matters. Giving the power to the people, enabling us all to decide on everything is a revolutionary step. But it can start small and grow as we learn how to get it right.

Finally, crowdocracy may also offer us a viable methodology for tackling the many other wicked problems we face. Chapter 9 will illustrate how crowdocracy could successfully accommodate the six characteristics of wicked problems to facilitate equally wicked, wise solutions.

It really matters who is in charge.

Not only could crowdocracy change the way we are governed, it may also change the way we relate to each other by bringing all of us together again, helping us to fully express our social nature and reinforce our interdependence.

Chapter 2:

Is Democracy Still Fit for Purpose?

'Democracy is the worst form of government except for all the others that have been tried from time to time.'[1]

– Sir Winston Churchill

There is little doubt that when Churchill made his comment about democracy he was right. The world had recently emerged from WWII and was acutely aware of the destruction that could be wrought by a determined dictator. The communism he witnessed when looking out into the world was not the pragmatic, progressive one-party system that is the Chinese experience today. While democracy was clearly flawed it was still considered preferable to 'all the others'. Even today, democracy is frequently held up as the best form of governance that we can hope for. In every non-democratic country there are activists aspiring to bring democracy to their region.

The appeal is obvious – democracy is rule by the people and it has given a voice to the voiceless over several centuries. As political scientist Hélène Landemore reminds us in her brilliant book *Democratic Reason*, the history of democracy is one of

---

[1] Churchill, W. (1947) House of Commons speech, 11 November.

increasing enfranchisement.[2] Initially only property-owning white men like Winston Churchill could vote. Over time that expanded to include men without property, non-whites and women, who were finally considered fit to cast votes on important issues.

But even with this positive evolution in the democratic process it is still necessary to choose our leaders. Of course, if a government, business, international body or any organisation is poorly led then the problems we face are compounded. In a rapidly evolving world we need leaders capable of understanding the complexity of the challenges they have to deal with. This means they must be almost superhuman in their ability to understand multiple disciplines, multiple dimensions and how to work with multiple stakeholders who often hold radically different views.[3] They also need to be able to broker agreements and rapidly reach a decision despite this level of change and complexity. But that is not all. We also need men and women who are sufficiently mature and sophisticated to see beyond their own personal interests. Our leaders need to be able to rise above their parochial concerns and chart a way forward that serves all of us not just some of us.

Even if we could find such superhuman leaders how do we ensure they work effectively together? How can we encourage them to identify answers that work for all of us rather than advocate a partisan or incomplete answer that only addresses a piece of the problem or keeps a minority happy?

These are the challenges of national governance – how to find the balance between the drive for control and power by individuals and groups and the greater good of the system including the individuals, communities and ecosystems within that system? While democracy may seek to strike some balance, we will argue

---

[2] Landemore, H. (2013) *Democratic Reason: Politics, collective intelligence and the rule of the many*, New Jersey: Princeton University Press.

[3] Wilber, K. *Superhuman OS*, accessed 18 December 2015, https://superhumanos.net

in this chapter that democracy is past its sell-by-date and we are in urgent need of more evolved governance. And we are not alone in our opinion.

On 28 July 2015, the thirty-ninth President of the United States, Jimmy Carter suggested, 'the USA is no longer a functioning democracy'.[4] Considering that the USA is 'the poster child' for democracy – that's a pretty damning statement.

In 2008 WorldPublicOpinion.org polled 17,525 people across 19 countries (China, India, the United States, Indonesia, Nigeria and Russia – as well as Argentina, Azerbaijan, Britain, Egypt, France, Iran, Jordan, Mexico, Poland, South Korea, Turkey, Ukraine, and the Palestinian Territories). While approximately 85 per cent of the populations in all 19 nations agreed with the democratic principle that 'the will of the people should be the basis for the authority of government', 74 per cent did not believe it did or at least thought that the 'will of the people' should have more influence than it currently does.[5]

Democracy Exposed

Clearly, both the system of governance whereby we elect representatives to make decisions on our behalf and the way those representatives behave and interact is in need of an overhaul. We suggest that overhaul is required for the following reasons:

---

[4] Zuesse, E. (2015) 'Jimmy Carter Is Correct That the U.S. Is No Longer a Democracy', *The Huffington Post*, accessed 18 December 2015, www. huffingtonpost.com/eric-zuesse/jimmy-carter-is-correct-t_b_7922788. html

[5] WorldPublicOpinion.org website (2008) 'World Publics Say Governments Should Be More Responsive to the Will of the People' , accessed 18 December 2015, http://worldpublicopinion.org/pipa/articles/governance_bt/482.php?lb=btgov&pnt=482&nid=&id=

1. Democracy is not majority rule.
2. Supreme power is held by the lobby and vested interests.
3. Democracy fosters superficial and inadequate focus on the issues.
4. Democracy fosters division.
5. Politicians are struggling under the weight of escalating complexity.
6. Democracy is not a meritocracy.
7. Politicians don't have a voice either – their vote is 'whipped'.
8. The system facilitates self-interest and scandal.

1. Democracy Is Not Majority Rule

In a democracy, the people rule – and most democracies opt for the principle of the rule of the majority. Of course, we can't all pitch up at parliament and shout our opinion so instead we have elected representatives to become our voice in the corridors of power. Those representatives are then meant to put forward the views and opinions of 'the people' they represent in deciding how the country is governed and what policies and laws are enacted. But do they really represent the views of the majority in practice? Professors Martin Gilens of Princeton University and Benjamin Page of Northwestern University decided to find out. They looked at more than 20 years' worth of data to answer the question, 'Does the government represent the people?' What they found was that, 'the preferences of the average American appear to have only a minuscule, near-zero, statistically non-significant impact upon public policy'.[6] The research shows that there is hardly any correlation between the opinions of the vast

---

[6] Gilens, M. and Page. B.I. (2014) 'Testing Theories of American Politics: Elites, Interest Groups, and Average Citizens ', *Perspective on Politics*, accessed 18 December 2015, http://scholar.princeton.edu/sites/default/files/mgilens/files/gilens_and_page_2014_-testing_theories_of_american_politics.doc.pdf

majority of the people – on any given subject. There was about a 30 per cent chance that any proposition would become law, whether the public agreed with this proposition or not. However, for the richest 10 per cent of Americans the outlook was quite different. Seventy per cent of laws were passed if the wealthy were in favour of a law while zero per cent of laws were passed when the wealthy were against that law. So, the richest 10 per cent of the US can effectively veto legislation, whereas the opinions of the other 90 per cent have no influence whatsoever. Clearly what the majority want has little to do with how politicians make decisions.

Organising a democracy so that the 'will of the people' can emerge has always been a challenge and in many countries a constant source of antagonistic debate. In multiparty systems with proportional representation (so no districts or political constituencies), such as Denmark, Sweden and the Netherlands, elections lead to the formation of coalitions – often leaving the voters disillusioned with the outcomes. While during election periods the differences between parties are accentuated and positions harden, politicians are often capable of making surprising U-turns when the coalition is formed and they have a chance to be part of the ruling government.

In systems with two main parties and voting by districts or constituencies, many citizens feel disenfranchised. As a result, in some of these countries, new parties have appeared on the scene, but the district, constituency voting system has not been adjusted, leading to very undesirable outcomes.

The 2015 UK general election is a case in point. For weeks prior to the election the media was rife with speculation over a hung parliament. This could have resulted in some sort of unholy alliance between any numbers of political party combinations. The UK electorate were staring down the barrel of endless post-election horse trading, secret deal making and behind closed-door concessions exchanged for political influence or a seat at the table. But the collective anxiety about what a patchwork alliance would do to the country was ultimately unnecessary because the pollsters got it wrong – very wrong. Of the 92 pre-election polls conducted in the six weeks before the election only three predicted a win by the Conservatives (or 'Tories') – although none got the margin correct. With less than 37 per cent of the popular vote, the Conservative Party won more than 50 per cent of the seats in Parliament. The UK Independence Party (UKIP) won 12.6 per cent of the popular vote, but got only one seat in Parliament. As the result was dissected the evidence suggested that the result was not down to a 'late swing' or 'shy Tories' not participating in the polls but rather masked a deeper, more problematic trend. This trend revealed that 25 per cent of the electorate did not vote for any of the main three parties (Tories, Labour or Liberal Democrat). In fact, this lack of support for the three main parties has doubled since 2010 when only 12 per cent voted for a party other than the big three.[7]

This significant surge away from the mainstream suggests that there may be a serious problem with the very idea of 'majority rule' inside a democratic system and therefore the legitimacy of any resulting government. This lack of legitimacy is much more profound than any of the main parties are prepared to admit. In their euphoria at the unexpected 'outright win' many Tories have, since the election, taken it as read that they have a significant mandate and a clear signal from the electorate. But is that really the case?

Let's apply the Tories' own logic to determine the degree of their legitimacy. Since the election one Conservative MP suggested plans to tighten up the law surrounding union activity. They have sought to criminalise picketing and make it illegal for workers to strike if the union does not have a 40 per cent mandate in favour of a strike. But by that exact logic the 2015 Tory government would be illegal as they only won 37 per cent of the vote. Nearly

[7] Cowling, D. (2015) 'Election 2015: How the opinion polls got it wrong', *BBC News*, accessed 18 December 2015, www.bbc.co.uk/news/uk-politics-32751993

two-thirds of the electorate either didn't vote at all or they voted for a different party – that is not majority rule! At an individual level only three MPs received more than half the vote in their own constituency and could legitimately state they were elected by the majority. The remaining 647 MPs were therefore elected because they won the largest share of the minority vote. 191 MPs were elected with less than 30 per cent support. One MP even broke the record for being elected on the lowest winning share of the vote in UK electoral history with just 24.5 per cent.[8]

All the other UK parties, except perhaps the Scottish National Party (SNP), have even more reason to be unhappy with the 'democratic electoral process'. The Greens and UKIP received more than 5 million votes but won only two seats between them. Labour's share of the vote increased but their number of seats collapsed. The Liberal Democrats won nearly 8 per cent of the popular vote but lost nearly all their seats (largely due to the policy U-turns of coalition governments we mentioned earlier). Even the Scottish National Party would have to admit there is something wrong when they received 50 per cent of the votes in Scotland but still won 95 per cent of the seats. The SNP won 56 seats with just 1.5 million votes and yet UKIP received 3.9 million votes and won only one seat! Millions of people in the UK feel that their views are marginalised or irrelevant. In fact it is estimated that 25.7 million people currently live in constituencies where voting doesn't even matter because these seats are very unlikely to change allegiance in an election. It is hardly surprising that just two weeks after the 2015 UK general election nearly half a million people signed a petition calling for electoral reform.[9]

---

[8] Garland. J. and Terry, C. (2015) *The 2015 General Election: A voting system in crisis*, accessed 18 December 2015, www.electoral-reform.org.uk/sites/default/files/files/publication/2015%20General%20Election%20Report%20web.pdf

[9] Garland, J. and Terry, C. (2015) *The 2015 General Election: A voting system in crisis*, accessed 18 December 2015, www.electoral-reform.org.uk/sites/default/files/files/publication/2015%20General%20Election%20Report%20web.pdf

This approach also bakes in dissent by encouraging divisiveness and polarisation rather than wisdom and maturity. Just think about it: anywhere between two-thirds to just under half the population are always unhappy with the result and permanently 'offside'. Or as Thomas Jefferson said, 'A democracy is nothing more than mob rule, where 51 per cent of the people may take away the rights of the other 49.'

Only now, 34 per cent of the population can take away the rights of the other 66 per cent.

There is little doubt that the current 'democratic system' in many places around the world is no longer an example of 'majority rule'. Rather it is a system where there is rule by the largest minority or swing voters. This is starkly apparent in the US Presidential election. There is evidence to suggest that the number of states that could actually vote for either party has been declining over the last 20 years. In 1992 there were 32 states that could realistically vote in either direction whereas in 2012 this number was down to just 14.[10]

In fact most commentators believe that just seven of the fifty-two states are now genuinely 'swing states'. In the 2000 Presidential election the outcome was determined by just five states and by a margin of about 1 per cent of the popular vote.[11] In Florida the vote was won by just 537 people or less than 0.01 per cent of the population. It is clearly not a majority rule system when less than 1 per cent of the population determine the destiny of the 'leader of the free world'. That means tens of millions of votes simply don't matter anymore.

It is therefore little wonder that in most democracies millions of

---

[10] Olson, R. (2015) 'The Shrinking Battleground: Every 4 years, fewer states determine the outcome of the Presidential election', accessed 18 December 2015, www.randalolson.com/2015/01/12/the-shrinking-battleground-presidential-elections/

[11] Swing States, accessed 18 December 2015, https://en.wikipedia.org/wiki/Swing_state

people don't bother to vote at all because they don't believe it makes any difference and they don't believe their government is listening to them. Certainly results in the UK 2015 election, US elections and the Princeton study would indicate they are right. The government doesn't listen to them, and political parties can come to power despite not being voted for by the majority of the population. Majority rule is a myth.

2. Supreme Power Is Held by the Lobby and Vested Interests

Money talks in politics. In the Princeton study the researchers showed that the 'economic elites, business interests, and people who can afford lobbyists carry major influence'. Different industries spend varying amounts to influence the US government. Over a ten-year period the top five spenders were:

- Financial sector: spending $4.3 billion
- Communications sector (including the media): spending $3.5 billion
- Energy sector (including big oil companies): spending $2.9 billion
- Pharmaceutical sector: spending $2.2 billion
- Defence sector: spending $1.3 billion[12]

To win a Senate seat in 2014, it was calculated that each candidate had to raise $14,351 every single day. Money wins elections as evidenced by the fact that 91 per cent of the candidates who

---

[12] Allison, B. and Harkins, S. (2014) *Fixed Fortunes: Biggest corporate political interests spend billions, get trillions*, Sunlight Foundation, accessed 18 December 2015, http://sunlightfoundation.com/blog/2014/11/17/fixed-fortunes-biggest-corporate-political-interests-spend-billions-get-trillions/
Data Set from OpenSecrets.org, accessed 18 December 2015, http://influenceexplorer.com/fixed-fortunes/

spent the most money were elected. Once elected those in Congress spend 30–70 per cent of their time fundraising for the next election. Where does all this money come from? It comes from 0.2 per cent of the population or those rich enough to donate to the campaign coffers. In fact the 'bigger donors' – those who donate more than $10,000 come from an even smaller percentage of the electorate – namely 0.05 per cent of Americans. The mega-donors are an even smaller elite still. The Koch brothers, two industrialists who would certainly fall into the category of mega-donors, have said they will spend $889 million on the 2016 Presidential election, in support of a Republican candidate.[13] Logic alone tells us that when individuals donate large sums of money to an individual politician then that politician is indebted to that donor because they helped to put them in the job. In the USA, there is even a tradition that the most loyal fundraisers go on to get a job as an overseas ambassador.[14]

It is not difficult to see why, in return for campaign donations, elected 'representatives' in the US tend to pass laws that are good for their mega-donors, regardless of the impact of those laws on the rest of the American population. As a result when US 'representatives' are not fundraising, they have 'no choice but to make sure the laws they pass keep their major donors happy — or they won't be able to run in the next election'.[15]

Whether due to outdated electoral systems or the concerted effort of lobbyists working on behalf of special interests, it would certainly appear that a small wealthy elite minority rules. This is

---

[13] Reston, M. (2015) 'Could Koch brothers take out Donald Trump?' *CNN Politics*, accessed 18 December 2015, http://edition.cnn.com/2015/08/03/politics/2016-election-koch-brothers-donor-retreat/

[14] McKelvey, T. (2013) 'Should political fundraisers become ambassadors?' *BBC News*, accessed 18 December 2015, www.bbc.co.uk/news/world-us-canada-22894459

[15] Represent.us website, 'Study: Congress literally doesn't care what you think', accessed 18 December 2015, https://represent.us/action/theproblem-4/

made possible by the fact that in a democracy it is perfectly legal to purchase political support through lobbying.

The lobby industry in the USA has been estimated to be worth $9 billion and involves approximately 100,000 lobbyists, although there are only 12,281 officially registered lobbyists. This is partly because lobbying activity is thought to be an increasingly 'underground' activity with those involved using 'increasingly sophisticated strategies' to obscure their activity.[16] In the last five years alone the 200 most politically active companies in the USA spent $5.8 billion influencing the US government. Those same companies got $4.4 trillion in taxpayer support – and that's just the top 200 companies![17] That's a pretty phenomenal rate of return.

After the US, Europe is the next largest users of lobbyists with an estimated 15,000 – 30,000 operating in Brussels. The UK is third in the lobbying league table with an industry estimated to be worth £2 billion. Lobbying is big business and takes many forms including the creation of briefs for politicians to help influence the narrative, conversation and vote through to the facilitation of a quiet word in an influential politician's ear and even helping to write the language of new laws, all of which is facilitated and smoothed through by what the late Nye Bevan MP referred to as 'gastronomic pimping'.[18] Dave Hartnett, the civil servant formerly in charge of the UK's tax system was famously known as Whitehall's most wined and dined civil servant – accepting the

---

[16] Fang, L. (2014) 'Where Have All the Lobbyists Gone?' *The Nation*, accessed 18 December 2015, http://www.thenation.com/article/shadow-lobbying-complex/

[17] Allison, B. and Harkins, S. (2014) Fixed Fortunes: Biggest corporate political interests spend billions, get trillions, Sunlight Foundation, accessed 18 December 2015, http://sunlightfoundation.com/blog/2014/11/17/fixed-fortunes-biggest-corporate-political-interests-spend-billions-get-trillions/

[18] Cave, T. and Rowell, A. (2015) *A Quiet Word: Lobbying, Crony Capitalism and Broken Politics in Britain*, London: The Bodley Head.

hospitality of the UK's biggest banks, law firms and accountancy firms 107 times. Hartnett was a pivotal figure in agreeing the 'sweetheart' tax deals with large corporations.[19]

Lobbying is, of course, more than just free meals at private clubs – it is access and the ability to present a case and influence the discussion. When Gordon Brown proposed a tax on the pensions of the country's top earners, The Multinational Chairman's Group swung into action. Following a meeting in Downing Street to discuss how government policy, specifically taxes, were affecting international corporations, this tiny privileged lobby group made up of CEOs of major multinational businesses were instrumental in persuading the Blair government to drop the proposal.[20]

Lobbying was even able to halt much of the proposed banking reform put forward in the wake of the global financial crisis (GFC). Have you ever wondered why the universal outrage never really translated into action and change? The reason is because the banking sector is a fearsome and influential player in politics. In the UK the close ties between senior politicians and senior bankers are too numerous to mention. In his first week as London Mayor, Boris Johnson, a vocal advocate of 'The City', and long -time friend of many senior bankers, received an invitation by financial lobbyist Roland Rudd to attend a dinner party at his home along with 19 chairman and CEOs who were keen to hear Johnson's plans for London. In fact, Boris Johnson pledged to do his 'utmost' to ward off banking regulation and was instrumental in shifting the narrative and therefore preventing tighter regulation.[21] That is the art of the lobbyist – they are adept at reframing a narrow, commercial interest as synonymous with the national interest. Boris Johnson for example frequently implied

[19] Cave, T. and Rowell, A. (2015) *A Quiet Word: Lobbying, Crony Capitalism and Broken Politics in Britain*, London: The Bodley Head.

[20] Cave, T. and Rowell, A. (2015) *A Quiet Word: Lobbying, Crony Capitalism and Broken Politics in Britain*, London: The Bodley Head.

[21] Cave, T. and Rowell, A. (2015) *A Quiet Word: Lobbying, Crony Capitalism and Broken Politics in Britain*, London: The Bodley Head.

that an unregulated 'City' was the engine of prosperity in the UK and hampering that engine was against the national interest![22]

These are not isolated incidents – they are 'business as usual' in our current democracies. UK Prime Minister David Cameron promised to 'sort it out'...

> 'We all know how it works. The lunches, the hospitality, the quiet word in the ear, the ex-ministers and ex-advisers for hire, helping big business find the right way to get its way. We don't know who is meeting whom. We don't know whether any favours are being exchanged. We don't know which outside interests are wielding unhealthy influence. This isn't a minor issue with minor consequences. Commercial interests – not to mention government contracts – worth hundreds of billions of pounds are potentially at stake.
>
> I believe that secret corporate lobbying... goes to the heart of why people are so fed up with politics. It arouses people's worst fears and suspicions about how our political system works, with money buying power, power fishing for money and a cosy club at the top making decisions in their own interest. It is increasingly clear that lobbying in this country is getting out of control. We can't go on like this.' [23]

But nothing changes and all democracies are 'going on like this'. Remember Jimmy Carter's quote from earlier in this chapter? During an interview on the Tom Hartmann show he was asked what he thought of the Supreme Court's 2010 *Citizens United* and the 2014 *McCutcheon* decision to allow 'secret funding' (including overseas money) to pour into political and judicial campaign funds. He suggested, 'The USA is no longer a

---

[22] Fison, M. (2009) 'Boris Johnson calls for "light regulation" of City', Citywire, accessed 27 December 2015, http://citywire.co.uk/money/boris-johnson-calls-for-light-regulation-of-city/a360248

[23] Cameron, D. (2010) 'Rebuilding trust in politics', speech, 8 February.

functioning democracy'.[24] Here is exactly what he said about the decision to allow this secret funding:

'It violates the essence of what made America a great country in its political system. Now it's just an oligarchy with unlimited political bribery being the essence of getting the nominations for president or being elected president. And the same thing applies to governors, and US Senators and congress members. So now we've just seen a subversion of our political system as a payoff to major contributors, who want and expect, and sometimes get, favours for themselves after the election is over… At the present time the incumbents, Democrats and Republicans, look upon this unlimited money as a great benefit to themselves. Somebody that is already in Congress has a great deal more to sell.'

A key problem with lobbying is that it happens behind closed doors, out of sight and is not subject to public scrutiny. It may not be corrupt but it is undoubtedly corrupting. It is in effect legalised bribery. Politicians and civil servants can be swayed away from what is truly in the public interests and influenced by well-funded special interest groups. This increases the risk of political corruption and also decreases the trust in the political process. Transparency International UK's report on corruption revealed that the public consider political parties to be the most corrupt sector in the UK and Parliament itself is seen as the third most corrupt – hardly a glowing testimonial for democracy.[25]

---

[24] Zuesse, E. (2015) 'Jimmy Carter Is Correct That the U.S. Is No Longer a Democracy', *The Huffington Post*, accessed 27 December 2015, www.huffingtonpost.com/eric-zuesse/jimmy-carter-is-correct-t_b_7922788.html

[25] Transparency International UK website, accessed 27 December 2015, www.transparency.org.uk/our-work/uk-corruption/lobbying

Lobbying Undermines Our Social Contract

Fundamentally, power in the hands of a few undermines our Social Contract, a concept that lies at the heart of our democracies.

Jean-Jacques Rousseau wrote about the philosophical principles of political rights and how best to establish a legitimate political community in his 1762 book which built on his *Discourse on Inequality* essay.[26] This book inspired political reform across Europe and shifted the power base from the monarchy to the people. Rousseau argued against the idea that monarchs were divinely empowered to legislate and that only the people, who are sovereign, have that all-powerful right and it helped form the basis for most modern democracies. The people therefore had a Social Contract with each other and they would delegate authority to their chosen leaders.

It is quite clear that the Social Contract that Rousseau advocated has run its course. We didn't contract with each other to hand power to a few entertainers, to the media or to the lobby and yet that is exactly what we have done. The new 'ruling class' – usually those with the most money or the most influence have created their power base in such a way that the next government is virtually always a variation on the previous one and the people's interests are not well served.

Not only has our relationship with our elected representatives turned sour as a result but perhaps more importantly the relationship among us, between our fellow citizens, has also been adversely affected. With the disappearance of the trust in our elected leaders, we are losing the trust in each other. At the same time, we know we trust each other more than we do our politicians. In the US, a Gallup poll showed that 61 per cent

---

[26] 'The Social Contract', Wikipedia, accessed 27 December 2015, https://en.wikipedia.org/wiki/The_Social_Contract

of the American people trusted 'the American people' to make judgements about political issues compared to just 46 per cent who trusted the 'men and women who either hold or are running for public office'.[27]

Our Social Contract is in urgent need of an upgrade so we can all become actors in the proposal and shaping of our legislation and decision-making. In doing so we re-energise the Social Contract that Rousseau envisaged where we all take individual and collective responsibility and accountability for each other and ourselves. Human beings are social creatures. We need each other; we thrive in groups and in communities. As we grow up we move from dependence to independence to interdependence. In the West especially we have often become stuck at independence and assumed that's the best we can achieve – that we each stand on our own two feet and contribute to the world. But our nature is social; we live and work in interdependent groups, communities, societies and cultures. We need to get back to that – working for the good of all of us, not the elite minority.

3. Democracy Fosters Superficial and Inadequate Focus on the Issues

Not only has democracy become the rule by the elite minority, the vested interest or the lobby, but also the democratic system fosters a superficial and inadequate focus on the real issues we need to address.

For a start the issues that politicians have to address are now significantly more complex than they were a generation ago. It is simply not possible for a few hundred individual politicians to find smart answers to an escalating number of highly complex

---

[27] Jones, J.M. (2013) 'In U.S., Political Trust in "American People" at New Low: Remains higher than trust in politicians', Gallup website, accessed 27 December 2015, www.gallup.com/poll/164678/political-trust-american-people-new-low.aspx

interdependent issues that they may know nothing or very little about (more on that in a moment).

But also the system itself is obviously built on regular free elections – otherwise it wouldn't be a democracy. Therefore, the goal for those in power understandably becomes staying in power while also keeping the donors and lobby happy (no easy task). For those in opposition the goal is to get into power so the ruling party and all the opposition parties frequently engage in adversarial politics. Or as the 'American Nietzsche' H.L. Mencken said, 'Under democracy, one party always devotes its chief energies to trying to prove that the other party is unfit to rule – and both commonly succeed, and are right.'[28]

No one is really interested in coming together for the greater good of the nation to solve the big issues. Instead the party in power simply naysays what the opposition are suggesting whether it has any merit at all and vice versa. At times such behaviour is akin to Monty Python's 'argument sketch'. [29] It would be funny if the issues in question were not so incredibly important.

On the night of Barrack Obama's inauguration in 2009, a group of prominent Republicans met in a hotel and agreed a plan to stop him.[30] That plan was to, 'show a united and unyielding opposition to the president's economic policies', 'Begin attacking vulnerable Democrats on the airway' and 'win the spear point of the house in 2010, jab Obama relentlessly in 2011, win the White House and the Senate in 2012.' It was not about the greater good and what was best for the American people even though a sweeping majority did elect Obama – it was a full-on assault against *anything*

---

[28] Mencken, H.L. (1956) *Minority Report: H.L. Mencken's Notebooks*, New York: Knopf.

[29] 'Argument Clinic', Monty Python's Flying Circus, accessed 27 December 2015, www.youtube.com/watch?v=kQFKtl6gn9Y

[30] Draper, R. (2012) *Do Not Ask What Good We Do: Inside the U.S. House of Representatives*, New York: Free Press.

that Obama proposed. Such was their desire to get Obama out that they took America to the edge of the 'fiscal cliff' in 2013. Politics stopped being about what was right for the country but how best to thwart any plans for recovery so the Republicans could blame Obama and wrestle back power.

In the US fundraising is such a major issue that it also prevents the politicians from really addressing the issues. Remember the statistics from earlier – once elected those in the US Congress spend 30 to 70 per cent of their time fundraising for the next election. Considering the escalating complexity of the challenges politicians face it is simply not possible to solve them when they only have 30 to 70 per cent of their time free to even consider them, never mind come up with shared, cross-party solutions.

To make matters worse, in the absence of any real solutions politicians spend what little time they have left explaining what went wrong in the past and trying to justify it. Finger pointing is often all they can do. They simply cannot understand the complexity of today's or tomorrow's challenges, so they use their already limited time to dig into the past and blame their predecessors for all the problems that they have encountered rather than actually seeking to solve those problems.

Politicians also need to keep an eye on the opinion polls so the whole political process degenerates into a personality based 'beauty contest' and spectator sport. Desperate to win votes and stay ahead in the polls, politicians resort to personal attacks on each other and attempts to manipulate public opinion by smearing individuals and negatively briefing against them. Of course, this sort of unsavoury behaviour only adds to the public's disengagement with the political process. In the UK in 2015 the controversial new leader of the Labour Party, Jeremy Corbyn is already very familiar with the media assault and character assassination that is now part and parcel of political life (certainly for those opposing powerful vested interests). Interestingly, as we write this chapter Bernie Sanders, a similar character to Jeremy Corbyn – older, unpolished, left wing socialist – is gaining ground on Hilary Clinton as the Democrat nomination for the 2016 Presidential campaign. He is attracting record crowds with his no-nonsense approach – going after billionaires to get their money out of politics, opposing free trade and advocating a publically funded system for healthcare, adding, 'What you are looking at is not called democracy. It is called oligarchy and we are going to end that… The United States and our government are not for sale!' [31] Meanwhile Donald Trump's ability to distract the electorate away from genuine policy debates on to personality issues is both impressive and terrifying. And the media seems all too willing to participate if not exacerbate the circus.[32]

The degradation of political discourse into puerile debate about personalities, how politicians dress or their hairstyle rather than their policies is one of many reasons why we are in desperate need of a new approach. We face many serious and complex challenges with far reaching consequences – imagine what could be achieved if politicians were able to redirect their time, effort and influence away from the toxic, adversarial point scoring and relentless fundraising into solving these issues for the greater good.

Without real change and an evolution of democracy that simply will not happen. As a result, in most developed nations, we have the sorry state of affairs with a largely disenfranchised population who are not even surprised by the lack of alignment between what the politicians say and what they then do. In order to get elected in the first place politicians need to make certain promises – promises that they will solve certain problems, address issues

---

[31] Usborne, D. (2015) 'US Presidential campaign 2016: Bernie Sanders – the socialist Senator going after billionaires and mega-banks – and garnering widespread support, *The Independent*, accessed 27 December 2015, www.independent.co.uk/news/world/americas/us-presidential-campaign-2016-bernie-sanders--the-socialist-senator-going-after-billionaires-and-megabanks--and-garnering-widespread-support-10379060.html

[32] For an example of how far this entertainment goes see the Jimmy Fallon sketch (2015) 'Donald Trump interviews himself in the mirror', accessed 27 December 2015, www.youtube.com/watch?v=c2DgwPG7mAA

and listen to the people. The people then vote for that party on the basis of those promises and the party gets elected. But once in power the party realises that they don't actually have the time to dig deeply into the complexity of those problems. They have no way of facilitating a shared cross-party solution that can be explained to the public so they never even get to formulate a viable and sustainable answer never mind implement it. They don't have time because almost all their attention is consumed by the political popularity contest. In the US they even have mid-term elections. Once in office the President has maybe 18 months to make an impact before having to get on the road again and campaign to win votes.

The Shortcomings of Dialectic Reasoning

Much of the often artificial 'naysaying' that permeates modern politics is based on the false belief that adversarial debate is the best way to reach a wise or high quality answer. Philosophically, our democratic processes have been based on the notion that 'dialectic reasoning' and debate will generate the best outcome. This idea has been central to European and Indian philosophy for centuries. It was made popular by Plato in the Socratic dialogues. Such 'dialectic methodology' and 'reasoned arguments' has been used to get to a 'truth' or resolve disputes since ancient Greece.

In theory the success of Socratic debate requires that those involved in the debate are not emotionally invested in their point of view because emotion tends to cloud judgement and lead to poor quality decisions. Unfortunately, most people simply do not operate at a level of maturity or ego development that enables them to debate alternative points of view without seeing a contrary view as a personal attack, wrong or – in a politician's case – a betrayal of their party. Even if an opposition party has something useful to contribute this can't be formally recognised as to do so would fundamentally go against the grain. Politician's normally take the view, particularly in public, that they can't be seen to be agreeing with the opposition. Occasionally some issues attract 'cross-party support', but this is the exception, not the rule.

In the Socratic approach the goal is to win the debate by persuasion – proving your own argument is correct and the opposition argument wrong. If one side cannot triumph then resolution often requires the winner to be determined either by a judge, a jury, or by group consensus. Such an approach is, we would suggest, profoundly simplistic and certainly not sufficiently sophisticated to deal with the complex wicked problems that most governments face.

The real problem here is a lack of development. Indeed the majority of people, politicians included, are operating from the level of development that believes that the world really is polarised into right and wrong, good and bad, better and worse. They adopt black and white or binary thinking where arguments have winners and losers. This is a perfectly adequate approach when dealing with simple problems but when seeking to resolve complex multi-dimensional wicked issues, align people or generate wise insightful answers, it fails badly. It is entirely possible for both sides to have a piece of the truth or both apparently contradictory perspectives to simultaneously have merit. However, our current political process doesn't allow for this.

The sort of adversarial conflict we see in the democratic political system where there is a government and an 'opposition' often does not generate wise or even innovative answers from such 'creative tension'. Real solutions or breakthroughs are extremely unlikely within such an adversarial environment and the whole notion of an 'opposition' being an adequate 'check and balance' is also very poor. As outlined in the first book of this *Wicked & Wise* series, we believe that complex and wicked problems require a much more sophisticated, more mature approach that involves more developed individuals who can focus on the issues rather than fighting each other.[33] Crowdocracy proposes a completely different way of reaching decisions that integrates the best thinking from diverse opinions rather than a muscled imposition of a singular view. This more integral approach is already working in various parts of the world and can generate wiser and better quality answers than the current adversarial approach.

4. Democracy Fosters Division

In the UK and the US where there are two, possibly three, main parties, millions of people feel unrepresented. In many European democracies such as Holland and Belgium they have a different problem – too many parties which leads to fragmentation and frustration. Of course, when people don't feel their voice is being heard because their views are not represented by the main parties or their voice is lost in the noise of too many parties, their attitude often hardens and arguments become even more polarised. Add the challenges of dialectic reasoning to the mix and their polarised views become harder and harder to reconcile further escalating division.

The suppression of expression promotes divisiveness in society.

As we wrap up this book, Paris is still reeling from the worst terrorist attack since the September 11 attack on New York. A few years ago ISIS, the group responsible for the multiple attacks across Paris killing 130 people, did not exist. So, where did it come from? ISIS is largely the product of genocide in Syria while the world stood back and watched. Over 200,000 Syrians were killed by their own government and millions more were displaced. Initially peaceful, Syrian protestors looked to the rest of the world for help. Fearful of getting embroiled in another war in the Middle East, the world was reluctant to get involved and the peaceful protest quickly turned into disenchantment, disillusionment and disenfranchisement. That polarised group was then radicalised

---

[33] Watkins, A. and Wilber, K. (2015) *Wicked & Wise: How to Solve the World's Toughest Problems,* London: Urbane Publishing.

and became violently militant. ISIS is the result.[34]

Following the twin tower attacks, Harvard Professor Cass R. Sunstein wrote a paper entitled, 'Why They Hate Us', which is sadly just as relevant today. In it he states, 'When group polarisation is at work, like-minded people, engaged in discussion with one another, move toward extreme positions. The effect is especially strong with people who are already quite extreme; such people can move in literally dangerous directions. It is unfortunate but true that leaders of terrorist organisations show a working knowledge of group polarisation. They sharply discipline what is said. They attempt to inculcate a shared sense of humiliation, which breeds rage, and group solidarity, which prepares the way for movement toward further extremes and hence for violent acts. They attempt to ensure that recruits speak mostly to people who are already predisposed in the preferred direction. They produce a cult-like atmosphere.'[35]

Although thankfully not as radical, extreme or violent, such divisions and the polarisation of views is a trend that is sweeping across Europe. Millions of people in modern 'democracies' feel they have no say in how their country is run which in turn is a breeding ground for dissent. In modern democracies this dissent has manifested in two ways, both of which further erode the legitimacy of democracy itself.

When people feel that a certain party no longer represents their own views then a new party is often born. A cursory glance at political history in many nations reveals this simple truth and the phenomenon continues today. In 1981 four Labour MPs in the UK felt that their party had become too left-wing and that their own

[34] Khedery, A. (2014) 'How Isis came to be', *The Guardian*, accessed 27 December 2015, www.theguardian.com/world/2014/aug/22/syria-iraq-incubators-isis-jihad

[35] Sunstein, Cass R. (2002) 'Why They Hate Us: The Role of Social Dynamics', 25 Harv. J.L. & Pub. Pol'y 429, accessed 27 December 2015, http://nrs.harvard.edu/urn-3:HUL.InstRepos:12921736

views were no longer being heard. This prompted Roy Jenkins, David Owen, Bill Rodgers and Shirley Williams to found the Social Democratic Party. In the 1983 and 1987 general elections they formed an alliance with the Liberal Party with whom they subsequently merged in 1988 to form the Liberal Democrats.

Similarly concerned with the UK's growing entanglement with Europe and potential loss of independence, historian Alan Sked founded the Anti-Federal League in 1991, which became the UK Independence Party (UKIP) in 1993. UKIP has gone on to attract many natural Tory voters who felt that their voice was not being heard inside the Conservative party. In the 2015 general election UKIP was the third largest party in the UK, eclipsing the Liberal Democrats and attracting 3.8 million votes or 12.6 per cent of the total. However, this only translated to winning one seat. UKIP's rise has signalled the end of the two or three party elections. The UK has become a multi-party battleground with six parties receiving a million votes or more in 2015.

When the values of a party no longer match the values of the members in that party or the people they represent political fragmentation occurs. What happened in Iceland is a classic example of this political fragmentation in action. Since the Global Financial Crisis (GFC), the collapse of the Icelandic banks and the consequent bankrupting of the country, the Icelandic people have been particularly disenfranchised with their politicians. This created the most tumultuous political upheaval (which we will discuss in more detail in Chapter 5) and the most incredible flourishing of new political parties all promoting different views.

Lack of adequate representation doesn't just create political fragmentation and divisiveness it also creates deep social divisions and an isolationist mentality. Part of the driving force for Scottish independence has been the fact that many Scots have felt that their voice was not being heard in Westminster. Despite the fact that Scotland rejected independence, 55 per cent to 45 per cent, when it was offered to them in the 2014 referendum, the problem has not gone away. In fact the UK is now in the grip of a constitutional crisis, which begs the question as to whether the 'democratically' elected UK government will even have a Britain left to govern by the end of this parliament. In addition to this constitutional crisis driven by the national divisions in the UK they are also facing a referendum of whether to separate from the EU. Not to mention the Human Rights problem, with the potential repeal of the 1998 Human Rights Act and the imposition of a British Bill of Rights, which duplicates some of rights of the European Convention on Human Rights and limits others. This later problem could itself drive another wedge between the nations that make up the UK.

Following the Scottish referendum result, David Cameron suggested that the Scottish devolution issue was now 'settled for a generation or perhaps a lifetime' but clearly it's not. Whilst the majority of Scots didn't want to break up the union, they do want change and they want their voice heard. If the promises made are not honoured then there is still a significant possibility that the minority in Scotland that still want independence will continue to pursue the divisive agenda. If, in the European referendum, most of the people in England vote to exit the EU and most of Scotland vote to stay then Scotland would again feel their views were being ignored. This would almost certainly reignite the whole Scottish independence problem as the SNP leader has indicated that Scotland will not accept being forced to leave the EU without its consent.

The divisions between the home nations in the UK borne of poor representation of certain sections of society will not go away. The growing constitutional crisis and whether there should be an 'English Assembly' to match the Scottish, Welsh and Northern Ireland Assemblies is currently under serious political consideration. As David Cameron also said immediately after the Scots rejected independence the 'voice of England should be heard'. But when you look at the options currently being offered in an attempt to overcome the constitutional mess that has been created, none of them look workable. We are staring down the barrel of the 'least worst option'. If we ignored all the lessons of history and chose to believe that society's evolution is best served by a separatist agenda where would this end? Would we end England itself as well as the UK? Should we devolve the county of Cornwall (and there are many in Cornwall that would like to do so); or devolve power to regional assemblies centred on the main cities? Fortunately when such divisive ideas have been put to the crowd, wisdom has prevailed with the people roundly rejecting such notions. If not devolution then what is the answer to the constitutional crisis in the UK? Various quasi federal solutions have been suggested. But there is no federal system on the planet that would work where one member (in this case England) has 85 per cent of the population. Furthermore the whole idea of a federal system for the UK was extensively explored and completely rejected as an option as long ago as 1973 by the Kilbrandon Commission, who said such an idea would be 'so unbalanced as to be unworkable'.[36] Nations have tried this and paid the price – look at the USSR, Czechoslovakia, Yugoslavia. If the constitutional crisis can't be solved by devolution or federalism, is there any alternative left? This is the question addressed by William Hague's Cabinet Committee after the Scottish vote. The three mooted options were:

1. English votes for English laws
2. All 'English' legislation should be considered by an English Grand Committee built on proportional representation lines
3. English legislation should be debated by all MPs but only be passed if there is a majority of English votes for that legislation.

Even though the third contortion to this constitutional mess is attracting the most support, it could easily become an

---

[36] Small, M. (2014) 'The F Word', Bella Calladonia, accessed 27 December 2015, http://bellacaledonia.org.uk/2014/06/14/the-f-word/

administrative nightmare.[37] We believe that the problem lies in the system itself. Democracy is no longer fit for purpose. It is not sufficiently sophisticated to deal with the problems that are arising. For example, the very same people who are passionate advocates for decentralisation are the exact same people who demand 'the government must do something' when the resulting local management fails. There is, however, no sense of inconsistency in their position. If we want decisions to be decentralised and made locally then one of the consequences is that the provision of services may vary by postcode, zip code or geography. We can't demand autonomy and then claim central government must do something when the autonomy we demanded fails. The system must address the likelihood of such inconsistencies. Such issues are one of the perpetual symptoms of a democratic system that is failing.

Arguably the most divided political landscape is found in Belgium. Next to the political ideological divide that is found in many countries (liberal, socialist, conservative, green) and the religious divide (catholic, reformist and humanist), there is also a linguistic divide (French vs Flemish and even small German-speaking parties). The different ideologies are all represented in separate linguistic parties (e.g., there is a French-speaking socialist party and a Flemish-speaking socialist party). There are no representative parties active in both communities. On top of this, important political decisions need to be approved at the national level and at the level of the Flemish and Walloon regional government. The leaders of the political parties wield enormous power in this system – more so than the ministers in the cabinet. The complexity this creates when it comes to creating coalitions can be mind-boggling. In 2010–2011, Belgium went without a

---

[37] Bogdanor, V. (2015) 'The Crisis of the Constitution: The General Election and the Future of the United Kingdom', The Constitution Society, accessed 27 December 2015, www.consoc.org.uk/wp-content/uploads/2015/02/COSJ2947_The-Crisis-of-the-Constitution_WEB_FINAL.pdf

government for 589 days. Many in the country expressed their view that in practice this made no real difference to their lives.

In all these complex political landscapes, the politicians would like us to believe that our views differ significantly from the views of our fellow citizens but the differences seem minimal. In the US, a 2014 joint study by the Voice of the People and the Program for Public Consultation (PPC) analysed 388 questions asking what the government should do in regard to a wide range of policy issues. What they found was that most people living in Republican districts or states disagreed with most people in Democratic districts or states on only 4 per cent of the questions. [38] While it makes sense that politicians overemphasise how strongly their views differ from others, because they need to differentiate to get attention, creating the sense of division where it is not really there, does not serve the public good.

5. Politicians Are Struggling Under the Weight of Escalating Complexity

In fairness to most politicians the problems that face governments are colossal, highly interdependent and complex. Many issues don't sit neatly within departmental or geographic jurisdictions. They are often wicked problems with multiple dimensions to consider, multiple stakeholders, multiple causes, multiple symptoms, multiple potential solutions and they are constantly evolving.[39] Interventions are too often compartmentalised because they are considered from a particular perspective by a particular government departmental with a particular agenda. As a result the best solutions politicians can come up with are nearly always partial, incomplete answers to more complex wicked issues.

---

[38] 'A Not so Divided America' (2014), accessed 27 December 2015, http://vop.org/wp-content/uploads/2014/07/Red-Blue-Report.pdf

[39] Watkins, A. and Wilber, K. (2015) *Wicked & Wise: How to Solve to Worlds Toughest Problems*, London: Urbane Publishing.

Take the Iraq War as a case in point. Whether you believe it was an illegal war or not, it was an extremely complex situation, shrouded in misinformation and propaganda on all fronts. Invading Iraq had serious and far-reaching consequences that were not properly considered. Indeed much of the problems in Syria, the rise of so-called Islamic State, can be traced back to that single political decision. In a brilliant reminder of the complexity of this decision, *Daily Mail* reader Aubrey Bailey wrote the following letter which was later published in the paper under the title, 'Clear as Mud'…

'Are you confused by what is going on in the Middle-East? Let me explain. We [UK] support the Iraqi government in its fight against Islamic State (IS/ISIL/ISIS). We don't like IS but IS is supported by Saudi Arabia whom we do like. We don't like President Assad in Syria. We support the fight against him, but not IS, which is also fighting against him.

'We don't like Iran, but the Iranian government supports the Iraqi government against IS. So, some of our friends support our enemies and some of our enemies are our friends, and some of our enemies are fighting our other enemies, whom we don't want to lose, but we don't want our enemies who are fighting our enemies to win.

'If the people we want to defeat are defeated, they might be replaced by people we like even less. And, all this was started by us invading a country to drive out terrorists who weren't actually there until we went in to drive them out – do you understand now?'[40]

Even now, years later, we can't really put our finger on what went wrong. The decision to go to war was not a reflection of majority rule which is, after all, supposed to be the hallmark of democracy. The vast majority of people in the US and Europe didn't want it.

[40] Heron, S. (2014) 'In case you are confused about what is happening in the Middle East', Newstalk, accessed 27 December 2015, www.newstalk. com/In-case-you-are-confused-about-what-is-happening-in-the-Middle-East

But when the President of the United States, George W. Bush is quoted as saying, 'I'm going to kick his [Saddam Hussein] sorry motherfucking ass all over the Mideast',[41] majority rule paled into insignificance. These are not the words of a mature, intelligent, visionary leader intent on finding a workable solution for all. These are the words of ego, hubris with an intent to 'win' at all costs. When individuals are insufficiently developed and unable to manage their emotions it can easily cloud their judgement resulting in poor quality decision-making. President Bush may have had every right to be angry but as the most powerful individual in the free world he also had an obligation to investigate the evidence rationally and clearly.

Unfortunately he was not alone. As a result, buoyed by a small group of like-minded politicians in the US, Europe and Australia, 'we' went to war with Iraq with devastating consequences. Those devastating consequences don't even consider the perverse economic incentives for going to war enjoyed by some of the key players.

Part of the problem is that the politicians we elect are asked to address problem areas where they may have little previous knowledge, experience or expertise. They are often expected to get involved and have an opinion on incredibly complex issues that they couldn't possibly understand without years of specialist knowledge. Consequently they may be completely out of their depth when it comes to really solving the issues they face. Very few politicians have deep experience with complexity theory. They are not schooled in wicked problems or trained to understand how to address the multiple dimensions of the issues they face. There is no 'political curriculum' that elected representatives can go through to get up to speed with the specifics of their areas of interest and deal with the 'wickedness' of the problems.

For example, UK MPs on the Culture, Media and Sport Select

---

[41] Isikoff, M. and Corn, D. (2006) *Hubris: The Inside Story of Spin, Scandal, and the selling of the Iraq War*, New York: Three River Press.

Committee issued a statement on blood doping in sport following revelations in *The Guardian*. To even understand what the revelations and blood tests meant, those MPs would have to have had years of specialist medical training *and* an in-depth knowledge of the individual physiology of the athletes the results related to. The MPs did not have that expertise and yet they still made grossly unfair comments, more or less naming an extremely successful UK athlete who they said was under suspicion.[42]

Like many of their corporate counterparts most political leaders are, as Professor Robert Kegan would say, 'in over their heads'.[43]

6. Democracy Is Not a Meritocracy

In days gone by people usually entered politics after a successful career in business or some other profession. They had life experience and were able to bring that acumen to the table. Today we are in a position where we have career politicians – those who enter lower level positions out of university or in their early 20s. As Robert Louis Stevenson once said, 'Politics is perhaps the only profession for which no preparation is thought necessary.'[44]

While we can debate the ideal preparation for a career in politics or how well prepared many politicians are before they enter into politics (some will say a business background is better, some will say the opposite), at least we can say that once in the system, there is often very little meritocracy in democracy – it is a popularity contest. Party rhetoric might say that the goal is to

---

[42] 'Paula Radcliffe denies cheating amid doping hearing', *The Irish Times*, 8 September 2015, accessed 27 December 2015, www.irishtimes.com/sport/other-sports/paula-radcliffe-denies-cheating-amid-doping-hearing-1.2344561

[43] Kegan, R. and Lahey, L. (2009) *Immunity to Change: How to Overcome It and Unlock the Potential in Yourself and Your Organization*, Boston: Harvard Business School Press.

[44] Stevenson, R.L. (1882) *Familiar studies of Men and Books*, London: Chatto & Windus.

solve certain problems but genuine problem solving is not really the objective – staying in power or getting back in power is the objective. The memoirs of most politicians are full of the politics within politics.

In addition, we don't know how suitable an individual really is to the position they've been appointed to and even if we did, those appointments change fairly frequently through cabinet reshuffles. For most of us, our vote is not based on a thorough assessment of the capabilities of the individuals involved and that assessment does not then occur once parliamentarians are inside government. We don't peruse someone's curriculum vitae before casting our vote for our representative. Besides we choose our representatives with virtually no regard to merit or the degree of wisdom our political representatives can bring to bear. In her TED talk, social psychologist Amy Cuddy reminded us that we make sweeping generalisations and assumptions based on nothing more than initial first impression. A researcher at Tufts University, Nalini Ambady, demonstrated that a doctor's likelihood of being sued was directly linked to his likeability and the assumption was made non-verbally within 30 seconds. Princeton researcher Alex Todorov has shown that our judgment of political candidates' faces in just one second predict 70 per cent of US Senate and gubernatorial race outcomes.[45]

That's pretty scary. How someone looks is important, or how confident they appear in interview is important, but whether or not they have the capability to do the job seems almost forgotten. Politics in a democracy therefore degenerates into spin, looking the part and winning the media directed popularity contest. But there are stunning examples from around the world where meritocracy does matter.

---

[45] Cuddy, A. (2012) 'Your body language shapes who you are', accessed 27 December 2015, www.ted.com/talks/amy_cuddy_your_body_language_shapes_who_you_are/transcript?language=en#t-653614

Singapore is an example of a country that describes meritocracy as one of its official guiding principles for domestic public policy formulation, placing emphasis on academic credentials as objective measures of merit. The People's Action Party (PAP) swept to power in Singapore in 1959 winning 43 of the 51 possible seats in the Assembly, and the party has been returned to power in every general election since. The PAP, inspired by its founder Lee Kuan Yew who held very strong views about meritocracy based on educational achievement and job performance, applies the merit principle to making appointments and promotions in government service, and civil service salaries.[46]

According to Transparency International 2014, Singapore is considered the seventh least corrupt country in the world.[47] The World Bank's governance indicators have also rated Singapore highly on rule of law, regulatory quality, control of corruption and government effectiveness.[48] Of course, Singapore has its opponents who believe their civil liberties, and political and human rights are lacking.[49]

If we set aside the idea that one ideological party can have the legitimacy to rule a nation, then China's Communist Party offers another interesting example of a political meritocracy. The Politburo is China's highest ruling body and has 25 members. The vast majority of senior Chinese officials have worked and competed over several decades to prove themselves competent in first running a village, district or business before ever reaching

[46] Mauzy, D.K. and Milne, R.S. (2002) *Singapore Politics Under the People's Action Party,* London; New York: Routledge, pp. 55-57

[47] Transparency International Corruption Perception Index 2014, accessed 27 December 2015, www.transparency.org/cpi2014/results

[48] World Bank Worldwide Governance Indicators, accessed 27 December 2015, http://info.worldbank.org/governance/wgi/index.aspx#reports

[49] *World Report 2014: Singapore*, Human Rights Watch, accessed 27 December 2015, www.hrw.org/world-report/2014/country-chapters/singapore

senior political positions.[50]

As Eric Li explains in his TED Talk, China's 'Organisation Department' functions like a giant human resource engine. It operates a rotating pyramid made up of three components: civil service, state-owned enterprises, and social organisations like a university or a community programme. These three 'tracks' form separate yet integrated career paths for Chinese officials. Graduates are recruited into entry-level positions in all three tracks. If they demonstrate ability they will get promoted through four increasingly elite ranks: fuke (deputy section manager), ke (section manager), fuchu (deputy division manager), and chu (division manager). The range of positions is wide, from running health care in a village to foreign investment in a city district to manager in a company. Once a year, the department reviews their performance. They interview their superiors, their peers, their subordinates. They vet their personal conduct. They conduct public opinion surveys. Then they promote the winners. Throughout their careers, these cadres can move through and out of all three tracks. Over time, the good ones move beyond the four base levels to the fuju (deputy bureau chief) and ju (bureau chief) levels. There, they enter high officialdom. By that point, a typical assignment will be to manage a district with a population in the millions or a company with hundreds of millions of dollars in revenue. In 2012 there were 900,000 fuke and ke levels, 600,000 fuchu and chu levels, and only 40,000 fuju and ju levels in this highly competitive meritocracy. Beyond ju levels the best move up several more ranks, and eventually make it to the Central Committee. The process takes two to three decades. It took China's new president, Xi Jinping 30 years to reach the top position. He started as a village manager, and by the time he entered the Politburo, he had managed areas with a total population of 150 million people and combined GDPs of 1.5

---

[50] Li, E.X. (2013) 'A tale of two political systems', TED, accessed 27 December 2015, www.ted.com/talks/eric_x_li_a_tale_of_two_political_systems#t-281011

trillion US dollars.[51]

Compare that expertise and decades acquiring and gaining experience to Barack Obama, François Hollande or George W. Bush or the regular 'Cabinet reshuffles' that put countless politicians in functioning democracies in senior political roles without the relevant experience. In most modern democracies candidate selection seems nonsensical. The highly meritocratic system used in Singapore and China ensures the most experienced people are making the decisions, having taken decades to acquire their knowledge and skill. They are also much less constrained by the endless politics of politics. The leaders of Singapore and China can take a long-term view on their policies and focus on finding the best solution and implement that solution fast.

7. Politicians Don't Have a Voice Either – Their Vote Is 'Whipped'

Even if politicians were schooled in years of meritocratic training or went through some sort of political curriculum and cultivated a deep understanding in complexity theory, developed their ego maturity and understood the neuroscience of decision-making, would it help? Actually, not really. In many democratic systems politicians have to commit to follow the party line. Their vote is managed by their party's 'whip' – essentially the party enforcer.

Many parliamentarians will turn up to vote on legislation they know very little about. Even if they read their briefing notes the information is almost certainly presented in accordance with the party line or via lobbyists presenting a particular spin so it is already a biased look at the facts. As UK Green Party MP Caroline Lucas states, 'No one knows. Which means that when you get there [to vote], the whips can very effectively just push

---

[51] Li, E.X. (2013) 'A tale of two political systems', TED, accessed 27 December 2015, www.ted.com/talks/eric_x_li_a_tale_of_two_political_systems#t-281011

you into one lobby or the other and when I say push – it's not a figure of speech, they literally do.'[52]

Even if an individual politician believes that what they are voting for is against the people's best interests the 'whip' will use threats, incentives or quid-pro-quo deals to ensure the politician votes the 'party line'. If they don't, they can quickly gather a reputation for being an outlier or troublemaker and they will be left permanently on the back benches or out in the cold a long way from the real power brokers and the governmental core. Dissent from the 'party line' more than once or twice is a serious 'career-limiting move'. Those politicians will go nowhere, they will have no influence and the people who elected them will be poorly represented.

In the Netherlands, much of the political decision-making gets set in stone years in advance. After an election, the parties that wish to form a coalition will have very detailed conversations and significant horse-trading will occur on many topics. Once that coalition agreement is signed by the parties, all the parliamentarians belonging to the coalition parties are essentially bound by this agreement – not in a formal legal sense, but politically this agreement rules. For the following years – until the next election – the political agenda follows the agreement. From a political point of view, it creates a lot of stability, but it renders the majority of the elected politicians without much of a voice.

Even with the best will in the world, with the best, most honourable intentions possible the democratic political system is designed so that once in power, politicians will as much as possible ignore the local community – especially if the wishes of the local community conflict with the 'party line'. Even if the politicians stuck to their guns and voted against the party, their dissent wouldn't even matter because the whip would probably

[52] Jones, O. (2015) *The Establishment: and how they get away with it*, London: Penguin.

have ensured a majority. When faced with the choice to conform (and potentially advance their career and end up with a lucrative private sector position) or to stand up for what the people want, it is hardly a surprise that politicians do what their party wants them to do.

8. The System Facilitates Self-interest and Scandal

Many of us, particularly in the West define ourselves individually. We look for ways in which we are different. We prize uniqueness and deride any sort of collective orientation as 'liberalism', 'touchy-feely', or even 'communist'. This is ironic given we can only truly understand ourselves in relation to others. The one thing that has enabled *Homo sapiens* to become the dominant species on the planet is our ability to act in concert with each other.[53] As a result, our idea of leadership is also highly individualistic and our leaders often act in their own interests first rather than the interests of all of us.

Virtually everyone believes that our political leaders serve their own interests first before the interests of their nation. For example, Transparency UK's 'Global Corruption Barometer' states that 90 per cent of respondents believed that the UK Government is run by a few big organisations that act in their own interest.[54] This is particularly surprising given the high international regard in which the UK parliamentary system is held and Britain's comparably good ranking in the Corruption Perceptions Index.

In many developed nations people are disenfranchised with politicians. What do we think of Italy's track record? A Google

---

[53] Israel, J. (2014) 'Bananas in Heaven', TED, accessed 27 December 2015, www.youtube.com/watch?v=YZa4sdIwV04

[54] Transparency International UK, accessed 27 December 2015, www. transparency.org.uk/our-work/uk-corruption/lobbying

search of 'Berlusconi' and 'scandal' brings up half a million search results. He has been accused of corruption, consorting with prostitutes and minors, yet still survived in political leadership roles for many years until finally being convicted of tax fraud.[55]

In the UK, political scandals are discovered on an almost weekly basis. In 2009, the MP's expenses scandal broke in the UK media revealing jaw-dropping expense claims for everything from second homes that didn't exist to moat cleaning costs, to the purchase of an ornamental duck house and online pornography. Almost every politician, in all parties was involved in what appeared to be, at least until *The Telegraph* got wind of it, a very private, very quiet in-house perk.[56] The view was that politicians were not paid comparable salaries with the private sector and were therefore perfectly entitled to inflate their earnings by defrauding the public purse.

In 2015, Lord Sewel resigned from the House of Lords after he was caught snorting cocaine with prostitutes, boasting about his importance and deriding the stupidity of many of his colleagues – ironic considering he was the Chairman of Committees, which amongst other things oversaw political standards and conduct![57]

Unsurprisingly, public trust of politicians is at an all-time low.[58]

[55] (2012) 'Silvio Berlusconi sentenced for tax fraud', *BBC News*, accessed 27 December 2015, www.bbc.co.uk/news/world-europe-20102215

[56] Winnett, R. (2009) 'MPs' expenses: how Brown and his Cabinet exploit expenses system', *The Telegraph*, accessed 27 December 2015, www.telegraph.co.uk/news/newstopics/mps-expenses/5293679/MPs-expenses-Gordon-Brown-and-Cabinet-face-questions-over-claims.html

[57] (2015) 'Lord Sewel resigns from House of Lords after drug claims', *BBC News*, accessed 27 December 2015, www.bbc.co.uk/news/uk-politics-33685519

[58] Mludzinski, T. (2011) 'The public do not trust politicians', Ipsos MORI, accessed 27 December 2015, www.ipsos-mori.com/newsevents/blogs/thepoliticswire/766/The-public-do-not-trust-politicians.aspx

In fact, there have been so many cases of flagrant self-interest and scandalous behaviour the stories have formed books in their own right.[59]

The human propensity toward self-interest also means that politicians in the democratic system are often focused on their 'end game'. Positions of power in the public sector frequently lead on to high paying positions in the private sector for those that want one. For example, Sir Sherard Cowper-Coles was thought to be key in ending the Serious Fraud Office investigation into BAE systems' dealing with Saudi Arabia in December 2006. In June 2010, he announced that he intended to step down from his role as the Foreign Secretary's special representative to Afghanistan and Pakistan. In February 2011, he was appointed by BAE Systems as an international development director, leaving in 2013 to become an advisor to the Board of HSBC.

Since leaving politics Tony Blair has become Tony Blair Associates. He has a large property portfolio and an estimated £80 million of earnings accrued in just a few short years. Besides an excellent state pension and twenty-four-hour security team, Blair enjoys the best contacts that money can buy. Needless to say, other people are prepared to pay for those contacts and Blair's clients can be found around the world. Despite a dubious record as peacemaker, his role as special envoy in the Middle East has brought him into contact with a variety of oil-rich individuals who have since become his most profitable clients.[60]

In the UK, one department that has a particularly active 'revolving door' between government and business is the Ministry of

---

[59] Cave, T. and Rowell, A. (2015) *A Quiet Word: Lobbying, Crony Capitalism and Broken Politics in Britain*, London: The Bodley Head.
Jones, O. (2015) *The Establishment: And how they get away with it*, London: Penguin.
Hughes, A.K. (2013) *A History of Political Scandals*, Barnsley: Pen & Sword Books Ltd.

[60] Beckett F, Hencke D and Kochan N (2015) *Blair Inc.: The Man Behind the Mask* John Blake Publishing London

Defence. Since 1996, officials and military officers have taken up more than 3,570 jobs in arms and defence related companies – 231 secured in 2011/2012 alone.[61]

But this revolving door is by no means confined to the UK. In the Netherlands, Camiel Eurlings, the 'crown prince' of the Christian Democrats and Minister for Transport, quit politics to become the new CEO of KLM Airlines. A role that would almost certainly not been available to him had he not first been Minister of Transport.

In the US, Tennessee Representative Jim Cooper told Harvard professor Lawrence Lessig that the chief problem with Congress was that members focused on lucrative careers as lobbyists after serving, instead of focusing on public service, stating that Congress was a 'Farm League for K Street'.[62] 'K Street' is the name given to the main thoroughfare in Washington DC known as a centre for numerous think tanks, lobbyists and advocacy groups. In other words, being a member of Congress was not about public service at all – it was a training ground for the extremely well-paid jobs those individuals could then secure with those prestigious think tanks, lobbyists and advocacy groups. These are not isolated incidences but par for the course because politicians, like most of us, are driven by self-interest. Democracy provides a lucrative and fertile ground to maximise that self-interest.

One might rationalise the parliamentary expenses scandal, the cash for questions scandal, the appointment of ex-politicians to high profile and highly paid 'advisory positions' in industry or various party funding scandals as human weakness. They are.

---

[61] Hopkins, N. (2012) 'MoD staff and thousands of military officers join arms firms', *The Guardian*, accessed 27 December 2015, www.theguardian.com/uk/2012/oct/15/mod-military-arms-firms

[62] Lessig, L. (2010) 'How to Get Our Democracy Back', CBS News, accessed 27 December 2015, www.cbsnews.com/news/how-to-get-our-democracy-back/

Unfortunately we currently have a political system that facilitates and often exacerbates these human weaknesses rather than mitigates them. And sadly such problems are endemic the world over.

In Canada in November 2012, Montreal's Mayor Gérard Tremblay resigned amid allegations that his party was taking a slice out of municipal construction contracts. His replacement, Michael Applebaum, lasted seven months before he was arrested and charged with 14 counts of corruption. *The Economist* noted that Applebaum's 'arrest brings to six the number of mayors and former mayors in Quebec facing charges of corruption, fraud, or gangersterism'.[63]

In 2005, former US Republican Congressman Randy 'Duke' Cunningham pleaded guilty in federal court to tax evasion, conspiracy to commit bribery, mail fraud and wire fraud. He was convicted of collecting $2.4 million in homes, yachts and gifts on a scale unparalleled in the history of Congress. In 2012, former Illinois Governor Rod Blagojevich was sentenced to 14 years in prison after being convicted of 18 counts of criminal activity including trying to sell the appointment to fill the US Senate seat vacated by Barack Obama.[64]

It is extremely easy to find examples of individual politicians behaving badly, whether lining their own pockets, peddling their influence or lining up a high paying job before leaving office. Scandals are certainly not a new phenomenon in politics or

[63] (2013) 'Canada's Misbehaving Mayors: The scandals keep on coming', *The Economist,* accessed 27 December 2015, www.economist.com/blogs/americasview/2013/06/canada-s-misbehaving-mayors

[64] (2015) 'CNN Politics Politicians in Hot Water', accessed 27 December 2015, http://edition.cnn.com/2013/08/14/politics/gallery/politicians-behaving-badly/index.html

business.[65] As Lord Acton once said, 'Power tends to corrupt, and absolute power corrupts absolutely.'[66] All these examples are really evidence of failed leadership and ultimately the failure of individuals in the 'I' dimension.[67] As Scottish comedian Billy Connolly puts it, 'The desire to be a politician should bar you from ever being one.'[68] In other words, the very people attracted to the bizarre pseudo-celebrity life that characterises our current political landscape probably shouldn't be in positions of power.

What these stories and countless others we *could* recount demonstrate is that there are a surprisingly large number of people inside the political system that don't have the maturity and cognitive sophistication to think from multiple perspectives or transcend their own self-interest. Even if they did, the political system they enter is so fundamentally flawed that if they could rise above self-preservation and seek to affect positive change for the many not the few, the system of government is so convoluted and obfuscated that it's actually almost impossible to know who is making the decisions and why.

In fairness, most politicians probably go into politics for all the right reasons – they believe passionately in the power of government to affect change and want to represent their constituents. Most become politicians because they genuinely want to make a positive difference. It is often only when they get into politics that

---

[65] Owen, D. (2012) *The Hubris Syndrome: Bush, Blair & the Intoxication of Power*, London: Methuen Publishing Ltd.
Isikoff, M. (2007) *Hubris the Inside Story of Spin, Scandal & the Selling of the Iraq War*, New York: Three Rivers Press.
Desai, M. (2015) *Hubris: Why Economists Failed to Predict the Crisis and How to Avoid the Next One*, New Haven: Yale University Press.
Vaknin, S. (2015) *Narcissistic And Psychopathic Leaders*, Seattle: CreateSpace, Amazon.com, Inc.

[66] Acton, J.E.E.D. (1887) written in a letter to Archbishop Mandell Creighton.

[67] Watkins, A. (2015) *4D Leadership*, London: Kogan Page.

[68] An Audience with Billy Connolly (1985) Channel 4

they realise a) how ill-equipped they are to affect that change and b) how incredibly difficult it is to affect change because even they are just one voice inside a noisy political machine. They soon realise that their power, reach and influence depends heavily on the relationships they have with other politicians and how well they learn to work the system itself.

Time for Change

There is now an urgent need for us to create a better way forward – one where people's votes actually count and their voices are heard, a system in which we can all participate in an effective manner, that doesn't encourage corruption and manipulation. A system that doesn't rely on any form of elite, be that a Chinese meritocratic elite, a financial American elite or a British educational and 'class' elite. A system sophisticated enough to embrace the diversity that exists in all nations. A system where the crowd decides its own future rather than that future being in the hands of a secret few or poorly-informed, ill-equipped and completely untrained individuals or immature corrupted self-servers.

Most of us know that democracy isn't working or at least suspect that it is not all it is advertised to be. But so far, our quest to improve the democratic process and make it fairer has revolved around how to find better representatives who will improve the outcome in the existing system or pushing for electoral reform. Without some sort of political curriculum and developmental manoeuvre the first is nearly impossible. Most of the efforts to reform democracy are effectively seeking to tweak a fundamentally broken system. Whilst the tweaks may result in some improvement, most of the endemic problems with democracy we've outlined above will stubbornly prevail. For example, even those changes are heavily influenced and ultimately determined by the lobby. In 1982, the UK sought to reform the first-past-the-post voting system (FPTP) in favour of the Alternative Vote (AV).[69] FPTP favours the big parties and means they can win a majority with less than a third of the vote. A change to AV would have been better for smaller parties and would also mean that the process was more democratic as the winner would have to gain more than half the vote to win. According to Peter Facey of Unlock Democracy who was involved in the pro-AV campaign, 'AV forces politicians to work harder to earn and keep their support.'[70] The 'No to AV campaign' – at least partially funded by the lobby group Taxpayers' Alliance (TPA) – focused on the cost of the change and ran expensive billboard adverts in the run up to the referendum with a picture of a sick baby in an incubator and the caption: 'She needs a new cardiac facility, not an alternative voting system'.[71] By spinning the narrative as though the status quo was in the national interest, a positive evolution in democracy was effectively stopped in its tracks. Democracy will not be improved by tweaking.

We need more radical change.

What makes our proposal different from the solutions put forward so far is that we are advocating that we actually make the political process available to *everyone* – that we dispense with elected representatives altogether and put the power in the hands of the

---

[69] According to the Electoral Reform Society, 'Alternative vote (AV) is a preferential system where the voter ranks the candidates in order of preference. Each voter has one vote, but rather than an X, they put a "1" by their first choice, a "2" by their second choice, and so on, until they no longer wish to express any further preferences or run out of candidates. Candidates are elected outright if they gain more than half the votes as first preferences. If not, the candidate who lost (the one with least first preferences) is eliminated and their votes move to the second preference marked on the ballot papers. This process continues until one candidate has half of the votes and is elected.' Accessed 27 December 2015, www.electoral-reform.org.uk/alternative-vote/

[70] Cave, T. and Rowell, A. (2015) *A Quiet Word: Lobbying, Crony Capitalism and Broken Politics in Britain*, London: The Bodley Head

[71] (2011) 'No to AV campaign reject rivals' "scare stories" claim', *BBC News*, accessed 27 December 2015, www.bbc.co.uk/news/uk-politics-12564879

people. But before we do that, we need to describe the evolution through which we now arrive at a point where crowdocracy is the logical next step.

Chapter 3:

A Brief History of Governance:
How Did We Get Here?

'L'état, c'est moi.'[1] (I am the State)

– Louis XIV, King of France 1643 – 1715

There is no doubt that democracy has been a very positive and powerful force in the world but it is not the most sophisticated decision-making process available to us. If we are right that democracy is already past its sell-by-date, the question arises what are the next evolutionary stages? Also what happened to all the other forms of government that Churchill equally disliked? Did preceding models of governance at some point emerge and then vanish? The answer is that many still exist in some part of the world and some of the best features of these previous decision-making models are carried forth in our current governance model. Democracy is, therefore, simply an evolutionary step on a never-ending and unfolding process of how we self-organise and govern ourselves. Every stage includes and transcends the

---

[1] Address to the Parliament of Paris (13 April 1655); Attr. by Jacques-Antoine Dulaure, Histoire de Paris (1834), vol. 6, p. 298; probably apocryphal.

Figure 3.1 The Evolution of Decision-making

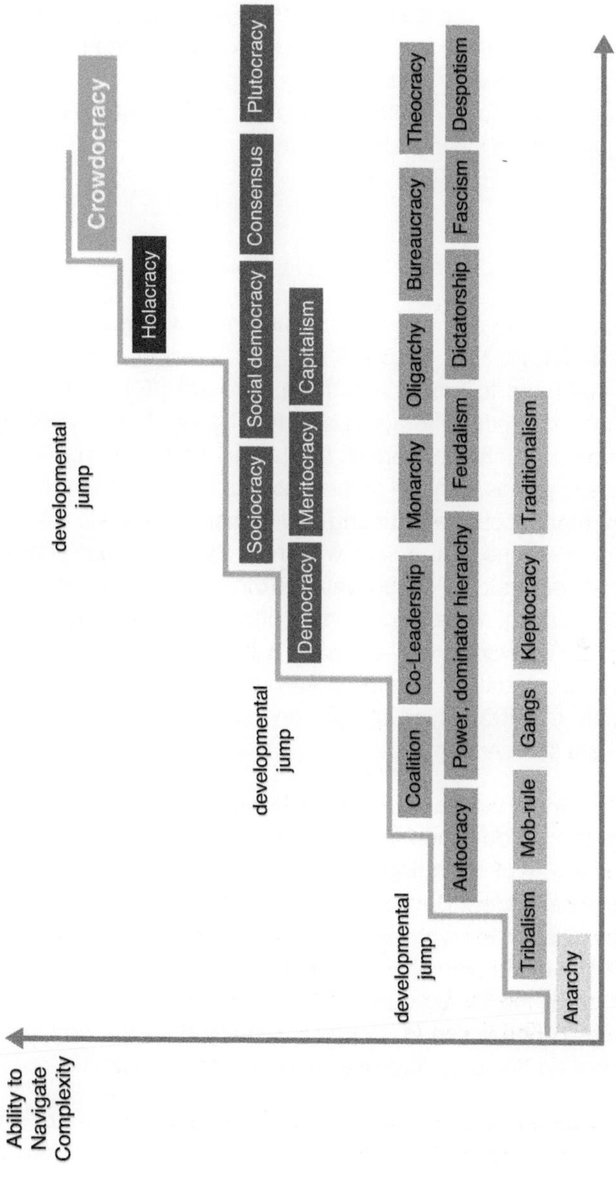

previous one – and so what we have today carries forward elements of the past. If we fully appreciate the evolution of decision-making (Figure 3.1) we can appreciate how we ended up here, how we created many of the wicked problems we face today and how we might evolve our way out of the problems our governance systems have created.

It Starts with Anarchy

Back in the day when the human race was grubbing around in the dirt, life was simple. It was just a matter of survival. People lived hand to mouth and there were only 'four F-ing choices' – fighting, fleeing, foraging and fornicating. It was every man (or woman) for him or herself. Virtually all decisions were focused on these issues with the greatest amount of time spent on foraging, or more accurately hunting and gathering. Anyone who has lived for any time in the wild will know that fire, fluid and food are the cornerstone, of survival. The other tasks, fighting, fleeing and fornicating, were largely intermittent activities. Hunter-gatherer societies were largely anarchic, with little organisational structure. Frequent battles would break out over food or fornication and only the fittest lived to fight another day. Virtually all decisions were self-serving.

Thankfully we have evolved, at least a little, since our early hunter-gathering days and most societies have moved beyond anarchy as a way of operating. However the idea of anarchy still appeals to a select few. But such misplaced primitivism is normally driven by disaffection with existing power structures and marginalisation in the decision-making process. Modern anarchists may want to disrupt the status quo but they rarely have any idea what they would rather see in its place. Usually their thinking doesn't go beyond the idea 'anything has to be better than this'.

This survivalist mentality and primitive decision-making exists when societies have not evolved beyond anarchy and can still be seen in many impoverished areas of the world today. It is prevalent in the poorest nations. People will sit at the roadside all day and watch the world go by. At this level of development people simply exist. They often experience strong feelings of helplessness. They placate themselves with the knowledge that at least they are alive and tomorrow is another, maybe better day.

It is also possible to find such hand to mouth existence in developed nations. The homeless often exist at this primitive level of development, as do many people with mental health problems, alcoholics and drug addicts. This stage of development is also where the long-term unemployed or the recently bankrupt operate. Individuals can only contemplate their own needs in their decision-making and getting through each day is the priority. Decision-making at this level is not complicated and there are few variables to deal with. All that matters is the personal survival needs of right now; there is no need for future planning. Time horizons are extremely short. The needs of others don't really factor into decision-making. The inability to deal with the future, other people and anything other than issues to do with personal survival means that people at this level simply can't handle any degree of complexity.

At some point it may start to occur to the individuals in the grip of this daily battle that they would do better if they ganged together. Thus anarchy eventually evolves and groups of individuals start to come together to form tribes.

The Emergence of the Tribe

This evolutionary step and the shift in focus from self-interest to collective survival requires a profound change in the way decisions are made because people now have to partially consider the needs of others if they want to survive. Individuals can no longer impose their will on other members of the 'community'. With the emergence of tribes comes the realisation that the collective is more powerful than any single individual.

The first version of tribal decision-making is mob rule. Small cliques emerge within the collective and will operate as a single 'alpha' unit imposing their will of the rest of the tribe. Mob rule is often violent and it is certainly unpredictable. Cliques are inherently unstable and allegiances can shift rapidly. Subtle changes in the pecking order could easily descend into a more primitive survival driven decision-making and show of strength. Eventually the people making the decisions for the tribe realise that stability of leadership is better for everyone than perpetual in-fighting.

Mob rule often leads to poor quality, emotion-fuelled decisions and there are numerous examples in the history of most countries of mobs lynching the wrong person. Over time, the collective pondered on how to stabilise the decision-making process and gradually traditions emerged. In many tribes, tradition honoured the decision-making prowess of the elders. This was a functional way of making decisions particularly if the elders regularly made the right call. Of course, no one is infallible and this system is always going to fail eventually, especially when the elders lack the capability or sophistication to make decisions around increasingly complex issues.

The primary dynamic in mob rule is an 'us versus them' mentality. If an individual is part of the 'in-crowd' then they will survive. On-going survival depends to a great extent on reinforcing membership of that elite group and polarising opinion against any outsiders. This manoeuvre creates stronger bonds between those who currently remain 'in-favour' and protects the individual from rejection. However, cliques, mobs and gangs are inherently unstable and people at this level of development live in perpetual fear of being usurped or rejected. This is one of the reasons they often have highly-tuned instincts on where threats, be they competitive, financial or physical may be coming from.

Tribalism is still common in most developed and emerging

nations. This is often referred to as ethnocentricity, although at times it manifests as sexism, xenophobia or borderline racism. A great deal of the conflict we see around the world today comes from such 'tribal wars'. The security of one tribe requires the demonisation of the other tribe. Politically speaking there has been somewhat of a resurgence of tribalism or 'us versus them' nationalism, particularly in Europe over the last 20 years. It often manifests as divisive devolution or a desire for separatism. In fact a number of political parties have heated up xenophobic nationalistic concerns particularly around the issue of immigration and made this an election platform. This is, for example, a significant part of UKIP's popularity and similarly, in the USA, Presidential candidate Donald Trump has suggested he will not only 'build a wall' to keep Mexican immigrants out but he will get Mexico to pay for it![2]

Ethnocentricity is even more prevalent in emerging nations who still operate on highly tribal or ethnic divisions. The population of Afghanistan, for example, is divided into a wide variety of ethnolinguistic clans. These include the Pashtun (40 per cent of the population), Tajik (22 per cent), Hazara (11 per cent), Uzbek (9 per cent), Aimak (1 per cent), Turkmen (2 per cent) Baloch (1 per cent) and Pashai, Nuristani, Gujjar, Arab, Brahui, Qizilbash and Pamiri (5 per cent).[3] Likewise many of the hostilities we still see in the Middle East today have their roots in this ethnocentric level of development.

The decision-making process inside the mob is unstable. Often no one is really 'in charge' and the mob can lurch from one reactive decision to another. For example, consider a gang of

---

[2] Balthazar, C. (2015) 'Donald Trump on Stephen Colbert: "We Are Going to Build a Wall, You Are Going to Pay for the Wall"', *Latin Post*, accessed 28 December 2015, www.latinpost.com/articles/81704/20150924/donald-trump-stephen-colbert-going-build-wall-pay.htm

[3] The Asia Foundation (2012) *A Survey of the Afghan People*, accessed 28 December 2015, www.asiafoundation.org/resources/pdfs/Surveybook2012web1.pdf

teenage girls out shopping on the weekend. One girl will suggest they hunt down a certain brand and the mob stampedes in that direction; a few minutes later a different girl makes an alternative suggestion and the stampede occurs in a different direction. While tribal mobs are, by dint of their collective intelligence, more successful than individuals they remain unstable and unpredictable in the direction they will take.

If the mob, gang or tribe survives long enough then a little degree of consistency often emerges and this is a stabilising force. But at this level of development there is still little real appreciation for how the world works and while conventions may start to appear, decision-making often comes down to strength in numbers, traditions, rituals or superstitions. Sometimes a smaller group of 'tribal elders' become the decision-making forum. But the inherent instability of mobs and the lack of a consistent direction eventually force the emergence of one of the most common decision-making methods in the world today in politics and business – autocracy.

The Need for Strong Leadership

The failure of the tribe or gang to make real progress is an important evolutionary stimulus. The lack of progress aggravates some tribal members to such a degree that they feel compelled to step forward and grab the reins. With the emergence of this developmental level, the pendulum swings back from collective mob rule to a single individual who asserts him or herself over the mob or tribe and controls its destiny.

This developmental jump signifies the emergence of what most people would recognise as leadership: a single individual taking charge and providing direction to accelerate progress. This is the emergence of autocracy. Of course, there have been autocrats since our hunter-gatherer days but modern day autocracy is a subtler version of its primitive ancestor. Indeed, autocracy is alive and well in virtually every nation on earth either in government, business or society in general.

One of the great benefits of autocratic leaders is they make things happen. Such individuals succeed because they are much more sophisticated than their primitive, aggressive autocratic ancestors. In hunter-gatherer days, autocratic leaders asserted their control through violence but over the centuries most learnt that the *threat* of violence was more effective and much less messy. Engaging in actual violence could result in injury, which would weaken the individual for any future power battles. Gradually intimidation became the currency rather than physical violence. The type of intimidation utilised by autocrats itself evolved and today it is the threat of the removal of sponsorship or patronage that many autocrats use to maintain their power base and control others. This is often the case in political systems where appointment to ministerial position may be the only real authority that politicians actually have.[4]

In their primitive form autocracies can be brutal and easily degrade into despotism, fascism, kleptocracy and dictatorship. There are still plenty of examples of all these versions in the world today such as President Mugabe in Zimbabwe. Mugabe, liberator turned dictator, is still in power despite being 92 years old and has vowed that only death will end his rule. His government operates much like a cult with Mugabe at the centre. A protective and loyal inner circle keeps him in power with the use of violence and intimidation to secure election victory. Zimbabwe is considered one of the most corrupt nations in the world, ranking 156th out of 174 countries on the 2014 Transparency International Corruption Perception Index.[5]

But strong leaders at this level of development are not all

---

[4] Powell, J. (2010) *The New Machiavelli: How to Wield Power in the Modern World*, London: Bodley Head.

[5] Transparency International Corruption Perception Index 2014, accessed 28 December 2015, www.transparency.org/cpi2014/results/

monsters. This level of leadership development has been a source of progress in many walks of life. One of the primary benefits of autocracy is the speed of decision-making. There are no tribal elders to consult. Power rests exclusively in one person who calls the shots. Such decisiveness is in fact extremely helpful in many situations. For example, in critical situations such as combat when decisions often have to be made quickly, there simply isn't time for consultation. The military often look out for autocratic leaders and promote them. In basic training they will often put recruits in unfamiliar circumstances and wait to see who steps forward to provide a way out of their predicament. This person is then often fast-tracked into leadership roles.

Business, when it seeks to open up new markets is often best served by sending a heroic, 'lead from the front' autocrat to break new ground, establish a new international office and bring the kind of drive, passion and urgency that is required to build something from the ground up. In fact, many entrepreneurial business leaders need to operate from this level of development when setting up their business. Nations in times of crisis can benefit from strong, single-minded, autocratic leadership. Leaders who are prepared to stand alone against the tyranny of other nations and meet strength with strength can be an incredible asset.

However, autocratic leaders tend to shy away from complexity and prefer to 'keep it simple stupid' which can drift into misguided oversimplification with declarations such as 'war on terror'[6] or 'build a wall'[7] becoming hollow, superficial sound bites rather than representing any useful policy statement. In fact, simplistic

---

[6] Transcript: President Bush's Speech on the War on Terrorism, *The Washington Post*, 30 November 2005, accessed 28 December 2015, www.washingtonpost.com/wp-dyn/content/article/2005/11/30/AR2005113000667.html

[7] Balthazar, C. (2015) 'Donald Trump on Stephen Colbert: "We Are Going to Build a Wall, You Are Going to Pay for the Wall"', *Latin Post*, accessed 28 December 2015, www.latinpost.com/articles/81704/20150924/donald-trump-stephen-colbert-going-build-wall-pay.htm

binary thinking is the norm with passionate, empty rhetoric reflecting spin over substance.

Autocrats demand intense loyalty. They will force choice – 'you are either with me or against me'. Any refusal to answer such a grossly simplified question is seen as opposition or worse a direct threat to their authority. They believe in very clear lines of accountability and build command and control hierarchies with themselves at the top. This enables them to know who they 'need to shoot' if things go wrong as one CEO put it to one of us.

They run their hierarchies through a 'hub and spoke' leadership model with individual meetings with each member of their core team. There is no interest or investment in the team. In fact many autocrats would see the team simply as something that slows them down. It is not uncommon for autocrats to deliberately undermine the team dynamic and create unhealthy conflict in a 'divide and rule' approach. This methodology strengthens their authority and ability to maintain control. Under pressure they will say, 'it's my way or the highway'.

Many people, particularly at lower levels of development, find the simplistic polarised clarity offered by autocrats refreshing. Meetings with ten people when all the power rests with one forceful leader is at least straightforward – effectively creating a one-versus-nine decision-making governance process. However, as the world speeds up and becomes more complicated, command and control approaches often fail.[8] They fail either because of their inability to handle complexity or understand the VUCA (volatile, uncertain, complex and ambiguous) conditions or they fail because they put far too much pressure on one person. This has been called the 'responsibility virus'.[9] If one leader creates a power hierarchy around themselves so they can make

---

[8] Seddon, J. (2003) 'Freedom from Command and Control: A better way to make the work work', Buckingham: Vanguard Consulting Ltd.

[9] Martin, R. (2003) *The Responsibility Virus: How control freak, shrinking violets - and the rest of us - can harness the power of true partnership*, New York: Basic Books.

all the calls then this often induces an accountability vacuum and passivity in others. Phil Clarke, the former CEO of Tesco is a classic example of an autocratic leader who systematically parted company with the cadre of senior managers who had run Tesco under Sir Terry Leahy.[10] The autocrats are not interested in succession or sustainability to any great degree; in fact they often take pride in how their system struggles once they have gone because this proves, in their mind at least, what a hero they were. Much has been written on some of the less positive personality traits of autocratic politicians and business leaders often referred to as the 'dark triad of narcissism, Machiavellianism and psychopathy'.[11]

Often enamoured with their own abilities, these hubristic leaders are the ones who are most susceptible to the corrupting nature of power.[12] It is no wonder that many politicians and celebrities get on very well with each other as they are often operating from the same level of development. In fact, it is not uncommon for politicians to move into the world of celebrity and vice versa.

Despite the massive benefits of strong leadership, and its accelerating nature on society it is often the excesses of the all-powerful leader that trigger a collective revolution that overthrows that leader and puts power back in the hands of the collective. The downside of any developmental stage always provides the evolutionary impulse for the emergence of the next stage in development – Coalition.

---

[10] Felsted, A. (2014) 'Philip Clarke failed to build on Leahy legacy at Tesco', *The Financial Times*, accessed 28 December 2015, www.ft.com/cms/s/0/34b67a7e-109e-11e4-812b-00144feabdc0.html#axzz3mjjKQxMV

[11] James, O. (2014) *Office Politics: How to Thrive in a World of Lying, Backstabbing and Dirty Tricks*, London: Vermillion.

[12] Desai, M. (2015) *Hubris: Why Economists Failed to Predict the Crisis and How to Avoid the Next One*, New Haven: Yale University Press.
Owen, D. (2007) *The Hubris Syndrome: Bush, Blair & the Intoxication of Power*, London: Politicos Publishing.

Coalition – Two Heads Are Better Than One

In the early days of the developmental move away from the absolute power vested in one autocratic individual, a number of forms of power-sharing emerged. When a society is mismanaged for long enough by a corrupt individual eventually the collective creates a mechanism to curtail their powers or at least share some of their powers with others. There was no doubt that some of the earliest sovereigns ruled as autocrats but eventually the power was diffused across the king and the queen. When threatened with complete removal of decision-making power it would be a relatively short step to acquiesce to power sharing with a spouse, because at least you keep it in the family or 'firm', as some royal families refer to themselves.[13]

The decision-making power being vested in the king and the queen was a very early form of coalition or co-leadership. But this evolutionary step from autocracy to coalition was a very significant change in the history of decision-making dynamics. It represented the shift away from having one individual with absolute decision-making power and it established the principle that sharing power may actually produce better results than restricting power to one person. Such dilution of power from the one to the two can take some time to become established in any system.

Coalitions, of course, create their own unique dynamics. Monarchy coalitions create a 'court' with an increasing number of people vying for favour and patronage by either the king or the queen or preferably both. When there are two decision-makers in play reaching a conclusion becomes much more complicated,

---

[13] Mendick, R. (2012) 'The Queen gets a £44bn valuation for family "Firm"', *The Telegraph*, accessed 28 December 2015, www.telegraph.co.uk/news/uknews/the_queens_diamond_jubilee/9292607/The-Queen-gets-a-44bn-valuation-for-family-Firm.html

particularly when there is a surrounding 'court' of advisers and influencers on both sides. The benefit, however, of a decision-making coalition is that two heads are invariably better than one and most 'pairs' can embrace a greater degree of complexity than any one individual. This greater ability to navigate complexity is possible because two people will have different life experiences and can bring different perspectives to the same issue. It enables any problem to be seen from more than one vantage point and this can generate a more accurate view of reality thereby increasing the chances of a more effective decision.

The emergence of coalitions with their ability to handle greater levels of complexity reflected and supported the increasing complexity of society. Prior to the emergence of coalitions as a way of deciding, an intermediary decision-making mechanism had already emerged. That mechanism was the feudal system. This was a sort of halfway house between original autocratic monarchical power and the emerging rule by a sovereign coalition. While not a formal political system in itself, the feudal system of the Middle Ages supported the semi-autocratic rule of a warrior king through a set of reciprocal legal and military obligations that hinged around a three-tiered hierarchy of lords, vassals and fiefs.[14] This three-tiered decision-making system was anchored to property rights and the ability of the monarch and the feudal system to control property. Many developed nations have experienced their own version of a feudal system. Feudal systems still exist today in the hands of local chiefs in large parts of Africa.

The basic dynamic of the earliest coalitions shifted the decision-making mechanism from the one versus nine vote seen in autocracy to a two versus eight vote in co-leadership coalitions. In the modern world, most people have experienced the upside and the downside of this form of decision-making system with

[14] Ganshof, F.L .(1944) *Qu'est-ce que la féodalité*, translated into English by Philip Grierson as *Feudalism*, with a foreword by F.M. Stenton, 1st edn (1952) New York and London: Harper; 2nd edn (1961); 3rd edn (1976).

their parents. This is the rule of 'Mum and Dad' (assuming you were brought up with both, otherwise it was most likely autocracy). While there are real advantages of such a process compared to the dangers of dominator autocratic hierarchies there are also problems with co-led coalitions.

Coalitions do establish the principle of power-sharing but they also plant the seeds of divisiveness. There are now two powerful views present in the debate, which can lead to divided loyalties. In fact, setting up a system that is 'parented' by two individuals who hold the decision-making power creates dependants or 'children' of the other possible stakeholders. As a result, one of the unintended consequences of such a system is that it can foster increased levels of immaturity. It also sows the seed of political manoeuvring as immature stakeholders seek to play one decision-maker off against the other; drive a wedge between the two or position themselves with the other 'children' in the system to create greater leverage on one of the coalition decision-makers.

One of the key features of the feudal system, a forerunner to the sovereign coalition, was the central importance of property and loyalty. When coalition emerged, loyalty became even more important to the decision-making process than it had been in feudal systems. Coalition can only work if people remain loyal to their side. Coalition, by definition, establishes the importance of political affiliation and the role of the court or lobby. While the society and the decisions required within that society remain relatively simple, the power of the lobby or court is not that great. However, as society evolves and the number and complexity of issues increases, the sovereign decision makers will invariably find themselves out of their depth – both in terms of time to address the issues and in comprehending the issues themselves. These twin challenges often spawned the advent of 'special advisers'. Those in charge, initially the king and the queen and subsequently the head of each coalition party, cannot be seen to lack knowledge and so would need to be 'briefed'. Of course, the quality of specialist advisers varies significantly. If the decision-makers themselves lacked maturity then the specialist advisers are often no more than cronies or 'yes' men and women who fluff up their ego and source or commission reports that simply validate the decision-makers' original opinion.

As the range of issues that need to be decided upon increased, rules had to be established to guide how decisions were reached and the role of the 'court' in those decisions. In the very early forms of coalition loyalty, the rules around participation were often seen as more important than the decision itself. Most gangs and mobsters operate under very strict and rigid rules and codes of behaviour – such as the Mafia's 'Omerta', or code of silence where members must not reveal or talk about the criminal network. The system depends on the brutal imposition of rules around loyalty and breaking the code is also usually met with swift and severe penalty – usually a flamboyantly sticky end!

There are, however, plenty of examples of healthy coalitions that work well in the modern world where two titular heads drive the system forward. In business, this can be the CEO and CFO or the CEO and COO. In government, this could be the Prime Minster and the Chancellor. It may be the President and the Vice President or the President and the leader of the House, or the First Lady.

There are a number of variants of coalition or co-leadership that have emerged in different parts of the world. When the decision-making is shared by more than a couple of power brokers it is quite common to find an 'oligarchy'. Russia is at times described as a Putin-led autocracy and at times a country run by a handful of rich oligarchs. As you will recall, former US President Jimmy Carter suggested that the USA is no longer a functioning democracy and has collapsed back into an oligarchy run by a handful of billionaires.[15] Some have argued that the entire planet

[15] Zuesse, E. (2015) 'Jimmy Carter Is Correct That the U.S. Is No Longer a Democracy', *The Huffington Post*, accessed 18 December 2015, www.huffingtonpost.com/eric-zuesse/jimmy-carter-is-correct-t_b_7922788.html

is run by a 'Super Class' operating at this level of development.[16] Given the level of inequality in more developed societies, it is not difficult to believe that we may be regressing from more evolved democratic systems into a planet run by the privileged few.[17] According to Winnie Byanyima, Executive Director of Oxfam International, 80 billionaires enjoy the same amount of wealth as the bottom half of the planet.[18] As well as the huge social and moral implications of such inequality it also poses a serious risk to economic growth.[19]

In other parts of the world, we have seen religious theocracies emerge, where the power is in the hands of a small coalition of religious leaders. Theocracies may be more dangerous to the future of the planet because the religious coalition often believes that it takes its authority from a divine leader, who by definition, cannot be mistaken.

The common denominator for all these political decision-making variants is the realisation that power must be shared by an elite and rules must be in place to prevent autocratic dominator hierarchies from developing. However, some of the less evolved versions of this level of political development are often held together by exactly that – an autocrat or dominating figure who the coalition has acquiesced to. But even these examples will

[16] Rothkopt, D. (2009) *Superclass: The Global Power Elite and the World They Are Making*, New York: Farrar, Straus and Giroux.

[17] Hanauer, N. (2014) 'The Pitchforks Are Coming... For Us Plutocrats', *Politico Magazine*, accessed 28 December 2015, www.politico. com/magazine/story/2014/06/the-pitchforks-are-coming-for-us-plutocrats-108014

[18] Byanyima, W. (2015) 'Richest 1% will own more than all the rest by 2016', Oxfam International, accessed 28 December 2015, www.oxfam.org/ en/pressroom/pressreleases/2015-01-19/richest-1-will-own-more-all-rest-2016

[19] Kennedy, S. and Martinuzzi, E. (2014) 'Davos Finds Inequality Its Business as Backlash Seen', Bloomberg Business, accessed 28 December 2015, www.bloomberg.com/news/articles/2014-01-23/davos-makes-inequality-its-business-as-political-backlash-seen

eventually mature as the collective gradually wrestle more power away from the autocrat and vest it in the coalition. One great advantage of the focus on rules is that it brings a degree of stability and sustainability. Change now requires not just a change in the opinion of the autocrat but a change to the rules and a change of the opinions of the members of the coalition. Often the decision-making power of the coalition is institutionalised in a constitution. Most developed nations have a constitution at the heart of their political system, with the exception of the UK, Israel and New Zealand.

The step change in stability and sustainability compared to autocracies meant that political systems at this level of development lasted centuries. Many countries are still largely operating from this level of development, albeit a slightly updated version. The primary learning from this level is that rules work. Over the years, such rule-based systems gradually develop by creating more and more rules to address the increasing complexity of the societies they are trying to govern. This resulted in the emergence of bureaucracies. Bureaucracies are the same developmental level as oligarchies, theocracies and coalitions but they are a slightly more mature version of this level of government in that they spread the decision-making power more widely within the political system. In bureaucracies the decision-making authority was no longer limited to the heads of an elite coalition, but spread across a number of bureaucratic divisions and they are alive and well in most modern societies.

Bureaucracies, like any new level of development, provide significant advantages over the previous level which is why they survive. But they also come with a new set of problems. As with every level, it is the problems of that level that provide the evolutionary stimulus for the emergence of a new form of government. The next level of governance was perhaps the most dramatic leap forward in the evolution of decision-making that the world had ever seen: democracy.

The Rise of Democracy, Freedom and the Final Frontier?

Most of us in the West have grown up with a story about democracy and how it is the most sophisticated governance system on the planet – the 'final frontier' and the ultimate form of governance. The narrative we have been fed is that all societies, as they evolve, will inevitably become capitalist, multi-party democracies, where all people vote and are 'free' to decide their own destiny along with many other untold benefits. Like all great stories, this narrative has some truth to it.

Democracy has delivered many wonderful things to the world including freedom in many dimensions, equality (at least in part) and improved civil rights. It is almost impossible to underestimate the benefits that democracy has brought to societies that have embraced this level of development. Democracy certainly allows a more sophisticated decision-making process than was available at the previous level of co-led coalition and its many variants; monarchy, oligarchy, theocracy, bureaucracy as well as other rule-constrained systems at this level such as Marxism, communism, socialism, totalitarianism or even a military junta. The evidence suggests that democracies are also, on average, richer than non-democracies, less likely to go to war and have a better record of fighting corruption.[20]

The narrative concludes that any nation that has not yet realised democracy is the answer has simply not yet seen the light. Given this story, it is not surprising that believers in democracy may want the world to benefit from it. The advocates of democracy have sought to export it to the world over the last 60 years. This export campaign has, in fact, been incredibly successful. The

---

[20] (2014) 'What's Gone Wrong with Democracy', *The Economist*, accessed 28 December 2015, www.economist.com/news/essays/21596796-democracy-was-most-successful-political-idea-20th-century-why-has-it-run-trouble-and-what-can-be-do

Figure 3.2 **The Evolution of Decision-making**

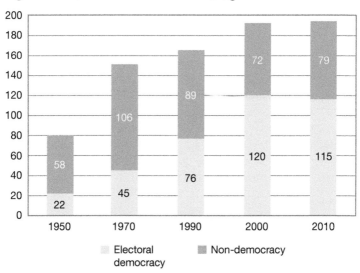

story of democracy became a best seller and has been exported by Western elites around the globe, sometimes by force. As a result, the number of 'democracies' on the planet increased from 45 in 1970 to 115 in 2010 (Figure 3.2).[21]

But the transition to democracy is often not that easy. There seems to be a dangerous pattern emerging in capital city after capital city. The people mass in the main square. The existing regime sends in its thugs to try to repel the crowd but if the crowd holds firm the thugs usually lose their nerve in the face of popular intransigence and global news coverage. The world then applauds the collapse of the autocratic or totalitarian regime and offers to help build a new democracy. But getting rid of a despot or a military junta is a lot easier than setting up a viable

---

[21] Li EX (2013) Li, E.X. (2013) 'A tale of two political systems', TED, accessed 27 December 2015, www.ted.com/talks/eric_x_li_a_tale_of_two_political_systems#t-281011

democratic alternative government. What normally happens is the new regime struggles, the economy flounders as the instability fails to attract desperately needed inward investment and the country descends into a worse state than it was before, frequently collapsing all the way back to mob rule. This has been the way with the Arab Spring and also to a large extent following the Ukraine's Orange revolution.

By the end of the twentieth century, we had seen the high tide mark for democracies. The story had taken hold in Germany after it had been scared by Nazism; in India, a rich country of poor people; and in South Africa, which had been disfigured by apartheid. As colonial powers withdrew from Africa and Asia, the number of democracies increased, although some embraced the story, rejected it and embraced it again. A number of autocracies, theocracies and oligarchies eventually gave way to democracy such as Greece (1974), Portugal (1975), Spain (1975), Argentina (1983), Brazil (1985) and Chile (1989) not to mention the immature democracies that emerged in Eastern Europe after the break-up of the old Soviet Union. At its peak in 2000, 63 per cent of the world had bought the democracy story.[22]

Since 2000, democracy has been losing much of its lustre. Besides Western Europe and North America, the commitment to democratic governance has definitely ebbed and flowed. Even in its stronghold in the West the narrative is looking increasingly outdated. As we pointed out in Chapter 2, whether many of the West's 'democratic elections' could even be described 'free and fair' is now highly debatable. Rather than the narrative being synonymous with freedom (which was a significant part of its appeal), Western democracy is looking increasingly synonymous with corruption, debt and dysfunction. Democracy is also guilty by association with its similarly tarnished sister – capitalism,

---

[22] (2014) 'What's Gone Wrong with Democracy', *The Economist*, accessed 28 December 2015, www.economist.com/news/essays/21596796-democracy-was-most-successful-political-idea-20th-century-why-has-it-run-trouble-and-what-can-be-do

itself increasingly under the spotlight and in urgent need of reinvention.[23]

There are probably two main reasons why the story of democracy is no longer selling: Firstly, democracy shot itself in the foot with the global financial crisis (GFC). Secondly, the rapid rise of an alternative narrative namely China and her escalating economic success.

For all its brilliance and its 'checks and balances', democracy failed to prevent the GFC. In Iceland, the people realised that this was not just a case of profound greed and self-interest in the banking sector but a fundamental lack of government attention, appropriate regulation and ethical commitment to the public good. Iceland took to the streets and the government fell – but more on that later.

The democratic narrative and the cause were not helped when most Western governments bailed-out their national banks on a massive scale. The lack of trust in elected representatives was further compounded when politicians refused to take a sufficiently tough line on bankers' pay and bonuses. All of this simply reinforced the sense of collusion in the public's mind and underpinned the fact that government, along with the media is one of the most mistrusted sectors in most countries.[24]

China too raises questions about the validity of democracy – certainly as an engine for economic growth and prosperity.

---

[23] Mackay, J. and Sisodia, R. (2014) *Conscious Capitalism*, Boston: Harvard Business School Publishing.

[24] Edelman Trust Barometer 2015, accessed 28 December 2015, www.edelman.co.uk/work/ and www.edelman.com/insights/intellectual-property/2015-edelman-trust-barometer/trust-around-world/

Chinese Bureaucratic Meritocracy

China is an incredibly interesting combination of two developmental levels. It operates a very rigid rule-based bureaucracy with lashings of capitalism and meritocracy thrown in for good measure. This very heavily managed bureaucratic meritocracy has enabled China to achieve a great deal in a relatively short space of time.

At the height of its power, American democracy doubled living standards in thirty years. By contrast, China has doubled living standards every ten years for thirty years. China is far from a Utopian paradise but according to political scientist Eric X Li, in the 30 years between 1970 and 2010, China went from one of the poorest agricultural countries in the world to the second largest economy. During the same time frame, 80 per cent of the world's poverty alleviation happened in China. Following the death of Chairman Mao, and the subsequent recognition of the failure of such an autocratic system, China has evolved and in so doing it created the circumstances that allowed 650 million people to lift themselves out of poverty. There is also an escalating middle class living in increasing prosperity. According to Pew Research Center, 85 per cent of the Chinese population are satisfied with the country's general direction compared to just 26 per cent in the US and 19 per cent in the UK. Seventy-five per cent of the population think they are better off than they were five years ago compared to just 28 per cent in the US and 22 per cent in the UK. Eighty-two per cent expect the future to be better compared to just 33 per cent in the US and 17 per cent in the UK. These statistics are telling in terms of China's on-going evolution.

From the outside, we often view China as still being a communist autocracy, a single party state. It is a single party state but it would be wrong to assert that it still runs as an autocracy. It is highly functioning because of its unique blend of bureaucracy, meritocracy and its clear common objective: the unity of the nation.

China's highest ruling body, the Politburo has 25 members. In the eighteenth Politburo, elected in 2007, just five members came from a background of privilege. The rest, including the President and the Premier, came from ordinary backgrounds. In the larger Central Committee of 300 members, the proportion of people born into power and wealth was even smaller. Most senior Chinese officials have worked for several decades to demonstrate their competence before ever reaching senior political positions.[25] In China, not only are the people making the decisions the best people to make those decisions, having taken decades to acquire their knowledge and skill, but they are unhampered by the endless politics of politics. They don't need to take their eye off the problem to campaign, 'press the flesh' or kiss babies. Instead they are free to focus on finding the best solution and implement that solution faster. The Chinese elite would argue that their model (with tight control by the Communist Party, relentlessly focused on recruiting talented people into its upper ranks) is more efficient than democracy and less susceptible to gridlock.

Of course, China is not without its problems including the continued suppression of free speech and all sorts of human rights violations as well as some questionable foreign policy issues but, in just two years China has extended pension coverage to 240 million people in rural regions – far more than the total number of people covered by America's entire public-pension system. China's success in tackling major issues over the last thirty years has even led to a number of Chinese academics advocating their system as a legitimate alternative to Western democracy. Although China's bureaucratic meritocracy has avoided a great many of the endemic problems that constrain democracies in the West, it is not an evolutionary step forward from Western democracy. But, it may partly explain why the Chinese model is so attractive to many emerging African nations – it presents a

[25] Li, E.X. (2013) 'A tale of two political systems', TED, accessed 28 December 2015, www.ted.com/talks/eric_x_li_a_tale_of_two_political_systems#t-336802

way to transition from the autocratic power in the hands of one to a strong bureaucracy, imposing some rules that make it less autocratic and more structured. This is a more logical evolution than going straight to democracy. In addition, China's greater collective orientation may resonate more deeply with Africa's strong tribal heritage than the more individualistic Western democratic model.

A system that is based on a majority vote, as we pointed out in Chapter 2, is highly susceptible to manipulation. In fact manipulation or 'gaming' the system is a predictable dynamic that occurs in any system at this level of development. Such a system naturally attracts gamblers and gamers, as well as sharks, bullies and autocrats, who all believe they are smart enough to 'beat the house'. In the West, most of the gamers of the system are big business and people with money.

In contrast, a bureaucratic meritocracy side-steps many of these issues, particularly when it is heavily controlled and has a healthy dose of rules (carried over from the previous communist levels of development). Together with the recruitment of the nation's best university talent, it can create powerful change capability. It is this blend of some of the more helpful elements of the previous levels of the decision-making system that have underpinned China's phenomenal success.

China's achievements are enhanced by comparison to the poor performance of a number of established and fledgling democracies which have shot themselves in the foot over the last 20 years. For example, after the fall of the Berlin Wall, Russia, under Boris Yeltsin, looked like it might stumble towards democratic process. But Yeltsin lost Russia to Putin in 1999 and the former KGB agent, with a penchant for baring his chest and pumping iron, muzzled the press, imprisoned his opponents and proceeded to take the country back to autocracy with him as the new tsar.

The Last Days of Democracy?

If we look around the world, there are a number of democratic systems that are under pressure. For example, the fledgling democratic forces in the Ukraine during the 'Orange Revolution' were usurped by Russian interference. In the 2013 elections, the people installed an oligarch in Kiev who has now become locked in an autocratic battle with the Russians over the annexing of the Crimea not to mention the Russian inspired ethnocentric violence in the east of the country. Similar problems with emergent democracies have followed Argentina and Venezuela.

In 1983, Argentines went to the polls and elected Raúl Alfonsin of the Radical Civic Union. Found to be fair and honest by international observers, Alfonsin won 53 per cent of the popular vote. Alfonsin marked a new era in Argentinean politics. He did however face considerable challenges to consolidate democracy, achieve economic development in a country devastated by military dictatorship, human rights violations, high inflation and huge external debts. Hopes for democracy were high but with such a mountain to scale progress did not go to plan.[26] Successive governments and leaders have appeared more autocratic than democratic with Alfonsin's successor Carlos Menem more than happy to push through his controversial agenda with the help of presidential powers and 'emergency decrees'. Various leaders have struggled to get a handle on grave economic problems, inflation and unemployment although the current Kirchner government has presided over economic improvement aided by the restructuring of foreign debt.

In Venezuela, Hugo Chavez was elected president in December 1998 based largely on three election promises: convening a Constituent Assembly to write a new constitution and improve the state, fighting poverty and social exclusion, and

---

[26] Tedesco, L. (1999) *Democracy in Argentina: Hope and Disillusion*, New York: Frank Cass Publishers.

eliminating corruption. So what happened? The Constituent Assembly became a vehicle to destroy all existing political institutions and replace them with a bureaucracy to exercise his wishes. Poverty and social exclusion remained a problem and government corruption was as high as ever.[27] Today, the nation is still essentially locked in a struggle between the defenders of democracy and current president Nicolás Maduro who leans more toward the autocratic leadership style of Chavez, who died in 2013 shortly after being re-elected. In February 2015, the Mayor of Caracas, Antonio Ledezma was arrested on Maduro's orders for 'crimes against the peace and security of the nation and against the constitution'. This move is widely seen as a sign of a regime losing its grip on power and desperately trying to reverse the tide by force.[28]

These nations and many like them disfigured their democratic process rather than replacing it, further undermining the global democratic narrative.[29] Hopes of democracy taking hold in Egypt after Mubarak's military junta was ousted in 2011 were short-lived when the Muslim Brotherhood reverted to ethnocentric aggression prompting the military to step back in, in July 2013. They arrested Egypt's first democratically elected president, imprisoned leading members of the Brotherhood and killed hundreds of demonstrators. Along with the civil war in Syria and the collapse into anarchy in Libya, the hope that the Arab Spring would lead to a flowering of democracy across the Middle East has been replaced with the realisation that democracy can

[27] Coronel, G. (2008) 'The Corruption of Democracy in Venezuela', The Cato Institute, accessed 28 December 2015, www.cato.org/publications/commentary/corruption-democracy-venezuela

[28] 'Sliding toward dictatorship', The Economist, 20 February 2015, accessed 28 December 2015, http://www.economist.com/news/americas/21644540-arrest-mayor-caracas-sign-regime-will-do-whatever-it-takes-hold

[29] Ferguson, R.J. (2002) 'The Struggle for Democracy: Chile and Argentina', accessed 28 December 2015, www.international-relations.com/WbLatinAmerica/Lec9.htm

only develop if the conditions are right. Similar stories on the failure of the democratic narrative can be seen in South Africa (one party state),[30] Turkey (autocratic corruption),[31] Cambodia,[32] Thailand[33] and Bangladesh.[34] Even in its European heartland, democratic forces are seriously suffering and are on the edge of collapsing. The European Parliament is widely despised; the UK is reconsidering their membership again; and the European centralists are seen as elitist and out of touch with popular opinion.[35] In many European countries, intended integration has instead ignited greater ethnocentric forces.

The danger in all this is that, as the democratic narrative collapses globally, we revert back to ethnocentric divisions and all the problems that *they* create. Given the crisis, a number of authors have advocated that we need to look again at the conditions necessary for democracy to properly take root, or alternatively we need to 'reboot' or 'rethink' democracy in some way.[36]

---

[30] Gevisser, M. (2009) 'South Africa: beyond a one-party state', *The Guardian,* accessed 28 December 2015, www.theguardian.com/commentisfree/2009/apr/20/south-africa-anc-election-democracy

[31] Vick, K. (2014) 'How Erdogan's Troubles Are Good for Turkey', *Time Magazine*, accessed 28 December 2015, http://world.time.com/2014/01/02/how-erdogans-troubles-are-good-for-turkish-democracy/

[32] Banyan Blog (2014) 'The future of democracy in Cambodia: Trying hard to smile', *The Economist*, accessed 28 December 2015, www.economist.com/blogs/banyan/2014/01/future-democracy-cambodia

[33] The Editorial Board (2014) 'Democracy in Thailand, Interrupted', *New York Times*, accessed 28 December 2015, www.nytimes.com/2014/02/04/opinion/democracy-in-thailand-interrupted.html?_r=0

[34] Ramachandran, S. (2014) 'Bangladesh: Democracy in Peril', *The Diplomat*, accessed 28 December 2015, http://thediplomat.com/2014/01/bangladesh-democracy-in-peril/

[35] Huhne, C. (2014) 'Our MEPs really are worth your vote', *The Guardian*, accessed 28 December 2015, www.theguardian.com/commentisfree/2014/may/18/mep-member-european-parliament-vote

[36] Arriaga, M. (2014) *Rebooting Democracy: A Citizen's Guide to Reinventing Politics*, London: Thistle Publishing.

The key challenge we face is that it is impossible to successfully skip a developmental level. Therefore, trying to install democracy in a society largely run by autocrats is almost certainly going to fail. There has to be a period where power is shared across a small group or coalition first (whether oligarchs, bureaucrats, theocrats, a communist politburo or a military elite.) This developmental power base will then create the societal structures that will ultimately be needed for democracy to function. Coalitions also create the societal rules that will provide an infrastructure that will prevent democracy from collapsing back to autocracy or tribalism. For example, coalitions break down complex problems into bite-sized pieces. They will, in time, reduce the monarchical 'court' into the three separate pieces, which eventually evolve into the three arms of government (legislature, the executive and judiciary). They will eventually see the value of the separation of church and state.

In addition to coalitions establishing the infrastructure that democracies will need, the dysfunction of co-leadership also creates the evolutionary momentum and internal motivation that spawns the evolution to democracy in the first place. The downside of a coalition is stalemate, as the two (or several) views in opposition to each other can't be reconciled. The deadlock slows decision-making to such a crawl that it creates a strong desire for change to overcome the perpetual logjams. If the frustration at the lack of progress doesn't provoke the desire to take a developmental leap forward then it is the tyranny of bureaucratic rules, excess process and procedures that sows the seeds for change.

If we understand the healthy precursors to democracy and make sure that when democracy starts to emerge we don't erode the infrastructures or deregulate the rules that provide societal or system stability then democracy is likely to sustain. If we also encourage meritocracy, greater pragmatism and inclusion then we may create the conditions for democracy to not only succeed but to create a platform for the next developmental leap beyond democracy – social democracy, or sociocracy.

Social Democracy and Sociocracy

The failures of democracy and its fall from grace need not result in a regression to an earlier form of governance and decision-making and all the problems that this would bring. Instead the failures of democracy could spawn, as did the shortcomings of every previous developmental level, a step forward into the next evolutionary stage.

At least this is true in principle but history has already shown us that the next stage of decision-making sophistication beyond democracy can itself be problematic and become entrenched in slow decision-making and stalled progress. This 'failure' can further reinforce the belief that we need to reinvent democracy because it may be the best available option we will ever find. However, take heart, a quantum leap forward awaits those that are prepared to look beyond democracy and its more sophisticated sister social democracy or sociocracy (more on that later).

Social democracy or sociocracy emerges out of dysfunction of the previous level, in this case democracy. Every new level inevitably transcends the problems of the previous level while including the benefits of each level. As we've explained, democracy is a system that can be gamed. In such a system, the currency often becomes Machiavellian manipulation and manoeuvring. There is a belief that the end always justifies the means. Anyone who disagrees with this 'do whatever it takes to win' philosophy is either accused of being 'out of touch with reality' (more specifically the reality at this level), a 'liberal' or weak.

Elitism abounds in democracy because there is now a malleable system that can be bent to the will of the few who know how to 'play the game'. Arguments are leveraged to make the case for control to be in the hands of the few so they can achieve their own personal objectives and the goals of the 'players' are usually money, power or possessions. This gaming of the financial systems is exactly what caused the GFC. In response to the economic crisis some suggested that we simply reimpose 'the rules'. This would have been a regressive step that would, in the absence of other measures, certainly have failed. The inherent financial inequity fostered by a democratic society leads to all sorts of global anomalies such as the prosecution of bankers in some countries (Iceland) but not other countries (USA, UK). Although regulation has tightened post 2008 little has really changed. The gaming continues,[37] Libor and other banking scandals continue and have now even appeared in the bastion of reliability: Germany's car manufacturer Volkswagen. Many of the conditions that caused the GFC in the first place still exist or are getting worse, causing some to suggest that we are in for another financial crisis driven by the excessive levels of private debt that exist in all developed economies.[38]

Sociocracy emerges in part to address all the inequities that democracy fosters. One of the driving forces for social democracy is the increasing abhorrence of the marginalisation of large sections of society and a realisation that if we continue to privilege the tiny minority excessively then ultimately this will destabilise the whole of society.[39] There is a wealth of data to suggest that societies with greater levels of inequality do badly on a whole raft of measures including educational attainment, infant mortality, adult health and happiness.[40]

---

[37] Duke, S. (2015) 'Standard Chartered faces new Iran fines', *The Sunday Times*, accessed 28 December 2015, www.thesundaytimes.co.uk/sto/business/Finance/article1603079.ece

[38] Dent, H.S. (2105) *The Demographic Cliff: How to Survive and Prosper During the Great Deflation Ahead*, New York: Portfolio Penguin

[39] Reich, R.B. (2012) 'Aftershock: The Next Economy and America's Future', accessed 28 December 2015, www.youtube.com/watch?v=f4ZTwPsmpnc

[40] Wilkinson, R. and Pickett, K. (2010) *The Spirit Level: Why Equality is Better for Everyone*, London: Penguin.

Social democracy seeks to build on the very positive aspects of democracy while also maintaining the rules and principles that made the earlier developmental versions of coalition effective and bring more sophistication to both. A number of countries have already developed versions of social democracy or established social democratic parties. Unfortunately, some of these parties and practices were nothing more than old school autocrats, bureaucratic oligarchs, or democratic gamers – wolves in sheep's clothing.

True Social Democracy seeks to involve many others in the decision-making process and is therefore more egalitarian than its democratic predecessor. At the collective, inclusive level of social democracy there is often a shift toward the 'green' environmental agenda as the collective seek solutions for the sake of everyone not just a select few. The approach is genuinely more caring, caring for people as well as caring for the planet.

There are many examples of this type of governance in continental Europe including Denmark, Sweden, Germany and the Netherlands. In the Netherlands for instance they use the 'polder model' – a term first used to describe the acclaimed Dutch version of consensus-based economic and social policy making of the 1980s and 1990s. It is described with phrases like 'a pragmatic recognition of pluriformity' and 'cooperation despite differences'.

In the 1940s, Holland was a fairly poor country. Then, in the 1950s, they discovered natural gas which turned the fortunes of the country around. The real consensual move that the Dutch government made at this time was to put those natural resources into the hands of the state – owned by everyone not private companies. Holland then used that revenue to build a welfare state and develop the infrastructure and services in the country for everyone.[41] Norway also did something similar and has an education system, welfare and reform system that is the envy of the world. In fact because the emphasis is on the collective good not the individual good, such governance systems tend to have a significantly superior social welfare, healthcare and education systems.

This consensus-based approach can also bring greater stability and minimise the combative and competitive aspects of democracy. But sociocracy *can* stifle progress. There are certainly many people around the world, especially those operating from the previous form of achievement-focused democracy, that look at the social democracy of some countries in mainland Europe and believe it is failing.

The main challenge slowing a more widespread evolution to social democracy is that those countries operating under social democracy have not produced results significantly better than democracy and so there is no compelling incentive to provoke a rethink of the democracy narrative. For most observers and commentators, the kind of government that emerges at this level is also not clearly distinguishable from what already existed. Despite its potential, sociocracy has not really produced a step change in the sophistication of decision-making and has not created a new system more capable of embracing the increased complexity of the planet.

In theory, successful sociocracies should create a mature coalition of forces that proactively seek to take a more pluralistic approach. The social coalitions that are created at this level of development are more complex than the coalition seen at the earlier level of development. They should be able to embrace more complexity than monarchy, oligarchy, bureaucracy, communism,

---

[41] It should be noted that the welfare state became much too large due to an overly optimistic view of the gas proceeds, causing significant economic and social issues in the 1970s. The Netherlands further built its wealth on a more competitive economic base, particularly in exports.

fundamentalism, or totalitarianism, and certainly more capable than the sort of two-headed dysfunctional pact that developed after the 2010 UK election. Real sociocracy is more nuanced than this because it is borne out of the failure of democracy. After the 2010 UK election, the British people experienced a 'hung parliament' – the first in 36 years. The Conservative party joined forces with the Liberal Democrats to gain a parliamentary majority ending 13 years of Labour government. Each party had, at times, very different views on policy but the way the democratic system was structured meant that the parties had to sit down and discuss the points of difference to come to some sort of compromise. But this was not a sociocratic integration of diverse perspectives. Rather it was either a democratic horse trade for the swing votes within the coalition, or if that failed it became a principled stand-off and ultimately an autocratic power battle with the Tories increasingly flexing their muscles. It was not a genuine coming together with a pluralistic desire to embrace the difference and generate a more sophisticated answer for the sake of the nation.[42]

The reason that many attempts at sociocracy fail to deliver on their potential is that they often get stuck in the swamp of consensus. A desire for inclusivity starts an endless debate to reach agreement but with no one able to drive integration of diverse opinion. As a result, discussions become circular with each party stating and restating their perspective in the hope that the other side will capitulate. Since there is often an implicit understanding that such capitulation would not be a good outcome, the conversation gets stuck. Part of the problem is that the protagonists are often insufficiently mature to appreciate that compromise normally means one side effectively imposes its view on the other side and they just surrender. Such a 'win-lose' dynamic ultimately results in a 'lose-lose' outcome. The side that surrenders never fully engages with the outcome and often secretly plots against it so the imposed outcome rarely comes to

---

[42] Personal conversation between Alan Watkins and Lord Owen (2013) on the internal dynamics within the UK coalition.

pass anyway so both sides lose.

For sociocracy to actually work it is necessary to create an integrated view that transcends and includes the diverse perspectives in the room, i.e. a natural hierarchy. Unfortunately the very idea of hierarchy repels most participants because they have only ever experienced 'dominator hierarchies', where one party held power over the other; where one side was in control and the other side was submissive.

But not all hierarchies are bad. Healthy 'growth hierarchies' exist in nature. Thus organisms transcend and include cells which transcend and include nuclei which transcend and include molecules which transcend and include atoms and so on. Molecules don't dominate or exclude atoms, they embrace and include them. Each higher level is therefore more and more inclusive and capable of an increasing embrace and increasing compassion. This is the exact opposite of a dominator hierarchy. If we were to look at a corrupt dictatorship, even in the modern world – the higher someone moves in those hierarchies, the more corrupt power they have, the more they can terrorise, oppress, dominate and control more and more people. All driven by the dictator's pathological power drives.

Social democracy can go one of two ways. It can collapse back and reinforce the validity of the democratic narrative in that democracy is the best we can hope for or it can set the stage for a monumental leap forward in the sophistication of decision-making. A level of sophistication that is both disruptive and transformational in equal measure. A system that when effectively installed can literally help reinvent governance and organisations.[43] This system is Holacracy.[44]

[43] Laloux, F. (2014) *Reinventing Organizations: A Guide to Creating Organizations Inspired by the Next Stage in Human Consciousness*, Brussels: Nelson Parker.

[44] Robertson, B.J. (2015) *Holacracy: The Revolutionary Management System that Abolishes Hierarchy*, New York: Portfolio Penguin.

Holacratic Governance

The term Holon was coined by Arthur Koestler to describe something that is itself a *whole* and simultaneously a *part* of some other whole.[45] Taken from the Greek word Holos meaning whole, a holon recognises that everything that exists, from a neutron to a nation, is not only a whole entity in its own right but it is also a part of something greater. This greater whole is itself a 'part' of something greater again. This whole/part relationship holds true up and down the scale and is deeply relevant to governance and decision-making. For example, a government think tank may be a separate entity in its own right but it is also part of a government department. That department is a whole entity in its own right, with its own budget and responsibilities but is also part of the larger government. Holacratic governance therefore offers a complete and practical system for honouring every aspect of the system, its wholeness and its parts. It enables more sophisticated decision-making to evolve in all areas of the system whether that system is a business, a school, a church group or a government.

Holacracy itself is a term coined by the founders of Holacracy One in the US. They describe it as a 'comprehensive practice for structuring, governing, and running an organisation. It replaces today's top-down predict-and-control paradigm with a new way of distributing power and achieving control. It is a new "operating system" which instils rapid evolution in the core processes of an organisation.'[46]

Over the last five years I (AW) have been helping organisations understand the principles of holacratic governance and embed some of the core practices within key executive teams. It has proved immensely helpful for speeding up decision-making, particularly on complex issues, and it helps to sort out many of

---

[45] Koestler, A. (1967) *The Ghost in the Machine*, Macmillan.

[46] Trademark of Holacracy One in the USA.

the chronic issues that have been slowing organisations down and reducing their effectiveness. Of course, these challenges are the same challenges facing government – the ability to make faster, higher quality consensus decisions in response to escalating complexity and a smorgasbord of wicked problems that desperately need resolution.

At the core, holocratic process requires an organisation to change the way they approach decision-making and governance. Most organisations already have numerous 'governance committees'. However, when you dig into the work that these committees are actually doing it is usually focused on compliance with various regulatory frameworks. If they are not embroiled in compliance work then the committees are often engaged in operational oversight to ensure projects are being managed effectively. Of course, businesses and government must operate within their own regulatory framework and comply with the law but this is not governance. Similarly, operational oversight is vital but it is not governance. Effective governance answers a series of specific questions including:

1. What decisions are needed?
2. Who will make these decisions?
3. How will the decisions be made?
4. What decision-making process will we follow?
5. What policies will guide our work together?
6. How can we change existing answers?

In many organisations and governments, it is difficult to figure out where the decisions get made. One of the problems with democracy is that decisions are made behind closed doors, out of sight and unreported. In businesses, the decisions are often made by the CEO in consultation with one or two others (chairman, a non-executive director, the CFO or COO) and not by the executive board. When the debate actually occurs at the executive board level it may already be a done deal. Or, if the decision is not already made but the debate gets stuck on a tricky issue, the CEO will suggest, 'let's take that one offline' – a euphemism for 'I'll decide later'. The leader will essentially subvert the decision-making process and the decision will be made elsewhere between themselves and one or two others.

Such obfuscation about who decides in government was clearly at play when a Freedom of Information request obtained by UK human rights group *Reprieve* revealed that British combat pilots had been covertly embedded in American and Canadian coalition forces bombing targets in Syria without democratic sanction.[47]

Answering the specific governance questions also creates a very specific output. They allow you to:

1. Clarify all decisions-making forums and create any new necessary sub forums.
2. Define remit and limit authority of all forums.
3. Define reporting process, frequency and quality standards.
4. Establish meeting discipline and way of working.
5. Create new roles.
6. Establish clear accountabilities and assign any new accountabilities to existing roles.
7. Establish new policies or changes to existing policies.

Holacracy seeks to clearly define where all the key decisions get made and delegate the decision-making authority as close to the action as possible. In order to handle the level of complexity that exists in government and business, there are a number of other key principles that make holacracy a more sophisticated system that can help us succeed in the VUCA world.

---

[47] Staples, D. (2015) 'UK pilots authorized to bomb Syria without democratic sanction – Reprieve', RT, accessed 28 December 2015, www.rt.com/uk/310080-uk-pilots-authorized-to-bomb/

Principles of Holacratic Governance:

- Must move from 'predict and control' to 'sense and response' to enable speed and agility.

- Appreciate that we can change any decision at any time.

- Solutions only need to be 'good enough for now' (not perfect).

- Change the way we see 'problems', people can 'hold tensions' on behalf of the team and organisation, they are not seen as 'Bob's problem' rather Bob senses a tension within the system. Thus tensions get channelled into organisational learning and a change in how things are done (organisational development).

- Appreciate that integration of multiple perspectives is not the same as forced inclusivity.

One of the core holacratic processes that facilitates faster, more sophisticated decision-making is 'integrative decision-making' (IDM). The value of IDM is that it transcends democratic process which often produces a 6v4 vote. The goal of the IDM process is to create complete alignment within a team and generate a 10v0 vote. This is achieved without getting stuck in the consensual hell of sociocracy. Being able to rapidly reach a genuinely collective, mutually agreed upon 10v0 decision within an executive board, a governmental committee, or any team, saves a huge amount of time and energy. It is no longer necessary to neutralise the effects of the minority that are unhappy with the decision because no one has to 'toe the party line' and therefore feels the need to plot against the outcome. Of course, many politicians and business leaders do not stick to such rules and often attempt to slow or subvert the outcome by working against the decision or blocking its implementation because they were outvoted.

Holacracy is however, more than just a decision-making process – it's a way of dealing with incredibly complex situations and decisions by facilitating a much greater level of inclusion, integration and feedback within the system.[48] Without IDM and many more holocratic processes, governance can so easily regress to simpler operational oversight conversations typical in democracies or compliance debates more common in bureaucracies or even provoke autocratic vetoes.

However, the downside of holacracy is that it can be quite complex and difficult to implement on a large scale. While it can be implemented within a government committee and can drive profound benefits for all those within the system, the decision-making power is still held by a few individuals. Crowdocracy transcends this and genuinely gives the decision-making power to all the people.

Crowdocracy

Crowdocracy includes the upside of holacracy while also honouring the benefits of all previous decision-making approaches from autocracy to democracy to holacracy. All these approaches can still be utilised when appropriate, and still exist in crowdocratic systems. But crowdocracy aims to take us from the 10v0 holacratic outcome to very high levels of alignment on a much greater scale. It taps into the wisdom of the crowd and avoids decision-making by an elite, a self-selected few, be they autocrats, democrats or any sort of 'representatives' – elected or otherwise. It offers us a new model for rapid decision-making on the wicked problems we face. But if we are to embrace crowdocracy and all the immense potential it brings we must, as with all previous levels of development, understand the

---

[48] Robertson, B.J. (2015) *Holacracy: The Revolutionary Management System that Abolishes Hierarchy*, New York: Portfolio Penguin.

conditions that have to be in place to make it work so it can deliver on its promise. A failure to do so runs the risk of crowdocracy going the same way of democracy. Like all government systems crowdocracy cannot be imposed; it must be embraced.

Of course, the logistics of such an idea have, until now, been utterly impossible. The democratic system we now find ourselves in is the direct result of that operational impossibility. We can't ask all the people because there are too many people to ask and even if we could, we couldn't coordinate the opinion to facilitate mutually agreed majority decisions. We elect representatives and cross our fingers that they actually represent us. They don't and often can't so we are constantly disappointed.

But the world has changed. The obstacles to mass democratic scale participation have been removed. Real majority rule, not hypothetical or ideological rule of the majority is possible. A government in which the supreme power *is* seriously vested in the people and exercised by them directly or indirectly through technology and a shared, mutually agreed and rigorously applied constitution is possible.

What we are suggesting is the end of politics as we know it – an evolution that will fundamentally change democracy forever. And it is only just become possible because of two separate emerging realities.

Access to More Developed Thinking

In 1887, when Lord Acton made his famous statement about power and suggested that 'Great men are almost always bad men' – he was probably right! But as a species we have come a long way since then.

Much has been written about the rate of change most modern

societies are going through.[49] We really do live in a VUCA world. The technological dimensions of this change are all around us. But there has also been an evolution in the sophistication of our thinking. This human developmental leap is partly accelerated by the fact that we all now have access to the smartest thinking around the world at the touch of a button.

In addition, an increasing number of individuals and organisations have realised that 'vertical development' rather than learning curves and learning organisations are the true source of competitive advantage in the VUCA world.[50] Horizontal development is the acquisition of skills, knowledge and experience or 'learning'. Learning may allow us to become more proficient but vertical development unlocks significantly higher levels of capability that can step change performance. Learning 'adds more apps' whereas vertical development upgrades our operating system.[51]

This human evolution significantly improves various human capabilities such as the quality of our thinking, the sophistication in our value systems, maturity of ego, the degree of emotional intelligence, behavioural effectiveness and the extent of our connectivity which cumulatively underpins the political systems and governance mechanisms we create in society. As a result, we are much better placed to not only develop a new way of governing but make such a system a reality.

Our development as individuals underpins the development of our social structures and the way we organise ourselves. Thus our evolution is both individual and collective. As we evolve through

---

[49] Kurweil, R. (2001) 'The Law of Accelerating Returns', 7 March 2001, accessed 28 December 2015, www.kurzweilai.net/the-law-of-accelerating-returns

[50] Watkins, A. (2015) *4D Leadership*, London: Kogan Page. Petrie, N. (2011) *Future Trends in Leadership Development: A White Paper*, Greensborough, North Carolina: Center for Creative Leadership.

[51] Watkins, A. (2015) *4D Leadership*, London: Kogan Page.

well-defined stages of adult development, we don't lose access to the capabilities of the previous level –we simple transcend and include them. Each new emergent level of development is not 'better' than the previous level. Each level has its advantages and disadvantages, but each new level has a much greater capacity to handle complexity. The more developed we become, the more sophisticated our thinking becomes and the more perspectives we are able to take.

What makes crowdocracy possible today and simply inconceivable just ten years ago is that there are now enough human beings who are capable of handling much greater degrees of complexity. When we reach higher levels of development, we are finally able to recognise that each of the previous levels is only partially correct and offers some benefits but also some limitations. As we develop, we transcend the 'right or wrong' binary thinking that constrains most political debates and we develop the maturity to recognise that every level suffers from some degree of myopia. But as we evolve to more advanced levels of development we become much more innovative, cooperative and inclusive and real change becomes possible. Globally, between 1 and 2 per cent of the population is now operating at this disruptive innovative level.[52] However, amongst certain influential populations such as business leaders the figure is closer to 10 per cent.[53] We both also believe that more of the younger generation (Gen Y and earlier) are operating from this level of disruptive innovation level. We have some evidence for this although we have yet to publish this data on the emergence of a plethora of young, innovative entrepreneurs who are changing

---

[52] Wilber, K. (2001) *A Theory of Everything: An Integral Vision for Business, Politics, Science and Spirituality*, Dublin: Gateway.

[53] Watkins, A. (2014) *Coherence: The secret science of brilliant leadership*, London: Kogan Page.
Laloux, F. (2014) *Reinventing Organizations: A Guide to Creating Organizations Inspired by the Next Stage in Human Consciousness*, Brussels: Nelson Parker.

markets, inventing markets and changing the game of business considerably.

For the first time in history, we have enough people who are able to conceptualise at an advanced level, embrace complexity, innovate around wicked problems and cooperate effectively. We are now able to formulate a better system than democracy and engage 'the crowd' to further improve democracy for the benefit of all.

When individuals are no longer driven by self-interest and the accumulation of power or money, they are liberated by the constraints of their own personal history to find solutions to the wicked problems, like democracy.[54]

Whereas the democratic system can exaggerate human failings while simultaneously stifling human ingenuity, crowdocracy does the opposite by unleashing human ingenuity while minimising the impact of human failings. When we include everyone the individual failings of a few self-serving individuals or minority groups gets cancelled out by the collective wisdom of the crowd.

But it is not just access to more developed thinking that makes crowdocracy possible. The real catalyst for change is the emergence of much more sophisticated technology.

Access to More Sophisticated Technology

Even before the Internet futurist and inventor Buckminster Fuller proposed 'the knowledge doubling curve' to explain how the volume of what we know has escalated rapidly. Essentially, the more knowledge we accumulate the faster we create more

---

[54] Watkins, A. and Wilber, K. (2015) *Wicked & Wise: How to Solve the World's Toughest Problems*, London: Urbane Publishing.

knowledge. Up until the 1900s, human knowledge doubled every one hundred years or so. By 1945, it doubled every 25 years. Today, knowledge doubles every 13 months and is expected to reduce to just 12 hours![55]

That's an unfathomable amount of data and it has been made possible by an explosion in technological capability explained by 'Moore's Law'. In the 1970s, Gordon Moore, one of the inventors of integrated circuits noticed that it was possible to squeeze twice as many transistors on an integrated circuit every 24 months. US inventor and futurist Ray Kurzweil points out that there will be 1000 times more technological change in the twenty-first century than there was in the twentieth century.[56] According to Kurzweil, even Moore's Law will be obsolete by 2019 because the rate of advancement will be even more rapid than the exponential growth it currently describes.

In his seminal essay, *The Law of Accelerating Returns*, Kurzweil states, 'There's even exponential growth in the rate of exponential growth. Within a few decades, machine intelligence will surpass human intelligence, leading to The Singularity – technological change so rapid and profound it represents a rupture in the fabric of human history.'[57]

That rupture is here and it presents an unprecedented opportunity to really express the true ideal of democracy. In the past it was physically, financially and logistically impossible to find out what

---

[55] Schilling, D.R. (2013) 'Knowledge doubling every 12 months, soon to be every 12 hours', Industry Tap, 19 April 2013, accessed 28 December 2015, www.industrytap.com/knowledge-doubling-every-12-months-soon-to-be-every-12-hours/3950

[56] Kurzweil, R. (2013) *How to create a mind: The secret of human thought revealed*, New York: Penguin Books.

[57] Kurweil, R. (2001) 'The Law of Accelerating Returns', 7 March 2001, accessed 28 December 2015, www.kurzweilai.net/the-law-of-accelerating-returns

the people wanted, what they felt about policy or legislation and what they wanted their government to do. Today it is possible because we have sophisticated social media platforms, open source software and mind numbing data storage and analytic capabilities. It is these innovations that could help make crowdocracy a reality.

Interestingly, Kurzweil also predicted that supercomputers would have the processing power of one human brain by 2010, and personal computers would have the processing power of one hundred human brains by around 2020. By 2030, it will take around 1000 human brains to match $1000 of computing power. Such is the speed of development brought on by knowledge doubling that by 2050, $1000 of computing power will equal the processing power of all the human brains on Earth.[58] This technological advance is already revolutionising our lives and when we combine collective intelligence with the data analysis and integration techniques of artificial intelligence then we can finally revolutionise democracy so that the people really do decide.

Let the People Decide

Whenever either of us mentions the idea of crowdocracy to senior leaders, politicians or intellectuals the immediate response is, 'Are you mad? You really want to let the people decide even though most of those people don't have a clue what they are deciding on?' Actually, the language of these conversations is usually much more colourful but the essence is the same. The assumption is that all the people can't really decide because

---

[58] Kurweil, R. (2001) 'The Law of Accelerating Returns', 7 March 2001, accessed 28 December 2015, www.kurzweilai.net/the-law-of-accelerating-returns

too many of them are too ill-informed. The average person simply doesn't have enough knowledge about the issues, their complexities or their implications.

But what if we told you that their level of knowledge didn't matter? What if we told you that just by opening up the decision-making process to *all the people* we would always get a better solution than relying on so-called 'experts'. This goes against everything we have been conditioned to believe but the fact remains that the 'wisdom of the crowd' is a robustly proven phenomenon in social science that we will unpack in detail in the next chapter.

Hundreds of years ago it may have been possible for one person or a group of really smart, experienced people to make more right decisions than wrong ones, but not today. The pace and speed of change, the complexity of the situations and challenges we face together with the proliferation of knowledge and data mean those days are long gone. Even if we sacked every politician on the planet and made their re-employment dependent on whether they were operating from a more mature, advanced level of thinking, they still wouldn't make better decisions than the crowd can make. No one person is ever as smart as all the people.

Solving the real social issues we face in government and beyond is therefore not about ferreting out the very best, very smartest people and expecting them to solve problems in a darkened room. It is about opening the problem solving process up to the collective and allowing the crowd to find the best solution. Technology is finally at a point where that is possible.

We have come a long way since Churchill took a swing at democracy. Even accounting for the fact that he had just lost the election and was feeling a little unloved despite his stellar wartime leadership – he was right. At the time there was no better form of government. There simply were not enough people capable of even conceptualising an evolutionary improvement never mind implementing that improvement. Today there are. We are now capable of creating a much more sophisticated answer. There is also a growing appetite for political change. Add those factors to the exponential growth in technology and we have the opportunity and the will to bring that more sophisticated answer to life.

For the first time in a very long time political transformation is possible.

Chapter 4:

The Wise Crowd or the Angry Mob?

'The many, who are not as individuals excellent men, nevertheless can, when they have come together, be better than the few best people, not individually, but collectively, just as feasts to which many contribute are better than feasts provided at one person's expense.'[1]

– Aristotle

When you have a big decision to make what do you do? Do you go it alone, disappear into a quiet space and simply hope that you will be blessed by a sudden flash of brilliance? Or maybe you phone a friend or 'ask the audience'? Should the big calls that affect our lives be made by us and us alone? Are two heads better than one? Are many better than two? These questions have been the source of much debate over the years and in many ways these questions remain at the heart of government and governance. Who decides our destiny? Who should be involved in the decisions that affect all our lives? Most modern societies have concluded that since we can't all be involved in every question, we must elect representatives that can make

---

[1] Aristotle (1941) *The Basic Works of Aristotle*, R. McKeon, Editor, New York: Random House.

decisions on our behalf. But as we pointed out in Chapter 2, when this smaller group of elected representatives get together they often don't come up with a better answer than any of us could individually. Often it is far worse. Is there wisdom in the crowd? Or do collectives become dumb and even descend into an angry mob?

If we are dissatisfied with the quality of decisions made on our behalf by our representatives is there anything we can do other than wait for a number of years, usually four, so we can vote them out and hopefully elect someone better? Even when we do elect someone new, we almost always end up regretting *that* decision too. There is certainly no guarantee that the newly elected representative will be any fairer, wiser or ethical than the last.

As we've mentioned, the most common response to the suggestion of crowdocracy is one of scepticism and disbelief. Most people, even the ordinary members of the crowd, assume that we simply can't leave the really important decisions to the general population because not enough of them are sufficiently informed to make the right call. Although difficult to corroborate, Churchill apparently said, 'The best argument against democracy is a five-minute conversation with the average voter.' George Bernard Shaw didn't think much more of the masses when he said, 'Democracy substitutes election by the incompetent many for appointment by the corrupt few.'[2] Oscar Wilde suggested, 'Democracy means simply the bludgeoning of the people by the people for the people.'[3] Hardly glowing testimony of democracy or the wisdom of crowds!

This inference of ineptitude is often the argument used against greater democratic participation. In 2017, those in the UK are likely to go to the polls to decide if they want to be 'in' or 'out' of the European Union. This is exactly the argument that is

---

[2] Shaw, G.B. (1903) *Man and Superman*, 'Maxims for Revolutionists: Democracy'.

[3] Wilde, O. (1891) *The Soul of Man under Socialism*.

being used against that referendum – the average person in the street has no idea what is involved in that decision, what the consequences would be and how they would really be affected by either eventuality. They are not well enough educated on the issues to make a sensible and rational choice. This position, also called the elitist view of democracy, has been around for as long as there has been democracy.

But, even if many people lack knowledge or sophistication, it doesn't matter. The fact that some people are not well educated on any issue will make the collective solution even better!

A Surprising Truth about Crowds

Charles Darwin's less famous cousin Francis Galton was one of the first to demonstrate the 'wisdom of the crowd'. In 1906, Galton attended the annual West of England Fat Stock and Poultry Exhibition – a local fair where farmers and townsfolk gathered to appraise the quality of livestock. His entire life up to this point was an exploration of breeding and how to measure and quantify that breeding. It was Galton who suggested that certain mental characteristics and abilities were inherited in the same way that physical traits were inherited. One of the examples he used to 'prove' his hypothesis was that wrestlers in the North Country tended to be the sons of other wrestlers from the North Country. He assumed therefore that the family had a natural talent for wrestling.[4] Of course, this theory completely missed the impact of environment. The son of a North Country wrestler was much more likely to be exposed to wrestling from a very young age, conversation in the house would have centred on wrestling, and the father would have probably wrestled with his son. It is also pretty likely that this early exposure to the sport coupled with

---

[4] Colvin, G. (2008) *Talent is Overrated*, London: Nicholas Brealey Publishing Ltd.

practice was what created the eminence not some mysterious 'wrestling gene'.

Galton's ideas, strengthened by Darwin's theories on natural selection led to an elitist viewpoint. He believed that there really were just a few people equipped to run companies and countries and that those people should be found and put in the top jobs. To be fair, a variation of that viewpoint still exists today for good reason – it appears rational and logical.

Unfortunately, it also happens to be false as Galton himself discovered at the local fair. Walking through the fair he discovered a weight-judging competition. A fat ox had been selected and placed on display and members of the crowd were invited to guess the 'dead weight' of the animal. In other words, once the animal was slaughtered and dressed ready for the butcher – how much would it weigh? The closest guess would win a prize. Eight hundred people at the fair paid their sixpence and made their guess on their stamped and numbered ticket. Many of the guessers were experts – butchers and farmers who logic would suggest had a better chance of getting the right answer. Most of the guessers were lay people who had absolutely no idea how much the animal would weigh.

The correlation of this experiment to politics and the notion of democracy was not lost on Galton who wrote later in the scientific journal *Nature*, 'The average competitor was probably as well fitted for making a just estimate of the dressed weight of the ox as an average voter is of judging the merits of most political issues on which he votes.' This was of particular interest to Galton because he believed that the average voter was capable of very little and this competition offered an opportunity to prove it. Unfortunately for Galton rather than proving his elitist view that we should leave complicated decision to the experts, he succeeded in proving the exact opposite.

Once he had thoroughly analysed the guesses received from the crowd and run extensive statistical analyses including calculating the mean of the crowd's guesses, Galton discovered that if the crowd was a single person they would have guessed that the ox weighed 1,197 pounds. The actual weight of the ox after slaughter was 1,198 pounds.[5] The farmers and butchers, who one would imagine would have the expertise to guess accurately didn't even get as close to the right answer as the collective wisdom of the crowd.

Galton had discovered, probably rather reluctantly, that *under the right circumstances* the crowd is often smarter than even the smartest people in the crowd. Although completely counterintuitive, this is true even when the people in the crowd know very little about the problem they are assessing!

The logical response to Galton's findings is that it was luck or that perhaps this collective wisdom is only useful when the challenge is simple like guessing the weight of an ox or guessing the number of jellybeans in a jar. When it comes to something more complex – like politics or military challenges –then it won't work – right?

Actually, no. In May 1968, the US submarine, *Scorpion*, disappeared after a tour of duty in the North Atlantic. The navy had no idea where it was. They knew the *Scorpion's* last reported position but that simply gave them a twenty-mile radius to search and that's a lot of ocean. Even within that search circle, the ocean was several thousand feet deep in places. Searching for a needle in a haystack would have been a piece of cake compared to this task. The most obvious solution would have been to track down some naval and submarine experts and see if they could shed any light on where the sub might be. Instead naval officer John Craven took a different approach. Craven came up with a series of scenarios that would explain the disappearance and then assembled a team including mathematicians, submarine specialists and salvage experts. But rather than ask them to

---

[5] Surowiecki, J. (2004) *The Wisdom of Crowds: Why the many are smarter than the few*, London: Little Brown.

confer and discuss the likely location of the *Scorpion*, Craven asked each to offer their individual best guess without conferring with their colleagues. Lured by the promise of bottle of Chivas Regal whisky this small crowd made their independent guesses on why the submarine had disappeared. They made guesses on things like the speed the sub was travelling at as it sunk to the ocean floor and the steepness of its descent.

Using a formula called Bayes' Theorem, which calculates how new information about an event changes pre-existing expectations, Craven was able to estimate the *Scorpion*'s position based on the collective but independent answers of his assembled 'crowd'. The location that emerged was not a location any individual member of the group had suggested. And yet, five months after the *Scorpion* disappeared it was found just 220 yards from where Craven's collective wisdom said it would be.[6]

What's remarkable about this is that the data that was fed into this group was minimal. No one knew what had happened, they didn't know how fast the sub was travelling before it disappeared or how steeply it fell or where it fell and yet the group as a whole 'knew'. This phenomenon is known as 'emergent intelligence' and it is fundamental to the understanding of collective intelligence. Collective intelligence or, as Assistant Professor of Political Science at Yale University Hélène Landemore calls it, 'democratic reason', comes in two parts.[7] First, there is the intelligence of the individual citizens in the crowd. This intelligence is not limited to intellectual intelligence but includes a wide array of different types of intelligence as identified by Gardner,[8] Sternberg,[9]

---

[6] Sontag, S. and Drew, C. (2000) *Blind Man's Bluff: The Untold Story of Cold War Submarine Espionage*, London: Random House.

[7] Landemore, H. (2013) *Democratic Reason: Politics, collective intelligence and the rule of the many*, New Jersey: Princeton University Press.

[8] Gardner, H. (1983) *Frames of Mind: The Theory of Multiple Intelligences*, New York: Basic.

[9] Sternberg, R.J. (1985) *Beyond IQ: A Triarchic Theory of Human Intelligence*, New York: Cambridge University Press.

Salovey and Mayer.[10] Collective intelligence includes combined intelligence that exists in the environment in which the crowd functions, which means that it is both the sum of the parts and more than the sum of its parts. In the natural world we see this all the time. For example in a colony of bees, individual bees will have different intelligence depending on their role in the colony and there will also be a 'hive mind' that only exists in the collective and can't be located in any single individual bee.

Even Machiavelli, the most famous of all political strategists, concluded from his historical observations that people were 'of better judgement' than princes.[11] Contemporary political scientists have statistical methodologies and tools that are now able to verify that claim.

The Maths of Collective Wisdom

In his landmark book *The Wisdom of Crowd,* author James Surowiecki states that at the heart of collective intelligence is a 'mathematical truism'. If we ask a large enough group of diverse, independent people to make a prediction or estimate a probability, and then average those estimates, the errors each of them make in coming up with an answer will cancel themselves out. Each person's guess has two components: information and error. Subtract the error and we're left with accurate information.

This mathematical principal was first described by Aristotle in the fourth century BC when he wrote in *Politics*, 'For each individual among the many has a share of excellence and practical wisdom, and when they meet together, just as they become in a manner

[10] Salovey, P. and Mayer, J.D. (1990) 'Emotional Intelligence' in Oatley, K., Jenkins, J.M. and Stein, N.L. eds *Human Emotions: A Reader*, Oxford: Blackwell Publishers, pp. 313–20.

[11] Machiavelli, N (1996) *Discourses on Livy*, trans. H. Mansfield and N. Torcov, Chicago: University of Chicago Press.

one man, who has many feet, and hands, and senses, so too with regard to their character and thought.'[12] In other words, a group of people can find the answer to a problem when each member knows at least part of the solution. In fact in the 2007 French presidential elections, the Socialist candidate Ségolène Royal campaigned on this very theme – referring to it as 'citizens' expertise'. Royal argued that in a complex and constantly changing world, every citizen holds a parcel of the truth and that the best source of enlightened political decision is to be found in the people themselves and not a small group of experts or professional politicians.[13]

Our reluctance to even consider this approach is largely down to our embedded belief that we should let smart, experienced people decide. Even in the popular TV quiz show *Who Wants to Be a Millionaire* the contestant who doesn't know the answer will almost always choose to 'phone a friend' before 'ask the audience' because they assume that calling their smart friend is going to give them a more accurate answer than asking a bunch of strangers who happened to fancy watching a TV quiz show that afternoon. The expert friend is however only correct 65 per cent of the time versus 91 per cent of the time when the contestant asks the audience.[14]

The collective is correct much more often than the individual expert or smart friend because of mathematics. Using an example created by social scientist Scott Page, say a contestant is asked 'Which person from the following list was not a member of the Monkees?'

---

[12] Aristotle (350 BC) *The Politics*.

[13] Landemore, H. (2013) *Democratic Reason: Politics, collective intelligence and the rule of the many*, New Jersey: Princeton University Press.

[14] Surowiecki, J. (2004) *The Wisdom of Crowds: Why the many are smarter than the few*, London: Little Brown.

a. Peter Tork
b. Davy Jones
c. Roger Noll
d. Michael Nesmith

Imagine there are 100 people in the audience. When asked to vote, seven of them loved the 1960s pop group so they know that Roger Noll (who is actually a Stanford economist) was not in the Monkees and vote c. Another ten people recognise Davy Jones and Michael Nesmith – two of the most well-known band members. Say half choose a. and the other half choose c. that's still another five votes for c. Another fifteen members of the audience only recognise Peter Tork so they guess equally between b., c. and d. but again that still gives c. five more votes. That leaves the remaining 68 people in the audience who don't even know the Monkees were a pop group never mind who was in the group, so they split between all four options equally. That gives c. another 17 votes. The maths looks like this...

a. 5 + 17 = 22
b. 5 + 17 = 22
c. 7 + 5 + 5 + 17 = 34
d. 5 + 17 = 22

If you asked the audience this question and took their advice you would win even though 93 per cent of the audience did not know the answer. As Page suggests, 'There is no mystery here. Mistakes cancel one another out, and correct answers, like cream, rise to the surface.'[15]

When left to our own devices, all our innate logic tells us to find the best in any industry or the expert for any challenge and ask them. Of course, it is this 'leave it to the experts' mind-set that has allowed the more toxic by-products of democracy such as lobbying and vested interests to flourish. Not to mention fuel our collective apathy and disengagement with the political process.

Even if by some miracle we could find enlightened, mature, smart and ethically superior politicians to fight our corner they still wouldn't make better decisions than the crowd can make. All of us will always be smarter than some of us.

There is also evidence from other completely unrelated areas of research to suggest that systems which create a 'pecking order' with the strongest or smartest rising to the top do much worse than systems where individuals work collectively and collaboratively with no pecking order. Margaret Heffernan makes a compelling case for the power of the collective in business and beyond, suggesting that teams without stars can often do a lot better than a team with stars. Heffernan states that, 'For the past 50 years we've thought that success is achieved by picking the superstars, the brightest men, or occasionally women, in the room, and giving them all the resources and all the power. The result has been aggression, dysfunction and waste. If the only way the most productive can be successful is by suppressing the productivity of the rest, then we badly need to find a better way to work and a richer way to live.' We couldn't agree more. Heffernan ends her TED talk by adding, 'We won't solve our problems if we expect it to be solved by a few supermen or superwomen. Now we need everybody, because it is only when we accept that everybody has value that we will liberate the energy, imagination and momentum we need to create the best beyond measure.'[16]

That is not to say that we don't need the innovators and the visionary system builders. We do; their adaptability, flexibility and cognitive sophistication is vital in designing a successful

[16] Heffernan, M. (2015) 'Why it's time to forget the pecking order at work', June 2015, accessed 29 December 2015, www.ted.com/talks/margaret_heffernan_why_it_s_time_to_forget_the_pecking_order_at_work/transcript?language=en#t-920919

transition from the flawed system we have now, to a better more egalitarian system. But beyond that – we need *everyone*. And we really do mean everyone. It is the smart thinking *and* the novel, naïve, crazy or half-baked suggestions of the many that will help to ensure that crowdocracy is effective, robust and very difficult to manipulate.

Characteristics of a Wise Crowd

Remember earlier when we said that *under the right circumstances* the crowd is often smarter than even the smartest person in the crowd? Different authors have suggested different characteristics or attributes that facilitate wise crowds,[17] many of which have merit. These are the four conditions we consider essential in the context of political governance and how to facilitate wise crowds:

1. **Diversity of knowledge and opinion** – where each person has some private information even if it is just their personal opinion or interpretation of the 'facts'.

2. **Independence of thought and collaboration** – so one person's opinion is not unduly influenced or coloured by other people's opinion.

3. **Decentralisation of power** – no power hierarchy exists where the 'boss' determines the answer so people can specialise and draw on local knowledge, data or information.

4. **Integration** – where a system or mechanism exists to turn private judgement into a collective decision. This mechanism requires us to integrate not aggregate information.

---

[17] Surowiecki, J. (2004) *The Wisdom of Crowds: Why the many are smarter than the few*, London: Little Brown.
Miller, P. (2010) *Smart Swarm: Using Animal Behaviour to Organise Our World*, Collins.

1. Diversity of Knowledge and Opinion

Diversity is often the characteristic that is the most counterintuitive. We find it hard to accept that the best result comes when everyone has a voice and everyone's opinion is considered – even the people who know virtually nothing about the decision being made. Scott Page, a professor at the University of Michigan, ran a series of experiments to demonstrate the positive effects of diversity. What he found was that groups that consist of smart people and not so smart people almost always did better than groups of just smart people.[18]

Organisational theorist James G. March puts it this way: 'The development of knowledge may depend on maintaining an influx of the naïve and the ignorant'.[19] The argument that we can't hand over power to the masses because they are ill informed simply doesn't stand up to scrutiny. As attractive as an elitist approach may be (whether an intellectual elite, a political elite or a financial elite) it is wrong because it is the diversity of opinion that actually facilitates a wiser decision. Cognitive diversity ensures that different types of people look at and approach the challenge from different directions and perspectives. They will interpret the 'facts' differently and present different potential solutions – this is what makes the difference. When this cognitive diversity is present, 'a randomly selected collection of problem solvers outperforms a collection of the best individual problem solvers'.[20] This is known as the Diversity Trumps Ability Theorem, which states that it is

[18] Page, S. (2002) 'Return to the Toolbox', unpublished paper.

[19] March, J.G. (1991) 'Exploration and Exploitation in Organizational Learning', *Organization Science*, 2, pp. 71–87.

[20] Hong, L. and Page, S. (2004) 'Groups of Diverse Problem Solvers Can Outperform Groups of High-Ability Problem Solvers', Proceedings of the National Academy of Sciences of the United States, 101, no. 46, pp. 16385–89.
Page, S.E. (2007) *The Difference: How the Power of Diversity Creates Better groups, Firms, Schools and Societies*, New Jersey: Princeton University Press.

often better to have a group of cognitively diverse people than have a group of very smart people who all think alike.[21]

Considering the political ranks of most nations or the corporate boards of most companies the men vastly outnumber the women, white men vastly outnumber those of ethnic backgrounds and those with privileged educational backgrounds usually outnumber those without. Those small collectives are therefore thinking alike – they are effectively looking at the problems they face through the same eyes and wondering why they can't solve them.

This is despite robust evidence, certainly in business, that proves the financial gains that diversity can bring. Research conducted in 2014 by the New York based Center for Talent Innovation (CTI), involving more than 40 case studies and 1800 employee surveys looked at 'inherent diversity' such as gender, race and sexual orientation and 'acquired diversity' such as experience and language skills. It found that publicly traded companies with inherent diversity were 45 per cent more likely than those without to have expanded market share in the past year and 70 per cent more likely to have captured a new market. When teams had one or more members who represented a target end-user, the entire team was as much as 158 per cent more likely to understand that target end-user and innovate accordingly.[22] A 2012 Deloitte report looking at 1550 employees in three large Australian businesses identified an 80 per cent improvement in business performance when levels of diversity and inclusion were high.[23]

[21] Landemore, H. (2013) *Democratic Reason: Politics, Collective Intelligence and the Rule of the Many*, New Jersey: Princeton University Press.

[22] Smedley, T. (2014) 'The evidence is growing – there really is a business case for diversity', *Financial Times*, 15 May 2014, accessed 29 December 2015, www.ft.com

[23] Deloitte (2012) 'Waiter is that inclusion in my soup? A new recipe to improve business performance', accessed 29 December 2015, http://www2.deloitte.com/content/dam/Deloitte/au/Documents/human-capital/deloitte-au-hc-diversity-inclusion-soup-0513.pdf

Clearly common sense must also prevail here in that we do still need the smart people in the collective but it's critically important that we don't limit that collective to just smart people. The group must also be large enough, coming from a deep enough pool of diverse individuals to ensure sufficiently different knowledge, opinions and perspectives emerge.

If diversity is so critical then we have to consider what sort of diversity matters. Is it age? Gender? Ethnicity? Sexual orientation? Educational attainment? Socioeconomic status? Political orientation? Geographic diversity including city dwellers and rural communities? Does diversity of morality or ethics matter? Do we need to ensure we have a spectrum of value systems present for optimal decision-making? Do we need people who operate from different levels of ego maturity? Does diversity of spiritual and religious practice matter? Where do we stop in our attempts to ensure we have a sufficiently diverse range of opinions? What is the process that a diverse collection of individuals go through in making a decision compared to a homogenous group? Does the diversity have to be 'representative' of the population the decision will affect in order for that decision to have legitimacy? If so should such representation be based on the number of different opinions or the spectrum of opinion? Thus if everyone in the population is an atheist except for one individual who is a religious zealot should both views be represented equally?

One of the problems with most modern democracies is that the only type of diversity being considered is the diversity between political parties, and even then the voting system is often constructed to minimise that diversity. Before elections, all the main parties remind us not to 'waste our vote' by voting for any of the smaller parties that are unlikely to win an outright majority. If we considered a broader range of diversity factors in selecting our representatives we may come up with better quality answers than we are currently generating.

That said, the whole idea behind crowdocracy is to hand power over to the people and let them determine the answers. We don't need to over-engineer the diversity using a quota system or some other manufactured way. When Iceland crowdsourced their constitution following the 2008 financial collapse they did virtually nothing to ensure diversity in their Constitutional Council and yet they still generated sufficient diversity and a much wiser answer than the politicians had created alone.

The wisdom of crowds will also be supported and facilitated by the creation of a user-friendly technology platform so that everyone can contribute their diversity to the debate. Just as we advocate trusting the crowd to come up with the wisest possible answers, we must also trust the crowd to show up and participate when they are finally given the chance. However, we envisage this will take time and it's why we advocate a gradual shift from where we are now to where we could be (more on that in Chapter 6). People will need to experience crowdocracy in action so that they begin to appreciate that they do genuinely have a voice – so long as they take up their right to make their voice heard. It will take time to reverse the widespread political apathy that exists in most modern democracies. Thomas Jefferson complained about it centuries ago, 'We in America do not have government by the majority. We have government by the majority who participate.' Apathy is still a challenge today but it is understandable. For generations, too many people have felt that their opinion and vote didn't matter so they simply stopped participating. Once they realise that their opinion does matter and they can air their views to influence the outcome, we envisage that apathy will dissipate.

2. Independence of Thought and Collaboration

In order to generate greater levels of wisdom, it is also important that the group doesn't interact too closely with each other. This is often the fear that sits behind some of the scepticism about whether such a new form of governance could actually work. We don't need to look far in human history to find deeply disturbing examples of what human beings are capable when they are whipped up by a charismatic leader or distorted ideology.

115

Think, for example, the lynch mobs of the Ku Klux Klan to the Nazi's under Hitler to the excessive, irresponsible capitalism that facilitated the global financial crisis. Human beings can be brutal, violent and can appear to drop to their lowest common denominator in a large group.

This phenomenon known as 'group think' was first coined by social psychologist Irving L. Janis and describes how people will naturally strive for consensus within a group. In their desire to 'fit in', be accepted and appear loyal, individuals will set aside their own personal beliefs, adopt the opinion of the rest of the group or simply remain quiet. None of which is helpful when seeking a wise answer.

Whether we like to admit it or not, we are influenced by other people. Robert B. Cialdini, Regent's Professor Emeritus of Psychology and Marketing at the Arizona State University identified six basic but powerful principles of psychology that can influence behaviour and inhibit our ability to operate independently of each other.[24] They are:

1. **Reciprocity** – we are influenced to return a favour. If someone is kind to us we are more likely to be kind back.

2. **Consistency** – we have a deep desire to be consistent so once we commit to something we tend to want to remain consistent with that choice.

3. **Social proof** – when we are unsure what we think or what to do we will be influenced by what others are thinking and doing.

4. **Liking** – we are more easily influenced by people we like and more easily disagree with people we don't like.

5. **Authority** – we are easily influenced by people in authority or perceived experts.

6. **Scarcity** – we are influenced to take action when not taking action might mean we miss out.

---

[24] Cialdini, R.B. (1993) *Influence: Science and Practice*, 3e, New York: HarperCollins College Publisher.

These principles can easily pollute the outcome of the crowd if the crowd is allowed to interact too closely. The two that are most likely to prevent the crowd from generating wise solutions are social proof and authority as evidenced by a CIA-funded experiment at Harvard.

In the experiment, four-person teams were tasked with assessing the data available around a fictional potential terrorist attack to see if they could identify the target and prevent the attack in time. Prior to the start of the challenge, all the students were given a battery of tests to identify key strengths such as verbal working memory or face recognition. The researchers then used the results to assign students to teams so that some teams had two experts – or students who scored particularly highly on relevant skills – and two generalists. This was important because they wanted to discover if a team's cognitive diversity affected its performance as strongly as its level of skills.

Researchers also wanted to see if a group's performance could be improved by taking the time to identify strengths and assign tasks and roles according to that strength – thus allowing the team to more fully exploit the diversity of knowledge and diversity of abilities.

Everyone in the various teams was told how each person in the team had scored in the tests. In half the groups, the team was then coached on how to best utilise those individual skills and the other half were simply told the scores and left to figure it out on their own. Perhaps unsurprisingly, the most successful teams at identifying the terrorist target and uncovering the plot were the teams who were coached on how best to use their individual strengths. What was a surprise however was just how badly the uncoached teams performed. When experts were identified in the team but the group was not coached on how to get the best out of both the experts and generalists, the experts simply took over. The generalists, who also had much to offer simply deferred to the experts and were unduly influenced by their elevated status (authority). These groups actually did worse than the groups that had no experts and were just made up of generalists.[25] The successful teams were able to draw on a wider range of opinion and experience. They pooled together a greater diversity of knowledge and skills than any one individual could offer on their own. As a result, they collectively compensated for their errors and arrived at the correct solution more quickly.

In addition to the potentially distorting nature of the expert leader, social proof can powerfully reduce independence of thought and lead to all manner of problems including the dumbing down of the crowd. Social proof is when an individual starts to believe that if others are doing something or thinking in a certain way then it must be right. Social proof is the driving force behind peer pressure and conformity. Both of these phenomena have been widely studied and have been shown to not just reduce the quality of an answer, but conformity can, on occasion, cause individuals and groups to create a completely false answer.[26]

In one now famous experiment called the Solomon Asch conformity experiment, the researchers asked a group of people to identify which of the lines in Exhibit 2 was the same length as the line in Exhibit 1 (Figure 4. 1.) Everyone in the group was however a 'stooge' and 'in on the experiment', apart from one person who did not know he was the only true subject. The researcher then asked each person in the group, starting with those that were in on the experiment, which line in exhibit 2 matched exhibit 1. Each person in turn identified the wrong line – either all 'C' or all indicating that 'B' was the same as Exhibit 1.

Both 'B' and 'C' are clearly wrong and yet a third of the time the true participant went along with the view of the group and agreed with whichever line the rest of the participants had identified. Had

[25] Miller, P. (2010) *Smart Swarm: Using Animal Behaviour to Organise Our World*, Collins.

[26] Cialdini, R.B. (1993) *Influence: Science and Practice*, 3e, New York: HarperCollins College Publisher.

Figure 4.1 Flashcard used in the Solomon Asch Conformity Study

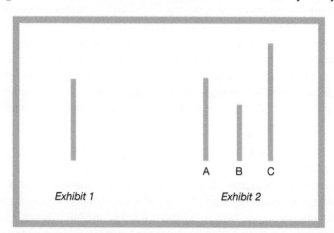

the participant been able to give their response without knowing what everyone else thought and therefore not then pressured to conform – even with an obviously wrong answer – chances are they would have been correct. In fact, in a control experiment where there was no pressure to conform and the participants were able to independently decide which line was the same, there was less than a 1 per cent error rate.[27]

This tendency to conform becomes greater as the crowd gets bigger and more and more people express an opinion that is different from our own. It is also more powerful when we are unsure of the answer or proposed solution. In a highly connected crowd facing a very uncertain situation there is therefore a real risk of the crowd dumbing down unless people are insulated to some degree from other people's opinion and are free to share their independent thoughts, whatever they may be.

Independence of thought and collaboration is essential in order to ensure that everyone contributes their unique insight without

[27] Asch, S. (1955) *Social Psychology*, New Jersey: Prentice Hall.

being unduly influenced by other people, whether they are experts in positions of perceived authority, or people they like and want to cosy up to or even people they don't like and want to reject. People participating in the decision must be free to change their mind if they want to and not be bribed by some form of reciprocity, social proof, authority or peer pressure. This independence of thought and collaboration can significantly improve the collective input and increase the likelihood of getting to the best solution.

It is, however, worth pointing out that independence of thought and collaboration must be distinguished from insularity. Insularity is often a predictor of future failure, particularly in a VUCA world. Insularity can also create the toxic cult-like 'group think' behaviour we see in terrorist groups such as ISIS. This is why constitutional design is so important to facilitate independence of thought and positive collaboration while minimising the potential for negative collaboration and group polarisation. Citizens in democratic nations are already susceptible to group polarisation and in truth it is not always a bad outcome. It is very possible that a movement in a more extreme direction, say regarding action to halt climate change could be a movement in a better, much needed direction. But only if that choice is the result of open exchange of diverse opinions and independent thought and not the result of a group of like-minded people controlling the narrative toward a preferred direction.[28] Independent thinkers are usually very open to information but are not excessively influenced by considering alternative points of view. This is key.

3. Decentralisation of Power

Another critical factor that promotes increased wisdom of the crowd is the decentralisation of control.

Power with the crowd can't reside in one central location. Instead

---

[28] Sunstein, Cass R. (2002) 'Why They Hate Us: The Role of Social Dynamics', 25 Harv. J.L. & Pub. Pol'y 429

important decisions must be made by individuals based on their own local and specific knowledge rather than by a planner or leader located hundreds, possibly thousands, of miles away from the area that will be affected by that decision.

Decentralisation fosters specialisation so individuals in the crowd build up areas of expertise that they can then add to the debate. In decentralised decision-making this vast reservoir of specialised knowledge, in terms of the experience, geographic location and area specific knowledge vastly improves the quality of output. In her TED presentation, Margaret Heffernan provides a brilliant example of the importance and speed of specialised knowledge. Arup, one of the world's most successful engineering firms had been commissioned to build the equestrian center for the Beijing Olympics. This was a huge project with a vast number of considerations – one of which was how to handle the manure created by two-and-a-half thousand highly strung thoroughbreds. The engineers could have spent months talking to vets, doing the research and tweaking spreadsheets but instead they found someone who had designed the Jockey Club in New York. The problem was solved in less than a day because of access to decentralised specialist knowledge.[29]

Decentralisation also increases what Friedrich Hayek calls 'tacit knowledge'. Tacit knowledge is knowledge that can't easily be summarised or described because it is specific to a particular role, industry or geographic location. This is the knowledge we have that we don't necessarily know we have or assume everyone has and yet it's incredibly valuable to the crowd. When the crowd is decentralised and power is not held in the hands of a few who can veto a decision they choose to, the crowd is more likely to contribute both specific and tacit knowledge to the debate. Paradoxically, while specialisation invariably narrows

---

[29] Heffernan, M. (2015) 'Why it's time to forget the pecking order at work', June 2015, accessed 29 December 2015, www.ted.com/talks/margaret_heffernan_why_it_s_time_to_forget_the_pecking_order_at_work/transcript?language=en#t-920919

and deepens *individual* knowledge when all the individuals come together in the collective and contribute their knowledge, the reservoir of potentially accessible knowledge is both vast and deep.

At the heart of decentralisation is the fact that those closest to the challenge, who probably have the most information or input to add and who will be most affected by the outcome, are most likely to find novel and creative solutions. American philosopher and pioneer in social reform John Dewey suggests that the public is definitely the best judge of where the problems lie and therefore must be consulted. In fact, Dewey suggested that the strongest case for democracy was that it involves, 'A consultation and discussion which uncovers social needs and troubles' which 'forces a recognition that there are common interests, even though the recognition of *what* they are is confused.'[30] This is logical; we know when something is wrong in our society because we often experience it in our daily lives. We may not know what's causing it but if we had a platform to raise the challenge and everyone could share their thoughts, ideas and insights then there is little doubt that the collective would come up with better, faster and more effective solutions.

The crowdocractic platform would therefore need to strike the right balance between making individual knowledge globally and collectively useful while still ensuring that the information was resolutely specific and local, not diluted or dumbed down.

Linux is a classic example of what's possible when the crowd is decentralised. The technology itself also holds a great deal of promise in the creation of The Crowd platform.

Linux

In 1991, Finnish computer programmer Linus Torvalds created his own version of the Unix operating system. He called it Linux and

---

[30] Dewey, J. (1927) *The Public and Its Problems*, Chicago: Swallow Press.

released the kernel source code to the public along with a note that said, 'If your efforts are freely distributable, I'd like to hear from you, so I can add them to the system.' Effectively he asked the crowd what they thought of his code and invited suggestions for improvement. Of the ten people who initially downloaded the kernel, five sent back bug fixes, code improvements and new features.

Linux is probably the most prominent example of free, open source software collaboration. The Android smartphone operating system is built on the Linux kernel, making it the largest installed base of all general-purpose operating systems. It's used on servers, mainframe computers and supercomputers but few desktop machines. It's also used in mobile phones, tablets, network routers, TVs, video game consoles and smart watches. The underlying source code can be used, modified and distributed commercially and non-commercially by anyone under license. But, no one owns it. If there is a problem with the software, the community is asked to find a solution and they do. Linux has nearly 12,000 contributors who have actively fixed or improved the operating system and they have done so free of charge. There are no offices, no organisational chart, no centralised power base and yet the crowd organises itself to provide the very best solutions.

The core promise of open source license is that *everybody* should have access to *all* the code *all* the time. But Linux has thousands of programmers making real time changes to the code from all over the world. What if two people are making the same changes or changing the same piece of code at the same time? Traditionally, this has been done by some sort of version control system but that only really works when there is some order in who is doing what, when. That order doesn't exist in Linux so they created 'git'.

Git is Linux's, distributed version control system and it allows the core promise of open source to be realised. But even more impressive is that any time any programmer makes a new file, modifies a file or merges some files, the change is given a unique identifier number. This means that two programmers in different locations can make changes to code that are then merged after the fact even if they don't know about each other. This, as Clay Shirky points out, is 'collaboration without coordination' and this has inspiring implications for politics.[31]

Technology makes decentralisation of power or collaboration without coordination possible and can happen in huge, complex communities - like say a voting population. In fact the 'Github' is already being used to gather opinion around political bills. The New York Senate operated 'open legislation' which is hosted on Github because of its fluidity and version control capabilities. You can login to the page, choose a senator and click on any number of bills they have sponsored and register your opinion. People on Github are already exploring the possibilities of how this type of technology platform could be used to further the development of legislation.

Figure 4.2 illustrates what is known as a 'dif' and shows the responses gathered from the crowd around the copyright debate that occurred in the US Senate in 2011. It lists the text that many people are editing, when the change was made, who made it and what the change is. The content in grey is what got deleted and the content in green is what got added.[32] And it's all being done by technology.

---

[31] Shirky, C. (2012) 'How the Internet will (one day) transform government', TED, September 2012, accessed 29 December 2015, www.ted.com/talks/clay_shirky_how_the_internet_will_one_day_transform_government/transcript?language=en#t-1375

[32] Shirky, C. (2012) 'Clay Shirky: How the Internet will (one day) transform government', TED, June 2012, accessed 29 December 2015, www.ted.com/talks/clay_shirky_how_the_internet_will_one_day_transform_government#t-897313

Figure 4.2 **The 'Dif'**

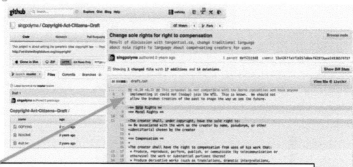

This proposal is not compatible with the Berne convention and thus anyone implementing it could not (today) join the WTO. This is known. We should not allow the broken treaties of the past to shape the way we see the future.

== Sole Rights ==

+== Moral Rights ==

The creator shall, under copyright, have the sole right to:

+* Be associated with the work as the creator by name, pseudonym, or other identifier(s) chosen by the creator
+
+== Compensation ==
+
+The creator shall have the right to compensation from uses of his work that:

* Produce, reproduce, perform, publish, or communicate (by telecommunication or otherwise) the work or substantial portions thereof
* Produce derivative works (such as translations, dramatic interpretations,novelizations, reuse of substantial character or plot content)
* Produce derivatives in alternate mediums (eBooks, audio books)

-* Be associated with the work as the creator by name, pseudonym, or other identifier(s) chosen by the creator
-and to authorize such acts.

Additionally, the fixed form resulting from the fixation of any work (such as a

performer's performance) is the sole creative property of the creator of the

+performer's performance) is considered a work of the creator of the original

work (such as the performer).

4. Integration

Once the crowd has generated a range of ideas, so it is necessary to integrate those opinions and ideas in a way that doesn't just choose the most popular version but seeks to integrate the very best of the best ideas into a coherent proposal that huge numbers of people can genuinely get behind.

The methodology for integrating different opinions and suggestions is absolutely crucial. If we were simply to take the 'average' view in a group then we may come up with a very poor answer. Likewise if we simply compromise or seek to generate some sorry consensus then we may end up with a 'camel' – which is a racehorse designed by committee.

When disparate views are present, the most important thing is not to take an 'either/or' mentality in the mistaken belief that there is a 'right' answer. For most complex and wicked issues such as political governance there is no 'right' answer, only a 'best answer right now' and therefore we need a more sophisticated methodology. What is really required is the ability to integrate the multiple perspectives rather than side with one specific view over another even though we only really agree with a part of that view. This requires us to transcend and include the various perspectives available.

Before we can integrate the diverse views that have emerged from independent thinkers in a decentralised way, we must start by flushing out the various perspectives of the specific issue in question. Everything from an idea to a business to a society evolves through a three-stage process of emergence, differentiation and integration (EDI).

The first stage is to ensure that the different views that have 'emerged' have done so as fully as possible. If we really want to leap forward into a better form of governance we must first arrive at the point where we are at least questioning the current approach. This is already happening with proposals for electoral reform, changes to the political decision-making system such as deliberative or direct democracy, citizen assemblies and a whole range of other inclusive participatory movements. This exploration is vital in helping all participants to feel that their perspective, idea or viewpoint has been heard and ensures they feel they have participated in the process.

With all the various views in play the next stage is differentiation, which involves assessing how the various approaches differ. This helps to ensure everyone has understood each of the various views so we can genuinely review how many distinct perspectives we have in the process and how many are closer to each other than we might initially imagine. Differentiation often requires us to unpack some of the perspectives offered in more detail to get to the underlying thrust of an idea or core driver. Or it may involve exploring the language used to express the idea – often what initially appears as two separate ideas are simply the same or very similar ideas expressed differently and obfuscated by language.

This differentiation step requires a high degree of capability, normally in the specific area in which the idea emerged. Such differentiation is vital to the emergence of the wisdom of crowds. Such differentiation can itself be done by the crowd as the multiple perspectives offered by the crowd are more likely to 'spot the difference' between the options than any one single individual could.

A great deal of the confusion we feel about the challenges we face, especially the really tough wicked problems such as political governance, climate change, poverty and rampant capitalism is down to the fact that we have been unable to clearly define and differentiate the issues we face. A lack of definition will often lead to an imprecise solution as evidenced by the countless failed attempts to solve these and many more complex challenges.

Once we have defined the various ideas or views in play we look to create proposals that can integrate as many of the perspectives as possible and create a workable (not necessarily optimum) way forward. Genuine integration of the best of many perspectives is achieved through a series of iterative conversations where each proposal is modified by determining what is stopping the proposal from being adopted. Objections are flushed out and integrated as much as possible. Ultimately, this generates a series of distinct proposals that are put to the crowd for a vote.

This final integration phase is critically important for evolutionary forward momentum. While it is entirely possible to break a new idea or system down into highly differentiated parts, unless there is integration with the best of what has gone before fragmentation or even dis-integration can occur pushing us backward not forwards. This dis-integration can be seen in modern scientific medicine.

Over the last 150 years, our understanding of the human body and human health has improved exponentially. In that time scientists and physicians have been unravelling the complexity of the human condition by systematically reducing it to increasingly smaller parts. This *systematic reductionism* has been the overriding approach to investigating human beings and it has been incredibly successful. Reductionism has shed new light on how the human body works. It has generated an enormous amount of new information, spawned whole new areas of medical research and created new languages to capture the myriad of discoveries being made.

But the unintended consequences of this incredible dissection and fragmentation of the human condition means that whilst we have largely mastered the emergence part of the evolutionary process, and we are pretty skilled at the differentiation element, we still have a very long way to go to master integration. In fact 'integrated care' and 'interdisciplinary research' has only really emerged in the last 20 years as a concept, let alone matured as a practice. Complex systems such as societies and governments can't be understood simply by understanding each part of that system because the whole is *always* greater than the sum of the parts. Integration is the final stage that allows emergence and differentiation to really bear fruit.

We need to integrate and understand how the new version of anything relates to what's already in place so we make genuine improvements rather than simply reshuffling the same tired old ideas. This requires us to develop our ability to integrate the new with the existing so we can transcend and include existing options and create new, improved inclusive scenarios. If we as individuals, groups, organisations or societies develop the ability to construct integrated answers that can embrace a wider set of phenomena then we are genuinely on the path to a wiser outcome, one that supports more of us rather than just the small elite.

Integration Fosters the Endowment Effect

One of the critical dimensions to the integrative process is that people feel their objections are heard and acknowledged in the construction of an evolving answer. If this is the case then they will often back the answer generated even if they did not completely agree with it.

In the field of behavioural economics this is known as the Endowment Effect. Basically, people tend to value what they choose or already own. This means that large-scale participation significantly increases the likelihood that people will execute the solutions they have a hand in generating.

One of the first people to write about the Endowment Effect was Professor of Psychology at Harvard University Dr Ellen Langer and her colleague at the time Judith Rodin in the 1970s. They conducted a now famous study in a nursing home. In one group, participants were encouraged to find ways to make more of their own decisions. For example, they were allowed to decide when they would see visitors or when to watch movies. Each participant was also encouraged to choose a house plant and the plant was then their responsibility. They could decide where the plant was to sit in their room and how often they needed to water it. The intention of the experiment was to make the residents of the nursing home more mindful of their day to day activities and help them engage with life more fully.

The second, control group were not given the same encouragement to be mindful and although they too had a houseplant they did not choose the houseplant themselves. Instead the plant was handed to them and they were told that the nurses would take care of it. A year and a half later, the residents from the first group were found to be more cheerful, active and alert as evidenced by the difference in a variety of test scores administered before and after the experiment. The study showed that those that were more actively engaged and felt more in control of their choices, even marginally, were also healthier than the other group. What came as a surprise however was that less than half as many residents from the engaged group died over the term of the experiment compared to the group who could not exert any control over their daily lives.

Langer and Rodin explained their results in terms of 'locus of control' or our need to have at least some say over the choices we make that affect us and the environment we operate in.[33] It's easy to see in this context why so many of us feel so disillusioned by the current political system – we feel we have no control.

Further studies into the Endowment Effect have verified these outcomes time and time again – we value, engage with and get behind ideas and solutions when we have been involved and allowed to contribute and participate on those ideas and

---

[33] Langer, E.J. (1975) 'The illusion of control', *Journal of Personality and Social Psychology*, 32, no. 2, pp. 311–28.

solutions.[34] Crowdocracy therefore allows us to activate the Endowment Effect around political governance and policy decisions because it provides us with a platform to participate so we can all have a hand in creating or choosing the policies we want to bring to life in the world.

People believe in what they create not in what is created and imposed on them by authority figures. When people are part of a process in which they have a say, they are far more likely to support the outcome, even if the final collective decision is not what they personally suggested or hoped for.

For example, when I (IS) lived in Lausanne, the capital of the canton of Vaud in Switzerland, the community was asked to vote on whether garbage bags should be taxed at eight Swiss francs per bag which is about £5 or €7 per bag. The purpose of this initiative was to gauge public support for a tax as a way to push recycling up and waste down. However, if a government department had tabled a meeting and decided to impose such a tax via a top-down initiative, the citizens would probably have been outraged. Five pounds per garbage bag is, after all, a pretty steep tariff. But the issue was put out to a public vote and it was voted in. Even those that voted against it bought the garbage bags for eight Swiss francs per bag because they felt they had been fairly consulted and were therefore part of the process.

Today Switzerland is one of the top recyclers in the world, with 66 to 96 per cent of recyclable materials being recycled. In many places in Switzerland, not just Lausanne, household garbage

---

[34] Kahneman, D., Knetsch, J. L., and Thaler, R. H. (1990) 'Experimental Tests of the Endowment Effect and the Coase Theorem', *Journal of Political Economy*, 98, pp. 1325–48.
van Dijk, E., and van Knippenberg, D. (1998) 'Trading wine: On the endowment effect, loss aversion, and the comparability of consumer goods', *Journal of Economic Psychology*, 19, pp. 485–95.
Knetsch, J. L., and Sinden, J. A. (1984) 'Willingness to pay and compensation demanded: Experimental evidence of an unexpected disparity in measures of value', *Quarterly Journal of Economics*, 99, pp. 507–21.

disposal is charged for. With the exception of dangerous items, such as batteries, garbage is only collected if a payment sticker is attached to the bag or the garbage is in an official bag with the surcharge paid at the time of purchase. This gives a financial incentive to recycle as much as possible, since recycling is free.[35]

Integration Facilitates Second Perspective

Integration is possibly the most challenging component for unlocking the wisdom of the crowd because we are so used to dialectic arguments of right and wrong. This binary position means that we are very familiar with arm wrestling others into our position or being convinced or brow beaten into a compromise position. In fact, we rarely consider there is another way. This is, at least in part, because we don't appreciate what perspective we are taking in a discussion. When someone is in first person perspective they are passionately advocating what they believe in. Many media opinions pieces are written from this perspective. Politicians may discuss issues from this perspective and lobbyists almost certainly advocate from this perspective. The most common alternative is third person perspective where an individual may helicopter up to become a dispassionate observer and explain the situation through data and facts. Often people will move between the two and will cherry-pick the data that validates their first person perspective but will package it up as third person perspective taking. Or they will use the third person data to validate their first person perspective.

What happens as a result is that when two groups get together, say to decide policy or debate an issue, the whole conversation gets 'dumbed down' as each side attempts to strong-arm the other into agreeing with their point of view. The side that then 'wins' effectively forces a surrender or negotiates a compromise. Neither is ideal.

---

[35] 'Switzerland – Energy, infrastructure, and environment', accessed 29 December 2015, http://country-stats.com

Genuine integration transcends and includes that simplistic approach to take the best of all input to create a new improved, shared position that most people can get behind willingly (taking second person perspective, by putting yourself in the shoes of the other(s)). Such integration, when done in a room full of protagonists requires very sophisticated facilitation, but it can be done by the crowd itself on the right technology platform. What technology does is remove the need for anyone to surrender or compromise. By collecting the wisdom of the crowd and integrating those ideas, a genuine shared solution that everyone can resonate with becomes possible because the first and third person perspectives are integrated. This is also helped by a greater individual understanding of the integrative process.

Smart integration will also diffuse the tendency for disagreement, conflict and 'posturing' whether it is political posturing or egoic posturing. It embraces the fact that we all have something valuable to add. If we follow the simple rules that guide this three-step evolutionary process then wisdom is much more likely to emerge. A point well made by James Surowiecki when he stated, 'Groups generally need rules to maintain order and coherence, and when they're missing or malfunctioning, the result is trouble.'[36]

These are the rules that will help us to avoid trouble as we differentiate crowdocracy from democracy and holacracy and seek to integrate it so that crowdocracy becomes the new best form of governance that transcends and includes all the best elements of previous forms of governance.

The wisdom of crowds can be a challenging concept to accept but it's worth remembering that at a time when the world is changing faster than ever before *innovation* is more important than ever. Genuine innovation is significantly amplified and accelerated by high quality differentiation and integration. The

---

[36] Surowiecki, J. (2004) *The Wisdom of Crowds: Why the many are smarter than the few*, London: Little Brown.

collective integration of all of our individual perspectives may help us solve wicked problems faster. Individual errors and self-interest will get cancelled out by the crowd so that the best solution for all of us emerges.

When we all participate and contribute our ideas, knowledge and diverse perspectives, then the wicked problem of politics may give way to a new level of crowd participation, a new level of engagement, a new level of community and a fundamental shift in our relationship with each other.

Chapter 5:

The Principles of
Crowdocracy in Action

'We are better off in our collective pursuit of truth if all of us are free to speak our minds.'

– John Stuart Mill[1]

Although we may not realise it, most of us are actually already very familiar with intelligent crowd-based processes. What we feel, think and do is already being captured in technology-based tools and devices that most of us use every day. Google's algorithms are based on crowd intelligence and rely on more than 200 unique signals or 'clues' that make it possible to guess what you might really be searching for amongst the billions of possible results. Spotify offers us playlists based on the preferences of all its users and how they are similar to ours – allowing us to find new music we might enjoy. Amazon's analytics offers us recommendations based on our buying behaviour and the wisdom of the crowd. Product advertising is also presented to us on the Internet based on our *collective* search requests and shopping behaviour.

---

[1]   Mill, J.S. (1859) *On Liberty*.

We are already using our collective intelligence in ways that were unimaginable before the technological advancements of the past 20 years. In this chapter we will share a few examples of how many of us are already collaborating online and offline to create products, services, organisations and even better governance. As such you will be able to see that crowdocracy is not a radical leap into the unknown but simply the next evolutionary iteration in a crowd-based revolution that is already quietly taking place all over the world.

There are many initiatives that aim to bring the wisdom of the crowd into the way we organise our businesses and our societies – each potentially a book in its own right. Technology has often been instrumental in the evolution of such systems. However, technology is rarely used to drive the transition from a system that includes the few to a system that is designed to embrace the many. We will highlight a few of the most inspiring examples that exist inside and outside the political arena that we believe are getting closest to the idea of crowdocracy. Specifically, we will explore:

- Crowd intelligence in products and services
- Crowd intelligence in research
- Crowd intelligence in organisations
- Crowd intelligence in governance
- Crowd intelligence in activism

Crowd Intelligence in Products and Services

In the last chapter we explored Linux as an example of technological decentralisation. Linux is widely used open source software that was made possible by the cooperation and participation of the crowd. Other examples include Wikipedia and Kickstarter.

Wikipedia

Founded by Jimmy Wales in 2001, the name 'Wikipedia' is a portmanteau of the Hawaiian word 'wiki' meaning quick and 'encyclopedia'. When Wikipedia began, there were already some serious online players in the market including *Encyclopaedia Britannica* and Microsoft's *Encarta*. At the time, Microsoft was still a hugely successful business with an almost omnipotent operating system. With such a direct line to the billions of computers around the world, Microsoft decided to enter the encyclopedia market. The intention was to produce a CD-ROM to sell to its users and later make it available online to download. It was, by all accounts, a smart business move.

Microsoft hired legions of professional researchers, writers and editors to craft articles on thousands of topics and employed well-paid managers to oversee the project. Yet on 31 October 2009, Microsoft pulled the plug on *MSN Encarta* after 16 years, stating, 'Encarta has been a popular product around the world for many years. However, the category of traditional encyclopedias and reference material has changed. People today seek and consume information in considerably different ways than in years past.'

Although not directly mentioning Wikipedia, it is widely acknowledged that Wikipedia killed *Encarta* in just eight years! By the time Microsoft bowed out, Wikipedia had more than 13 million articles in some 260 languages, including 3 million in English alone.[2] But Wikipedia didn't employ professional researchers, writers or editors, instead the content was written collaboratively by largely anonymous volunteers who were not paid or incentivised in any way. People of all ages, cultures and backgrounds can add or edit an article, the references, images or other media on Wikipedia.

---

[2] Pink, D.H. (2009) *Drive: The surprising truth about what motivates us*, New York: Penguin.

Anyone with Internet access can write and make changes to Wikipedia articles, although there are limited cases where editing is restricted. There are no managers, no schedules, no deadlines or even any requests – it's all done by the crowd when the crowd feels like it. Users can contribute anonymously, under a pseudonym or their real identity.

Again, it's the wisdom of the crowd that makes Wikipedia possible. The diversity of the crowd ensures that errors get cancelled out. If, for example, someone in London looks up the Wikipedia page for Harrods and as a London resident notices that something is inaccurate they can change it. When enough eyes are on the content and those eyes can change the content if it is wrong then the mistakes are picked up quickly and fixed. Even if there are no errors, human knowledge is constantly evolving and expanding, situations are changing so a live, continually created and updated information source is always going to be superior to a static, albeit beautifully bound physical book. Often, details of historic events appear on Wikipedia within minutes, rather than weeks, months or even years.

Wikipedia is built on five pillars or fundamental principles, stated as follows:

- Wikipedia is an encyclopedia: It combines many features of general and specialised encyclopedias, almanacs and gazetteers. Wikipedia is not a soapbox, an advertising platform, a vanity press, an experiment in anarchy or democracy, an indiscriminate collection of information, or a web directory. It's not a dictionary, a newspaper, or a collection of source documents, although some of its fellow Wikimedia projects are.
- Wikipedia is written from a neutral point of view: We strive for articles that document and explain the major points of view, giving due weight with respect to their prominence in an impartial tone. We avoid advocacy and we characterise information and issues, rather than debate them. In some

areas there may be just one well-recognised point of view; in others we describe multiple points of view, presenting each accurately and in context rather than as 'the truth' or 'the best view'. All articles must strive for verifiable accuracy, citing reliable, authoritative sources, especially when the topic is controversial or is on living persons. Editors' personal experiences, interpretations, or opinions do not belong.

- Wikipedia is free content that anyone can use, edit, and distribute: Since all editors freely license their work to the public, no editor owns an article and any contributions can and will be mercilessly edited and redistributed. Respect copyright laws, and never plagiarise from sources. Borrowing non-free media is sometimes allowed as fair use, but strive to find free alternatives first.

- Editors should treat each other with respect and civility: Respect your fellow Wikipedians, even when you disagree. Apply Wikipedia etiquette, and don't engage in personal attacks. Seek consensus, avoid edit wars, and never disrupt Wikipedia to illustrate a point. Act in good faith, and assume good faith on the part of others. Be open and welcoming to newcomers. If a conflict arises, discuss it calmly on the nearest talk pages, follow dispute resolution, and remember that there are 5,015,900 articles on the English Wikipedia to work on and discuss.

- Wikipedia has no firm rules: Wikipedia has policies and guidelines, but they are not carved in stone; their content and interpretation can evolve over time. Their principles and spirit matter more than their literal wording, and sometimes improving Wikipedia requires making an exception. Be bold but not reckless in updating articles, and do not agonise about making mistakes. Every past version of a page is saved, so any mistakes can be easily corrected.[3]

[3] Wikipedia's Five Pillars, accessed 25th November 2015, https://en.wikipedia.org/wiki/Wikipedia:Five_pillars

These five pillars form a sort of 'Wikipedia constitution'. And clearly it's working – as of June 2015, there are now more than 73,000 active contributors working on more than 35 million articles in 290 languages. Every day, hundreds of thousands of visitors around the world collectively make tens of thousands of edits and approximately 750 new articles are added per day to further advance the reach and scope of Wikipedia.

Kickstarter

Kickstarter was founded in 2009 with a mission to bring creative projects to life. Kickstarter was a little different from the get-go because it was founded as a B-corp (Benefit Corporation). A B-corp is a company whose legally defined goals include making a positive impact on society and the environment in addition to profit.

Kickstarter and other crowd-funding websites such as Indiegogo, RocketHub and FundRazr use crowd wisdom in a reverse way. Individuals or businesses propose their ideas to the crowd. Based on their reactions (mostly financial pledges) the initiators make a decision to go ahead with their idea or not.

For a start-up initiative or enterprise, Kickstarter has huge advantages. If, for example, you have an idea about creating a new line of T-shirts, you can figure out whether there will be a market for your idea very quickly and inexpensively based on a few computer drawings and maybe a couple of samples. Moreover, you can get the funding from the advance sales of your product, rather than selling the shares in your company to a venture capitalist. Today, entrepreneurs can better appreciate their idea's market potential *before* they've sunk thousands of hours into the project and remortgaged their home. Often the initial exploration phase can cost as little as a few thousand dollars.

As of November 2015, 9.9 million people have backed a project on Kickstarter since inception. Over two billion dollars have been pledged and 96,167 projects have been successfully funded across categories as varied as film, music, stage shows, comics, journalism, video games, technology and food-related projects.[4]

Crowd Intelligence in Research

When Raphael Silberzahn and Eric Uhlmann published research suggesting that noble-sounding German surnames, such as König (king) and Fürst (prince), could boost careers,[5] another psychologist, Uri Simonsohn at the University of Pennsylvania in Philadelphia, asked for their data set. Simonsohn was skeptical. Courageously, the researchers agreed in their first unplanned experience of crowdsourced research.

Although re-running the analysis using the same methodology yielded the same results, Simonsohn's alternative analytical approach showed no connection between powerful sounding surnames and career advancement. But rather than sweep the findings under the carpet or get upset even though they had recently announced their findings to the media, Silberzahn and Uhlmann acknowledged that Simonsohn's technique showing no effect was more accurate and all three wrote a new piece contrasting their analytical approaches and presented a joint conclusion.[6] This collaboration led to new improved insights into research methodology.

---

[4] Kickstarter website, accessed 23 October 2015, www.kickstarter.com/about?ref=nav

[5] Silberzahn, R. and Uhlmann, E. L. (2013) 'It pays to be Herr Kaiser', Psychological Science, 24, pp. 2437–44 .

[6] Silberzahn, R., Simonsohn, U., and Uhlmann, E.L. (2014) 'Matched names analysis reveals no evidence of name meaning effects: A collaborative commentary on Silberzahn and Uhlmann (2013)', Psychological Science, 25, pp. 1504-5.

In the world of research where analyses are run by a single team the researchers take on multiple roles and those roles are often conflicting. For example, the researcher must first be an inventor who creates ideas and hypotheses, then an optimistic analyst who scrutinise, the data in search of confirmation and finally they must play the role of devil's advocate and seek to reveal flaws in the findings. There is clearly a conflict of interest in this set-up because the same team that has just invested serious time and effort proving a hypothesis is then charged with disproving it. Logic alone would suggest that the efforts to disprove it are often less rigorous than the efforts to prove it.

Silberzahn and Uhlmann's experience working with Simonsohn and collaborating to get to a better outcome resulted in the proposal of an alternative set-up – where the part of 'devil's advocate' is played by other research teams or a wider research crowd. What these researchers acknowledged and subsequent experiments demonstrated is that any research can be interpreted a number of different ways which means that taking any single analysis too seriously could be a mistake. This is, however, exactly what is happening in the current system of scientific publishing and media coverage. Once published, a hypothesis can soon morph into scientific law and is therefore rarely questioned, sometimes with far reaching consequences.

Crowdsourcing the role of devil's advocate can reveal how conclusions are contingent on analytical choices. Providing a crowdsourcing framework also provides researchers with a safe space in which they can vet analytical approaches, explore doubts and get a second, third or fourth opinion.

Finally, as the researchers acknowledge, 'Crowdsourcing also reduces the incentive for flashy, [tweetable] results. A single-team project may be published only if it finds significant effects; participants in crowdsourced projects can contribute even with null findings. A range of scientific possibilities are revealed, the results are more credible and analytical choices that seem to sway conclusions can point research in fruitful new directions. What is more, analysts learn from each other, and the creativity required to construct analytical methodologies can be better appreciated by the research community and the public.'[7]

While not all researchers will be as open and transparent as Silberzahn and Uhlmann, and may not wish to share data they have painstakingly collected, there is little doubt that the results are improved by sharing it with the crowd. Considering that scientists around the world are hungry for more reliable ways to discover new knowledge, opening research up to the research crowd and possibly beyond may just be the answer.

Research by Sheer Numbers in the Crowd

The sheer numbers of the crowd, together with technological innovation are also providing exceptionally novel solutions to long-standing intractable challenges.

In one such example, game developers in Dundee collaborated with scientists at Cambridge University to create a gaming app similar to the retro computer game 'space invaders' called *Genes in Space*. To the gamer, it looks like they are navigating through stars and galaxies but what they are actually doing is navigating through graphics made up of the DNA information of thousands of tumour samples.

In its traditional form, this data is displayed on a computer screen as a series of dots in various peaks and troughs of differing concentrations. It was the job of researchers to assess those images to find anomalies that could then be analysed but this was notoriously difficult and time consuming. *Genes in Space*

---

[7] Silberzahn, R. and Uhlmann, E.L. (2015) 'Crowdsourced research: Many hands make tight work', *Nature*, 7 October 2015, accessed 29 December 2015, www.nature.com/news/crowdsourced-research-many-hands-make-tight-work-1.18508

now means that gamers identify the anomalies by navigating their battleship through densely concentrated areas of the galaxy. Each level the gamer then completes means that one DNA sample has been mapped and the data is automatically sent back to the lab for analysis.

According to the leader of the research team, Professor Carlos Candus, the lab received 1.5 million analyses in the first month following the release of the game. In other words, gamers had generated their own interpretation of the data 1.5 million times. Without the game it would have taken the research team 125,000 non-stop hours or 14 years to cover the same amount of data that the gamers had covered in just one month![8]

This type of collaboration between technology and members of the public is creating an explosion of 'citizen science' initiatives where ordinary people are collaborating with scientists to provide data around particular issues. This is happening via specially designed games such as *Genes in Space* or through providing data from their geographic area. For example, data on butterfly numbers, bird populations across a region or wildlife numbers can be provided in a fraction of the time and budget by ordinary citizens who can then send the data back to scientists for analysis using a specially designed app or website.[9]

Crowd Intelligence in Organisations

In organisations, particularly business, tapping into the intelligence of the crowd is a fast growing phenomenon as well. This happens in two ways: incorporating stakeholders' such as employees, customers and shareholder views in the decision-making processes and reducing or eliminating hierarchy in

---

[8] BBC One (2014) *Bang Goes the Theory*: *Big Data*.

[9] Citizen Scientist website, accessed 29 December 2015, www. citizenscientist.org.uk/welcome/

organisations to empower groups of people to self-govern.

Informing Decision-making

According to IBM's 2008 Global CEO Study, 83 per cent of CEOs and senior leaders expected substantial change – up from 65 per cent two years earlier. Unfortunately, those reporting that they had successfully managed change in the previous two years rose only 4 per cent, up from 57 per cent to 61 per cent.[10] This 'Change Gap' or the disparity between the expected change and the ability to manage it nearly tripled between 2006 and 2008.[11] The same study two years later identified escalating operational complexity in a VUCA world as the primary challenge. An alarming number of CEOs reported that they still felt ill-equipped to succeed in this drastically different corporate landscape.[12] In 2012, the challenge was still change. This time it was how to adequately manage and capitalise on the convergence of the digital, social and mobile spheres and how to connect customers, employees and partners to organisations and to each other in new ways.[13]

Leaders of organisations clearly recognise that the challenges they face in a highly competitive and volatile environment are severe with no sign that they will slow down any time soon. No one leader or even a small group of executives could possibly have all the answers to these challenges or be able to effectively navigate the changes they will bring. Smart leaders are already turning to their stakeholder crowd for help: gathering information, opinions, and advice. Not only are they then more likely to find innovative solutions and ideas that the executive team would never have thought of but they also facilitate greater engagement

---

[10] IBM Global CEO Study (2008) 'The Enterprise of the Future'.

[11] IBM Making Change Work (2008), accessed 29 December 2015, www-935.ibm.com/services/us/gbs/bus/pdf/gbe03100-usen-03-making-change-work.pdf

[12] IBM Global CEO Study (2010) 'Capitalizing on Complexity'.

[13] IBM Global CEO Study (2012) 'Leading Through Connections'.

from the various stakeholder groups. Remember we tend to value what we have had a hand in creating or influencing. When employees feel valued and listened to they are much more likely to engage their discretionary effort. When customers feel valued and listened to they are much more like to increase their loyalty – both of which can significantly influence the bottom line.

Globescan, a Canadian polling company with offices across the world, specialises in helping its corporate and non-corporate clients tap into the wisdom of its stakeholders. For example, when Unilever announced its bold sustainability programme in 2010, Globescan helped a global crowdsourcing of ideas from about 500 stakeholders (many of them sustainability experts) in an online lab. This helped Unilever gain 1750 comments and ideas from this (invitee only) crowd and at the same time built a larger engagement in the programme.

Prediction Markets

Some companies take a more technical approach to crowdsourcing, by setting up an internal market for ideas. In his book *Smart Swarm*, author Peter Miller tells the story of electronic superstore Best Buy vice president Jeff Severts who created some crowdsource experiments in the business after seeing a presentation by James Surowiecki – the author of *The Wisdom of Crowds*. Severts wondered if he could tap into his Best Buy employee crowd to facilitate better decisions and so he sent emails to several hundred employees throughout the company asking them to predict sales of gift cards in February. He received 192 replies and in early March compared the average of the 192 estimates with the actual sales figures. The collective estimate was 99.5 per cent accurate and five per cent better than the estimate produced by the sales forecast team. In an operation the size of Best Buy an improvement of inventory management of 5 per cent can equate to huge money.

Severts was so impressed with the result of the crowd over the small team of 'experts' that he and his team began experimenting with *prediction markets* – a more sophisticated way of gathering forecasts about company performance from employees. A prediction market, also known as a predictive, information or decision market, is a market that's created for the purpose of trading the outcome of events. The market price therefore indicates what the crowd believe the probability of that event occurring is and contracts are traded between 1 and 100 per cent. Employees at Best Buy were able to use play money to bid on the outcome of questions such as 'Will our first store in China open on time?' A correct bid paid $100, and an incorrect bid paid nothing. If the current market price was $85, for example, then collectively the group thinks there's an 85 per cent chance that the store will open on time. If an employee thinks there is actually a 95 per cent chance the store will open on time then he or she can place the bet seeing an opportunity to make an additional $10.

Best Buy were due to open a new store in Shanghai and for many months the prediction market hovered around $80, then eight weeks before the scheduled open date the price took a dive to $50 – meaning half the crowd didn't believe the store would open on time, despite official forecasts stating everything was on track. In the end the store opened a month late.

Severts stated, 'The first drop was an early warning signal. Some pieces of new information came into the market that caused the traders to radically change their expectations.' What's especially interesting in this context is that it actually didn't matter what the new information was or where it came from, the prediction market had proven its ability to integrate information from diverse, anonymous sources in a decentralised way so as to sound an alarm – assuming anyone was listening. As such the prediction market overcame the many barriers to effective communication that exist in a large company.[14]

---

[14] Miller, P. (2010) *Smart Swarm: Using Animal Behaviour to Organise Our World*, Collins.

In a typical commercial environment, even if someone knows that something was going wrong or suspects that something is off-track they are usually reluctant to raise it. Although we are told 'don't shoot the messenger' – we often do! Potentially, a prediction market allows the crowd to bring crucial information to light without finger pointing and accusations. This new data can then help to rectify the situation before it morphs into a major issue.

Self-Organisation

There is clearly a valuable role that the crowd can play in informing decision-making. But some organisations take the wisdom of the crowd to a whole new level and leave all the decision-making to employees. These enlightened and innovative organisations have realised that the traditional power hierarchy does not serve the full development of its people, or the full development of the company itself. In his book *Reinventing Organization*, author Fréderic Laloux describes a number of these companies, some of which have been around for a long time. They take the approach that the organisation is a living organism in itself, rather than a lifeless building, an organisation chart and a set of processes. Laloux's 're-invented' *living* companies all embrace three core principles:

– self-management: governance based on peer relationships without hierarchy or consensus building
– wholeness: people are invited to bring their whole self to work (and not hide behind a 'professional mask')
– evolutionary purpose: the organisation has its own purpose and direction that wants to emerge and they embrace the concept of evolutionary purpose

FAVI, one of the examples Laloux describes, is a French brass foundry that produces things like gearbox forks for cars. The company has around 500 employees, many of whom have little formal education. There are no managers, no central functions like

HR or finance. Everyone operates in teams, and everyone has full authority to make any decision they want, as long as they consult anyone else who may be affected by the decision. Throughout the organisation there are coaches, who can support teams with any tensions that they experience. This empowering consultative process ensures that the wisdom of the entire organisation is tapped into and the results are stunning. FAVI prides itself on never having missed an order in 20 years. Employee engagement is exceptionally high and staff turnover is negligible. FAVI is highly profitable, despite a very competitive marketplace.

The other organisations that Laloux describes share similar stories and demonstrate similar results. Laloux found, that the most powerful common denominator in all the companies he studied was trust. 'If you view people with mistrust and subject them to all sorts of controls, rules and punishments,' he writes, 'they will try to game the system, and you will feel your thinking is validated. Meet people with practices based on trust, and they will return your trust with responsible behavior. Again, you will feel your assumptions were validated.'[15]

This is stark contrast to most traditional organisations where formal leaders still live in the paradigm that they need to come up with all the clever ideas and that the people 'below' should follow and execute – or at least that they cannot be left with decision-making power.

What we find particularly interesting, and once again validates the wisdom of the collective, is that the individuals in the crowd don't need to be highly developed or even highly intelligent, and yet they are perfectly able to operate in the enlightened forms of organisational design. In other words, as long as the system is robustly designed anyone, regardless of their individual enlightenment, can operate within it. Of course, this is directly

---

[15] Schwartz, T. (2014) 'Putting Soul Back Into Business', *New York Times*, 19 September 2014, accessed 30 December 2015, http://dealbook. nytimes.com/2014/09/19/putting-soul-back-into-business/?_r=0

relevant to the new form of governance that we are proposing because the primary challenge that we hear is, 'Yes, but the people are not ready for this, they are not smart enough'.

So long as the governance system is fit for purpose, the people are ready for this and there is now overwhelming evidence to support that fact.[16] In an increasingly competitive and fast-moving corporate environment, harnessing the wisdom of the crowd may be the single biggest opportunity to future-proof a business.

Crowd Intelligence in the Political Arena

Crowd intelligence powered by technology has given great impetus to renewed initiatives in participatory democracy, deliberative democracy and direct democracy. These philosophical streams have been around for a long time, with limited influence in the actual processes of democracy. Participatory democracy emphasises the broad participation of constituents in the direction and operation of political systems whereas deliberative democrats are interested in the quality of communication and debate to ensure the development of more considered preferences in the political decision-making process.[17] While the two concepts are different, they are often mistakenly used interchangeably. In both concepts, the focus is on better decision-making by the representative politicians through the

---

[16] Arriaga, M. (2014) *Rebooting Democracy: A citizen's guide to reinventing politics*, London: Thistle Publishing.

[17] Floridia, A. (2013) 'Participatory Democracy versus Deliberative Democracy: Elements for a Possible Theoretical Genealogy. Two Histories, Some Intersections', 7th ECPR General Conference, accessed 30 December 2015, http://ecpr.eu/filestore/paperproposal/71d7f83c-3fe4-4b11-82a2-c151cd3769f4.pdf

inclusion of the views of those affected by the decisions.

Direct democracy goes a step further than participative or deliberative democracy. It advocates decision-making directly by the people, overriding the views of the representative politicians. The most common example of direct democracy is the use of the referendum: a direct vote by the people on a certain topic or piece of legislation. The right to launch a referendum exists in the legislation of many countries – although it is rarely used. The process can take a long time, it requires many people to support it and the chances of success are often not very high.

There are numerous initiatives across the world of participatory, deliberative and direct forms of democracy. More than 500 studies and organisations that use some form of the above three options have been described by academics on www.participedia.net.

Below we've highlighted a few that we think are particularly insightful in light of crowdocracy, which in essence is the next evolutionary step of direct democracy.

Iceland

In October 2008, Iceland's banking system completely collapsed. In 2003, Iceland's three biggest banks had assets of a few billion dollars which was about 100 per cent of the country's gross domestic product (GDP). Over the next three-and-a-half years the banking assets grew to over $140 billion. The banks went on a lending spree and Icelanders borrowed to buy shares and real estate. Between 2003 and 2007 the value of the US stock market doubled. The value of the Iceland stock market increased ninefold! Icelandic real estate prices tripled. It wasn't long before Icelanders had amassed debts amounting to 850 per cent of their GDP. With less than 350,000 inhabitants, the Icelandic people had somehow 'organised themselves to commit one of the single greatest acts of madness in financial history'.[18]

What followed was a severe depression. The three banks were nationalised, the stock market plummeted, unemployment tripled and there was even fear that the supermarkets would run out of food. The collapse was so catastrophic that many Icelanders considered emigrating.

Confusion quickly turned to anger, conversation turned to demonstration during a period of significant political unrest. After just five months of sustained and vocal demonstration, the protesters' got the result they demanded – the government, the head of the Central Bank and the director of the Financial Supervisory Authority all resigned.[19] The new left-leaning coalition government that took over set up an investigations office with the power to prosecute bankers and government officials. And they did. Many of the bankers involved were sent to prison for up to five and a half years for their role in the collapse.

Not only is this a pretty swift demonstration of people power in action but what Iceland has done since is nothing short of revolutionary and offers us real hope for global political change.

In March 2015, the International Monetary Fund (IMF) which helped Iceland after the crash praised the country for being, 'one of the top economic performers in Europe over the past several years in terms of economic growth [with] one of the lowest unemployment rates', and for being on course to pay back its IMF loans early.

So, how has Iceland done it? Iceland's significant achievements

---

[18] Lewis, M. (2011) *Boomerang*, London: Penguin.

[19] England, P. (2015) 'Iceland's "pots and pans revolution": Lessons from a nation that people power helped to emerge from its 2008 crisis all the stronger', *The Independent*, 28 June 2015, accessed 30 December 2015, www.independent.co.uk/news/world/europe/icelands-pots-and-pans-revolution-lessons-from-a-nation-that-people-power-helped-to-emerge-from-its-2008-crisis-all-the-stronger-10351095.html

post-financial crash were made possible by a politically re-engaged electorate that pressed for significant change and made use of innovative technology to change the political landscape. As a fledgling example of what can be achieved through a crowdocratic process of sorts, the Icelandic population stopped being political spectators and started a cluster of citizens' initiatives dedicated to improving the way democracy works. They were not interested in banking reform. They knew that such a band-aid solution would only lead to a new crisis down the track. Instead, they were after full-blown political reform so they could treat the disease instead of simply addressing the symptoms. The population wanted a new social agreement with its politicians that would change the context in which politicians operated so they could never again sell the country down the river. With a new Social Contract in place, citizens could build a new democracy. And part of this process took the form of writing a new constitution for the country.

The drafting and redrafting of the constitution was completely transparent and socialised on the Internet. The text was made public each week and the country was invited to offer comments and suggestions on an interactive website specifically designed for the purpose. Hundreds of citizens did and many suggestions were included in the developing constitution.[20] This may have been one of the crucial factors that increased the wisdom of the crowd. All comments, contributions and amendments from the wider community were taken on board in subsequent revisions. Despite considerable constraints, which we will outline in more detail in Chapter 7, the resulting document, while still not without its flaws, is considered the world's most inclusively and transparently written constitutional text and an inspiration for people around the world intent on writing or rewriting their own

---

[20] Gylfason, T. (2014) 'Events in Iceland show that a UK constitutional convention should involve politicians as minimally as possible', OXPOL, The Oxford University Politics Blog, 3 November 2014, accessed 30 December 2015, http://politicsinspires.org/events-iceland-show-uk-constitutional-convention-involve-politicians-minimally-possible/

social contract.[21]

The new Constitution put human rights at the heart of Icelandic democracy; it recognised the rights of nature and gave citizens the right to call referendums, block legislation, table bills and present issues for consideration providing there was enough support for the issue.

Researchers from the Comparative Constitutions Project considered the crowdsourced draft to be tremendously innovative and participatory. Adding, 'Though squarely grounded in Iceland's constitutional tradition as embodied in the 1944 Constitution, the proposed draft reflects significant input from the public and would mark an important symbolic break with the past. It would also be at the cutting edge of ensuring public participation in ongoing governance, a feature that we argue has contributed to constitutional endurance in other countries.'[22]

According to the 2010 Democracy Index, Iceland was ranked second in the world behind Norway based on five categories: electoral process and pluralism; civil liberties; the functioning of government; political participation; and political culture.[23] In 2011, Iceland was also ranked thirteenth in the world for government transparency.[24] Considering where it was just a few short years

---

[21] Landemore, H. (2014) 'We, All of the People: Five lessons from Iceland's failed experiment in creating a crowdsourced constitution', Slate, 31 July 2014, accessed 30 December 2015, http://www.slate.com/articles/technology/future_tense/2014/07/five_lessons_from_iceland_s_failed_crowdsourced_constitution_experiment.html

[22] Elkins, Z., Ginsburg, T. and Melton, J. (2012) 'A Review of Iceland's Draft Constitution', accessed 30 December 2015, http://comparativeconstitutionsproject.org/wp-content/uploads/CCP-Iceland-Report.pdf

[23] Democracy index 2010 'Democracy in retreat', Economist Intelligence Unit, The Economist, accessed 30 December 2015, https://graphics.eiu.com/PDF/Democracy_Index_2010_web.pdf

[24] Corruption Perceptions Index 2011, accessed 30 December 2015, www.transparency.org/cpi2011/results/

ago – these rankings are incredibly impressive.

Sadly, the crowdsourced Constitution has yet to be fully adopted as politicians from various parties have done their best to block the will of the people. In an attempt to break the deadlock, the Social Democrats managed to put the matter back in the hands of the people and ask them whether the Constitution should be adopted. Despite further political attempts to rig the question put to the people, a national referendum produced a whopping 67 per cent in favour of the new crowdsourced Icelandic constitution being adopted. Amazingly at this time (2015), politicians are still resisting the will of the people.

What happened in Iceland is both an inspiring glimpse of what's possible if we evolve democracy and a compelling reminder of the urgent need for change. Anthony Barnett, founder of the Open Democracy website also believes that what happened in Iceland demonstrates that we can and should trust citizens to determine how they are governed adding: 'Iceland shows that regular people have the wisdom to do this just as juries have the wisdom to come to views in trials. You cannot leave it to parliament on its own to rewrite a system in which it has this enormous vested interest.'[25] What happened in Iceland has also inspired many around the world, including us, to see what is possible if we have the courage to work collectively on the complex and wicked problems we face.

Argentina

In 2012, the Argentine political activist Pia Mancini and a group of friends discussed their political system. They wanted to have much more direct influence in their political system and believed

---

[25] England, P. (2015) 'Iceland's "pots and pans revolution": Lessons from a nation that people power helped to emerge from its 2008 crisis all the stronger', *The Independent*, 28 June 2015, accessed 30 December 2015, www.independent.co.uk/news/world/europe/icelands-pots-and-pans-revolution-lessons-from-a-nation-that-people-power-helped-to-emerge-from-its-2008-crisis-all-the-stronger-10351095.html

they were not alone. Their vision was to harness the power of technology to help them achieve that goal. They designed and developed a piece of software which they called DemocracyOS – an open-source web application that is designed as a bridge between citizens and their elected representatives.

Enthusiastic about their software, they reached out to traditional political parties and offered them DemocracyOS. The platform would allow political parties to open up two-way communications with their constituents to find out what the people really wanted and how they really felt. The result? They were unilaterally dismissed and called naïve. When you consider human evolution and the levels of development this response is hardly surprising. Too many people, including those in politics are still addicted to the idea of power rather than the power of ideas. Such people are quite happy with the status quo because it allows them to manipulate the narrative and maintain power and control.

That said, Mancini readily admits in her TED talk that in hindsight, they were naïve, 'Because the challenges that we face, they're not technological, they're cultural. Political parties were never willing to change the way they make their decisions.' We would add that those challenges are essentially developmental.

To combat the resistance they experienced, they founded their own political party, El Partido de la Red, or the Net party in the city of Buenos Aires and ran for elections in October 2013. The political message was simple – if elected, your representative will always vote according to what the citizens decided on DemocracyOS. Every single project introduced in Congress, the Net Party would vote according to what the majority of citizens decided on the online platform. The Net Party recognised that the only way to change the system was from the inside so they played by the rules, while also hacking that system.

Despite the Net Party being only two months old, they gained 22,000 votes (1.2 per cent of the vote) and came second for the local options. In such a short time, this result is significant and demonstrated a distinct appetite for political change. While it wasn't enough to win a seat in Congress, it was enough to gain political attention and become part of the conversation. In November 2014, for the first time in Argentina's history, Congress launched a DemocracyOS technology platform to discuss key pieces of legislation with the electorate. This means that the people are informed. Every new project that is introduced in Congress immediately gets translated and explained in plain language on the platform. Today, Pia Mancini is inspiring similar movements across the world – and we want to credit her for being one of the main inspirations for this book.

Today, we find similar strategies in Sweden, where they have 'Aktiv Demokrati'. There is the Online Direct Democracy movement in Australia and Party for Accountability, Competency and Transparency in Canada,[26] to name a few.

United States of America

In the US, an organisation called Voice of the People, has started organising Citizen Cabinets, to better inform political representatives of what the people would decide if they were in charge. Its founder, Steven Kull, political psychologist at the University of Maryland, has extensively researched the differences between what politicians believe their constituents think and what they actually think.

Kull's research shows that politicians are far more polarised than citizens and Voice of the People aims to share these views and better inform Congress directly. Voice of the People ultimately seeks to create a large standing national Citizen Cabinet of over 100,000 Americans, all connected by the Internet, with a representative sample in every state and district. It will also be operated by a congressionally-chartered National Academy for

[26] For more on these and many other initiatives and movements, please refer to participedia.net

Public Consultation. To get this underway, in the interim Voice of the People is establishing Citizen Cabinets in several states and districts.

This movement believes that a large representative sample of citizens is a better way forward than involving the entire crowd, because random choice would achieve a guarantee of diversity. Leaving the crowd to self-select carries two risks – apathy among the many and high involvement of the interested few – including the lobby and special interest groups. While we agree that diversity is critical, we believe that the crowd can be trusted to show up when it will actually matter that they do. Also, a Citizen Cabinet may never bring all the variety of ideas and opinions that the entire crowd could (this is the argument of decentralisation: people have tacit knowledge that needs to be unlocked). Lastly, we believe that the lobby will have a harder time manipulating the entire crowd than a small group of randomly chosen representatives (the larger the group, the larger the campaign needs to be).

In California, citizens have had the right to initiate legislation since 1911. California allows citizens to use the initiative process to create laws or statutes, and to amend the state constitution. Initiatives need only a simple majority of the vote to pass, and they usually pass only by narrow margins. The process is subject to significant debate, and many of the issues that have been put forward by citizens attract a lot of attention. Proposals that have been voted on include issues such as whether to increase taxes, mandate spending, reinstate the death penalty, legalise medical marijuana, authorise embryonic stem cell research, and allow same sex marriage. In a little over 100 years, Californians have adopted 115 initiatives, including 64 laws and 42 constitutional amendments. Although this may not seem a lot in the time frame, it is encouraging to see that new laws have been created by the people and it also serves to demonstrate that the people don't go crazy when given the power to legislate and will only initiate legislation that really matters.

Europe

Similar to California, although only since 2012, there has been a law in Finland that makes it possible for citizens to propose new legislation. If the proposed legislation is supported by 50,000 signatures from others, it is considered to have enough support that parliament is legally required to discuss the legislation and vote on it. To support citizens in this process, a not-for-profit organisation called Open Ministry offers help in drafting the legislation and setting up the campaigns necessary to garner support and collect the signatures of those who agree with the proposed legislation.

So far, seven proposals have reached the threshold of 50,000 signatures and six have made it to parliament. The seventh was submitted at the time of writing of this book. The proposals have dealt with a broad range of issues including copyright, gender-neutral marriage, bullying in schools, open data, one official language. All six have had delays in the discussion in parliament (with arguments that 'the agenda is set already' and 'there is not enough time for this').[27] All six have been rejected by parliament, which has led to significant disappointment among the initial enthusiasts.[28] While we cannot point to Finland as a shining example of crowdocracy in action, the seeds have been planted. With the right structure, better use of accessible technology and continued push, change is around the corner and Finland may well be one of the first places for crowdocracy to take root.

---

[27] Yle (2014) 'All six citizen's initiatives have failed – activists accuse Parliament of intentionally slowing the process', 13 October 2014, accessed 30 December 2015, http://yle.fi/uutiset/all_six_citizens_initiatives_have_failed__activists_accuse_parliament_of_intentionally_slowing_the_process/7525779

[28] Moody, G. (2014) 'Finnish Parliament Refuses to Consider Crowdsourced Copyright Law – or Any Other Bill Drafted by the Public ', Techdirt, 17 October 2014, accessed 30 December 2015, www.techdirt.com/articles/20141016/09594728848/finnish-parliament-refuses-to-consider-crowdsourced-copyright-law-any-other-bill-drafted-public.shtml

In Switzerland there is a long tradition of direct democracy, giving its citizens the right to corrective referenda and the right to an initiative at federal level and at the level of the cantons. Switzerland is divided into 26 cantons that have a high degree of autonomy. At a federal level, there are three forms of direct democratic choices:

- popular initiatives – where at least 100,000 citizens must support a proposition
- compulsory referenda – amendments to the constitution require popular support, and
- optional referenda – corrective propositions on any legislation, at the request of at least 50,000 citizens.

In each of these, the representative government has significant influence in both the process and the content. They are allowed to debate the topic and start campaigns to influence the population one way or another. While few matters make it to an optional referendum (the process is cumbersome and can take years) and a government position is rarely reversed through any of the forms of referendum, the very existence of the referendum has a significant influence on the democratic process. Those in power know that they have to take into account that a referendum could be raised – and thus they try to integrate the different views when they come to their decisions, effectively creating a negotiation democracy.[29]

Denmark also engages in various forms of collaborative governance. In one example, a project was initiated by the Albertslund municipality in 2010 to develop a new innovative citizen involvement policy. Rather than develop the policy in a standing political committee, which was normal practice, the City Council formed an ad hoc committee composed of six politicians, six citizens and three public administrators and they

29 Kriesi, H. (2005) *Direct Democratic Choice: The Swiss Experience*, Lanham, Maryland: Lexington Books.

were given one year to prepare the policy proposal.

The outcome was innovative policy content that redefined the overall purpose of citizen involvement in Albertslund. Emphasis was put on citizen involvement as a means to innovate public policy and services and the format was chosen deliberately to reach new audiences other than the public authorities themselves. A short policy pamphlet in simple, easy to understand language explained the problem and was supplemented by videos of interviews with citizens about the benefits of citizen involvement. A manual was also created describing the methods for citizen involvement to be used by the public employees. Instead of running a series of traditional meetings with a fixed agenda and structured debates between the members, the committee decided to invite different policy experts to their meetings, host an innovation camp and a workshop with relevant and affected stakeholders and minutes were replaced by mind maps.

This process also changed the people involved, further emphasising our point that crowdocracy will not only change the way we govern but will change the way we relate and interact with each other. The citizens began to see the municipal actors as collaboration partners and themselves as capable co-producers of policy ideas. The politicians discovered that they could develop new ideas in discussion with citizens and other relevant stakeholders, and found this approach much more satisfying than defending fixed policy positions. Also, the administrators gradually changed from controllers to participants in the discussions. Compassion, openness and genuine discussion and debate altered the nature of the debate and reduced conflict during the process.

Once complete, the committee presented the policy proposal at two meetings in the City Council, and the proposal was passed without changes.[30]

---

[30] Sørensen, E. (2015) 'Enhancing policy innovation by redesigning representative democracy', *Policy & Politics*.

Crowd Intelligence in Activism

Crowd intelligence can also be seen in 'crowd activism'. Activism has been around since the dawn of time but it is technology that allows the crowd to organise much more rapidly and push through change.

#TakeItDown

On 17 June 2015, Dylan Roof opened fire on a bible study group in Charleston, South Carolina, killing nine people, including a state senator. It was confirmed as a racially motivated attack. The same evening, a 59-year-old New Yorker, @lifeandmorelife used the Twitter hashtag #TakeItDown in relation to the Confederate flag flying above a South Carolina Capital building.

The Confederate flag is viewed by many as a symbol of white supremacy and racism which encourages the type of racial extremism demonstrated by Roof. To many, flying the flag on a government building implied government approval of such toxic beliefs.

Under the username 'BlackLivesMatter', the hashtag was retweeted through 1,661 Twitter followers. A day later, MSNBC anchor Chris Hayes suggested South Carolina cover up the Confederate flag in front of its Statehouse. Another tweeter replied, 'No, Chris, we should #TakeItDown.' Hours later, Hayes was demanding South Carolina Rep. Mark Sanford remove the 'symbol of tyranny', from government property. Within days, everyone from Mitt Romney to Michael Moore was using the hashtag.

Less than a week later, a #TakeItDown rally was held at the state capitol in Columbia and the hashtag was transformed into a protest chant. In a single day #TakeItDown was tweeted 17,000 times. Seemingly overnight, public opinion on the flag shifted.[31] A flag that had flown above the Capitol building for more than 50 years was removed just 23 days after the Charleston massacre. The crowd had 'spoken' and lawmakers in South Carolina's House of Representatives followed the state Senate by passing a bill to remove the flag, which was permanently removed on the 10 of July 2015.

When we bring large, diverse groups of people together, using technology as the intermediary to spread and integrate information we give people a voice. People also clearly believe in what they create, and engage with the system. When these systems are governed by principles that are strictly upheld, the community self-governs or appoints its own process guardians. When the collective is involved, the few tend not to be able to get away with bad behaviour – as Dr Walter Palmer found to his cost.

When Dr Palmer, a dentist from Minneapolis, Minnesota, US, killed Cecil, a protected lion in Zimbabwe in July 2015, he probably didn't expect to face a global wave of Internet outrage. Cecil normally lived in Zimbabwe's Hwange National Park – a 'free roam' park where hunting is illegal. He was however lured out of his protected territory by Palmer's local guides, hunter Theo Bronkhorst and local farmer Honest Trymore Ndlovu. Palmer is thought to have paid approximately US $50,000 to shoot the lion with a bow and arrow. After tracking the injured animal for 40 hours, Cecil was then shot, beheaded and skinned. At which point the hunting party must have discovered that Cecil was wearing a tracking collar. Thirteen-year-old Cecil was a major tourist attraction at the park and was being monitored as part of an Oxford University study into lion conservation. Dr Palmer was identified and forced into hiding, his business was closed and his picture, business and home address were posted and

[31] Sobel Fitts, A. (2015) 'How Black Twitter Helped Take Down The Confederate Flag', *Huffington Post*, 10 July 2015, accessed 30 December 2015, http://www.huffingtonpost.com/entry/black-twitter-confederate-flag_559fe8c2e4b05b1d02902eb1

reposted online. Some 400,000 people signed a petition calling on Zimbabwe's government to stop issuing hunting permits for endangered animals.[32] Interestingly, when the glare of global media was on the notoriously corrupt Zimbabwe government they were calling for Dr Palmer's extradition to face illegal poaching charges. When the furore died down, the government, did a mlraculous about-turn, dropping all charges and stating that Dr Palmer was welcome to return[33] – a stark reminder of how, in our current system at least, the power and wisdom of the crowd can so easily be overruled by a few corrupt politicians.

Change.org

This form of activism has in the past few years seen more structure and organisation. As of 2015, the place to go for anyone with a cause to bring to the crowd is the platform Change.org. Charge. org, like Kickstarter, is a B-corp (Benefit Corporation) which has a bigger agenda than just profit. Originating in the US, at the time of writing it has well over 125 million registered 'members' globally.

Following the death of Cecil the lion and the global outcry that followed, it was Change.org that petitioned airlines to stop transporting the animal trophies of big game hunting. Focusing on Delta Airlines, the only US carrier with direct flights to South Africa, the response was so significant that in August 2015, Delta banned the shipment of all lion, leopard, elephant, rhino and buffalo trophies worldwide as freight. Since that initial

---

[32] 'Cecil the lion: Zimbabwe hunter bailed over killing', *BBC News*, 29 July 2015, accessed 30 December 2015, www.bbc.co.uk/news/world-us-canada-33699346

[33] Onishi, N. (2015) 'Zimbabwe Won't Charge Dentist Who Killed Cecil the Lion', *New York Times*, 12 October 2015, accessed 30 December 2015, www.nytimes.com/2015/10/13/world/africa/zimbabwe-will-not-charge-dentist-who-killed-cecil-the-lion.html?_r=0

crowd inspired decision, nine other airlines also chose to ban the transport of certain animal hunting trophies – British Airways, Lufthansa, Emirates, Qantas, Qatar, Etihad, Iberia, Singapore and Brussels Airlines.[34]

Anyone can post a petition and ask the crowd to endorse their cause. The editors of Change.org are there to assist the petitioners (by shaping and editing their stories to appeal to a larger audience). According to their website, more than 125 million people from 196 countries are actively participating to push through change they feel passionate about. So far 15,424 petitions have led to the changes that the petitioners wished to see.[35] The driving force of this appears to be public pressure on politicians.

Crowd Insights

All these different initiatives in different domains clearly demonstrate that the crowd is already using its collective intelligence and its collective power in many ways.

The crowd has also shown that it is perfectly capable of organising itself within often loosely defined principles. Many organisations and societies have far more rules and procedures than some of these well-functioning crowd platforms that operate with only a small set of core principles. Also, in many of these examples, the crowd does not need overall coordination or someone to set an agenda. From the types of enlightened organisations described

---

[34] Green, C. (2015) 'VICTORY! Delta takes a stand against trophy hunting!', Petition Update, Change.org, accessed 30 December 2015, www.change.org/p/delta-air-lines-end-the-transport-of-exotic-animal-hunting-trophies/u/11615784

[35] Change.org website, accessed 25 November 2015, www.change.org/impact

by Laloux to Wikipedia, Kickstarter and Change.org, there is no one person or small group controlling what makes it on to the agenda, what gets written about or what gets funded. The crowd is fully empowered to take the initiative and action what it wants to action through a process of self-selection based on what the crowd deems as the most important issues.

As we have discussed, the crowd is already moving towards the realm of governance in many places around the world from the Icelandic constitution to DemocracyOS and beyond. We believe the evolution towards a fully empowered crowd governing itself is already well underway and crowdocracy is not a huge leap from where we already are.

The most important and potentially dangerous insight for us is the fact that in the political arena, crowd activism appears to be much more effective than any form of participative or direct democracy. None of the participatory and direct initiatives scale to a level where they are the dominant way of decision-making in a society. All the case studies that we have read or heard about face challenges – mainly in the form of resistance from those already in power. As Pia Mancini found out the hard way, 'Political parties were never willing to change the way they make their decisions.'

But politicians do appear willing to change their decisions when their arm is twisted – responding to large numbers of petitioners making a lot of noise online. While we can sympathise with a lot of the causes that the crowd gathers around, these developments challenge the fundamental democratic principles. A large vocal group of petitioners is fundamentally no different from a smaller, perhaps quieter but equally powerful lobby (unless, of course, the large group represents the majority opinion).

If politicians start to govern based on whoever makes the most noise and threatens their 'reputation', there is a real risk of sliding down to mob rule. Crowd activism is turning politics into reverse populism: politicians responding to the popular voice of the crowd. Take the European refugee crisis as a case in point. The UK had been resolute in their position that they would not take any more refugees into Britain. Then a picture of a two-year-old Syrian refugee washed up drowned on a Turkish beach was broadcast around the world which led to Britain agreeing to take 'thousands more'.[36]

Whatever you may think about this outcome – whether or not it was the right call or not, it is not an example of crowdocracy – it is an example of mob rule. Enough people were upset and angry enough to make their voice known so as to force a change in political direction, aided no doubt by a large slice of parental guilt. But it wasn't a considered, integrated choice – rather it was a knee-jerk reaction to popular opinion. That's no way to create policy – even if the outcome is one we believe is right. Such knee-jerk reactions designed to buy off public opinion certainly haven't solved the problem of immigration and they are no way to run a country.

In terms of people power, social media and the ability for ordinary citizens to voice their opinion – the genie is out the bottle. There is no going back – people are used to and expect to be able to express their opinion on just about anything. And they do. While there may still be people who fundamentally believe that 'ordinary' citizens are poorly informed, have no serious interest in public affairs and are generally ill-equipped for political participation, the evidence would indicate otherwise.[37] It is therefore vital that we start to organise this development, and the desire and willingness to participate, so that we can give the crowd a forum to make their voice heard. This forum must exist within a strong and ethical governance framework, underpinned by democratic

---

[36] Landale, J. (2015) 'David Cameron: UK to accept "thousands" more Syrian refugees', *BBC News*, 4 September 2015, accessed 30 December 2015, www.bbc.co.uk/news/uk-34148913

[37] Kriesi, H. (2005) *Direct Democratic Choice: The Swiss Experience*, loc 227 (Kindle edition), with a reference to Schumpeter, J. (1942) *Capitalism, Socialism and Democracy,* New York: Harper & Row.

principles that cannot be swayed simply by whatever hot topic ignites the crowd at any given time or whatever section of the crowd shouts the loudest. Without that framework, including a strong constitutional guide book that all participants co-create and adhere to, we won't actually evolve to a better system. Instead we will simply have a noisier version of what we have now.

Crowdocracy would facilitate the very best of what the crowd has to offer while mitigating our less helpful group behaviour such as group think, conformity and bullying. We will explore how it may work in practice in the next chapter.

Chapter 6:

How will
Crowdocracy work?

'If the idea is not at first absurd, then there is no hope
for it.'

– Albert Einstein[1]

So far, we've sought to ignite your interest in a new form of
governance and government that really puts the power in the
hands of the people – all the people. The burning platform for
reform of our political process is the fact that democracy, in its
current form, is failing huge numbers of people. We explained
why collective wisdom, while counterintuitive, is none the less
real, valid and scientifically robust. In the previous chapter,
we shared examples of how the crowd's collective wisdom is
already functioning successfully in many areas including in the
political arena, where citizen participation initiatives are being
tried, tested and honed around the world.

In this chapter, we will go a step further and explain how
crowdocracy *could* work in practice on a small or large scale.
We will do this by first setting out the fundamental systemic

---

[1] This quote is widely attributed to Einstein but no official source could be
located.

elements of effective governance, namely the separation of powers and other underlying principles. Then we will explore a number of practical examples to demonstrate how crowdocracy might work in practice. These examples are real world scenarios that we believe could reveal how such a fundamentally different system could work in your church group, football club, business, multinational corporation or your nation.

The Separation of Powers

The system of democracy that many currently hold up as the epitome of political maturity and progress emerged in its initial form in Ancient Greece. During the Enlightenment of the eighteenth century, French political thinker Montesquieu proposed that government should be divided into branches that keep each other in balance – the 'trias politica':

- The Legislative

- The Executive

- The Judiciary

As we explained earlier the ability to differentiate, in this case, sources of power in a society, is a sign of evolution and maturity. It may be a separation of church and state; a class separation of monarchy, aristocrats and commoners; or a separation of the three arms of government that exists in most modern democracies. How such democratic differentiation is supported differs significantly from one country to the next. In the UK, it is facilitated by one person/one vote. In Iceland, most of the people live in towns and cities so their voting system weights rural votes so rural communities are not ignored or marginalised in favour of a purely urban agenda. In the US, the value of votes also varies because of the Electoral College. Ordinary US citizens do not elect the President and Vice President; instead, they directly elect designated intermediaries called 'electors'. These electors however have almost always already pledged to vote for a particular candidate, who is selected according to the particular laws of each state.

There are also a variety of voting systems from the first-past-the-post (FPTP) system to various types of proportional representation. The way politicians get elected or appointed, the way legislation is drafted and enacted, the existence and role of the constitution, and the way democratic process is protected all vary in shape and form across countries and yet all may be classed as democratic. At its heart, each democracy has the same fundamental philosophy: the rule of law and ultimate authority is meant to rest with all the people, through some form of voting of elected representatives.

Montesquieu's theory on the separation of powers had a profound impact on most democracies. Montesquieu advocated a strict separation of power where sufficient checks and balances were in place to ensure the people's interests were genuinely served. Over the years, however, the lines between the legislative, executive and judiciary arms of government have become blurred in many countries.

For example, in the US, the President, head of the executive arm of government, appoints the highest ranking members of the judiciary. As of November 2015, in his time in office Barack Obama has confirmed 317 judges, including two justices to the Supreme Court of the United States, 54 judges to the United States Courts of Appeal, 259 judges to the United States district courts and two judges to the United States Court of International Trade.[2]

In the UK, the executive office dominates the policy agenda and therefore has a disproportionate influence on what the legislative

---

[2] List of federal judges appointed by Barack Obama, accessed 30 December 2015, https://en.wikipedia.org/wiki/List_of_federal_judges_appointed_by_Barack_Obama

arm of government does. One of the complaints, certainly in the UK, is that decisions are made by committees behind closed doors. We don't know who is on those committees or why and it is rarely just elected representatives who attend these meetings. In Brussels, and the US too, decisions are made by committees full of unelected civil servants, and, more disturbingly, the lobby.[3] Often, legislation even appears to be directly written by corporations who have a seat at the table via their lobbyist. This blurring of the lines between the various arms of government often makes a mockery of the checks and balances that prompted the separation of powers in the first place.

This separation of powers was designed to maintain a balance in power, in order to protect the interests of individual citizens and the collective. It is supposed to stop a powerful individual or powerful group, even an elected group from dreaming up laws that serve and protect the few and then passing those laws without its citizens ever even knowing. Which is, of course, exactly what's happening. For example, one bill that sailed through the House Financial Services Committee in the US in May 2013, despite objections from the Treasury Department, was essentially Citigroup's. Recommendations from Citigroup were reflected in more than 70 lines of an 85-line bill which would exempt broad swathes of trades from new regulation. According to the *New York Times,* two crucial paragraphs, prepared by Citigroup in conjunction with other Wall Street banks, were copied nearly word for word.[4]

Sure, the separation of power slows down decision-making capability – but that's the point. It forces debate and discussion before laws are passed and then executed. Needless to say, those

---

[3] Represent.us 'Study: Congress literally doesn't care what you think' accessed 30 December 2015, https://represent.us/action/theproblem-4/

[4] Lipton, E. and Protess, B. (2015) 'Banks' Lobbyists Help in Drafting Financial Bills', *New York Times*, accessed 30 December 2015, http://dealbook.nytimes.com/2013/05/23/banks-lobbyists-help-in-drafting-financial-bills/?_r=2

Figure 6.1: Visual illustrating how separation of power will look from democracy to crowdocracy

Government arm	Governance form	Who	Appointed by	Role/responsibility
Legislative	Democracy	Elected politicians ('parliamentarians')	All citizens (elections)	• Propose and approve laws • Check Executive
	Crowdocracy	All citizens	n/a	• Propose and make laws • Make policy decisions • Check executives
Executive	Democracy	Appointed/elected (president/mayor/ministers and civil servants)	Legislative arm or directly by citizens	• Make policy • Propose laws • Execute a policy
	Crowdocracy	Appointed officials	All citizens	• Execute a policy
Judiciary	Democracy	Appointed or elected judges (professional and lay persons)	Judiciary, the Executive, the Legislative or citizens (elections)	• Protect rule of law • Judge after the fact
	Crowdocracy	Appointed judges (professional and lay persons)	Judiciary and all citizens	• Protect rule of law • Judge after the fact • Guardian throughout the crowdocractic process

173

in power prefer to consolidate power; it makes their decision-making easier and faster. The legislative is therefore not always looking out to the wider world to see what policy and legislation is needed but rather they are being spoon-fed the policy and legislation that is wanted by powerful interests, which have often helped to draft the legislation in their favour. This legislation is then passed into law and executed by the same people who proposed it in the first place.

In crowdocracy, we return to a much stricter interpretation of the separation of powers and a far stronger role of the legislative, made up of all citizens. The essence of the structure of crowdocracy is as follows: the crowd becomes the legislature with the power to propose and draft policy and make all policy decisions. The executive officers get appointed by the crowd and execute that policy within the delegated authority of the crowd. The independent judiciary adjudicate and act as the guardians of the crowdocratic process. See figure 6.1 for a visual summary of the proposed structure.

Legislation by the Crowd

The legislature is the law-making body of government and would remain so in crowdocracy. Perhaps the biggest shift we propose is that in a crowdocracy, the crowd – all citizens in a community, city or country – collectively take over all legislative powers. This entails taking the initiative for creating policy, shaping all policy and voting on proposals.

Crowdocracy would no longer function in a physical place like a Parliament building. We would move the process online, through a purpose built technology platform (The Crowd). We envisage this system to be a hybrid between the concepts of Change.org (for raising proposals), Wikipedia (for collaboratively writing laws, regulations and other policies), and Kickstarter (for voting on the proposals).

Technology has levelled the playing field and it is technology that could finally allow all of us to participate in a way that simply wasn't possible even a decade ago. Anyone who can read, write and has access to the Internet can get involved in crowdocracy. Needless to say, the collaborative platform needs to be accessible to all, easy to use and very well protected against cyber-attacks and manipulation. We acknowledge that these two elements (access and cyber security) pose significant challenges for the implementation of crowdocracy.

The system itself will operate as an open source Linux-style platform. This means that no one will 'own' crowdocracy or the platform and it will be available for any community or organisation in the world to use and improve while being protected by all of us. As discussed, we already embrace open source as a collaboration that creates better software that improves our everyday lives. This is simply a political extension of this idea which would remove many of the toxic side effects of elected representation such as vested interests, cliques and rule by the elite minority.

Anyone who wishes to contribute will be able to take the lead and create a policy proposal in a certain area. Those that initiate policy discussions may be called the 'Shapers'. Other people will then participate, ask questions, raise objections, and suggest alterations or improvements to the original policy. Anyone can be a Shaper and anyone can provide feedback on the proposed policy.

This feedback would then need to be integrated to accommodate the best ideas from the crowd. We do not live in a black and white world so binary yes/no, like/dislike responses are too simplistic. We need nuanced co-creation where Shapers and citizens alike are always encouraged to improve proposals rather than simply accepting them or rejecting them. If someone really disagrees with a proposal, then they have an option to either vote against it, or to create a counter proposal.

Ultimately, anything can be changed but there is a process for creating changes to avoid endless tinkering with something that is already working. Governance like all wicked problems is constantly evolving. As such our equally wise solution must also constantly evolve. The primary criterion for adoption is that the proposal has to be 'workable' – not perfect. It also has to be an improvement on what currently exists. As a result, continuous improvement is baked into the crowdocratic process.

Once proposals have been shaped (through a process which we will describe shortly), the crowd decide the legitimacy of the policy by voting. Each proposal that is passed by the necessary majority, allowing for a reasonable minimum turnout, will then become a new law/rule/order or decision and is ready for execution. Every piece of policy will need to include how that policy will be executed. Most policy will be executed by the executive office, but it may well be that some execution is passed to civil organisations, volunteer groups or even the private sector.

In crowdocracy, everyone participates. The crowd becomes responsible for all aspects of legislation, because there will be no other authority. This is where we move significantly beyond all existing projects, theories and experiments that we know of in the world today. Most of the alternatives are designed to inspire, inform, or correct the failings of representative government. We advocate replacing legislative government with all of us – and really trust the crowd to govern itself.

Indeed, this means that we suggest sending our elected officials home, or rather, back to the crowd. For diversity, we do need the people who are actively engaged in the political process – yet we no longer want them as our elected representatives. Many politicians of today may well be key Shapers of the future – or part of the executive or judiciary. There would still be politicians but significantly fewer and the politicians that were left would move to the executive arm to execute the laws that were proposed, drafted and passed by the people or they would become guardians of the process in the judiciary. This revolutionary next step would finally facilitate what Abraham Lincoln discussed in the Gettysburg Address back in 1863 – 'government of the people, by the people, for the people'.

For many, this idea will sound ridiculous. Are we seriously suggesting that we let the people create the law? Indeed, we are. In the previous chapter, we outlined how the wisdom of the crowd can emerge. Within a proper structure and process, everyday citizens are perfectly capable of suggesting, assessing, collaborating and deciding on complex matters of public policy. In a comprehensive survey of empirical studies into citizen deliberation, Professor John Dryzek, Centenary Professor at the Centre for Deliberative Democracy and Global Governance at the University of Canberra's Institute for Governance and Policy Analysis stated that: 'The most obvious finding is that, given the opportunity, ordinary citizens can make good deliberators. Moreover, issue complexity is no barrier to the development and exercise of that competence.' After two decades of running citizen participation panels, James Fishkin, Janet M. Peck Professor of International Communication at Stanford, concluded that: 'The public is very smart if you give them a chance. If people think their voice actually matters, they'll do the hard work, really study… ask experts smart questions and then make tough decisions… Citizens can become better informed and master the most complex issues of state government if they are given the chance.'[5]

The crowd may well decide that it needs to be informed on certain elements, such as a factual basis for its policy and decision-making. The crowd may want institutions like state councils, universities, or NGO's to inform them – it is up to the crowd to design its own process. As information technology progresses, particularly artificial intelligence, the crowd will also be more and more informed by technology itself. The crowd will create an ally in the technology that can help it analyse complicated or wicked

---

[5] Arriaga, M. (2014) *Rebooting Democracy: A citizen's guide to reinventing politics*, London: Thistle Publishing.

problems and formulate solutions.

The crowd will debate its issues and solutions online, on a semi-anonymous basis (we will explain why later). Everyone can form their independent view and make their independent contribution. The diversity needed to truly unlock the wisdom of the crowd will occur naturally once enough people participate. Indeed, this requires that the apathy that we see today disappears. While we see the challenge, we are optimistic about participation in the future.

For years, people have longed to be involved. When asked, most of us have views on many aspects of our public life. Other than discussing them with our friends over dinner or complaining about them 'down the pub' however, we have no chance to channel our ideas or opinions and no chance of really being heard. Very few of us would like to devote our entire lives to being a politician but crowdocracy would allow all of us to devote a small part of our lives to public governance. There are enough of us to find the answers to everything. It would, therefore, be totally acceptable if we wanted to devote our attention to certain areas of personal interest only (as long as the voting gets enough representation).

An Empowered Executive Office

Policy needs execution. Garbage needs to be collected, streetlights need to be changed, electricity needs to be produced and distributed, roads need to be built and policed, and the military needs to be commanded. We are always going to need an arm of government that executes the policy and laws that the legislative arm creates.

Today, the executive branch has the authority and responsibility for the daily administration of the state. It executes or enforces the law and policy but it does not make the law or policy, that's the legislative arm. The executive doesn't interpret the law or policy – that's the job of the judiciary. The executive branch of government consists of key appointments and leaders of office, such as head of state or government (prime minister or president), defence minister, interior minister, foreign minister, finance minister, justice minister, etc. In most democracies, the executives are not directly elected by the people, rather they are chosen by the elected legislature. Exceptions are the directly elected presidents and mayors – but the vast majority of ministers, civil servants, and other officers have been appointed, not elected.

In crowdocracy, we will continue to have an executive arm. Creating enlightened, collaborative policy for the benefit of many is one thing, executing that policy requires a different skill set. It takes real ability to execute policy. While diversity of input and collaboration from the crowd will immediately start to change the quality of political contribution, the crowd can't execute that policy. As a result, the crowd needs to delegate authority to executive powers. But the crowd is, at the same time, free to shape how that executive arm is structured.

The executive office may well take the shape of an elected cabinet with ministers and civil servants to support them, but it may also be very different in the future – because executives are no longer creating policy, they are creating reality from policy. We imagine that the executive office will be much more decentralised. Why would a handful of people need to oversee all policy execution? Ministries and institutions could easily operate in a meritocratic fashion next to each other without the need for ultimate authority in the hands of a few.

Although the executive office will not directly take part in the shaping of policy, it will need to be able to give input. Knowledge, practical experience and a view on the feasibility of implementation (for example, on budget implications) may well be available within the executive office. In the process that we outline later in this chapter, we will describe how this input could be incorporated.

This means that today's politicians in the executive arm need to come to terms with a change to their role: executing policy generated by the people, rather than selling their policies to the legislature or to citizens directly. They would no longer have to worry about their next election, toeing the 'party line' or whether their actions will impact their ability to get re-elected in the endless political beauty contest. Instead they simply implement the policy the crowd has chosen and are therefore accountable only for their ability to execute.

One of the biggest challenges in politics right now is that policy is created and executed but the feedback loop between those affected and those who create the policy in the first place is either very slow or non-existent. Those affected often feel the effects of the policy or legislative change relatively quickly but there are few channels for them to voice their feedback and propose change. They could go to their local representative who may raise a question in parliament but nothing actually happens, if change does occur it often takes years. Crowdocracy closes the feedback loop so the crowd who created the policy or the executive officers who implemented it can then raise issues on the crowdocratic platform around how the policy is working in the real world. Thus, a new debate can open up, new Shapers can propose alterations to counter the negative impact of the policy, or any unintended consequences and revisions can be made much quicker to improve the policy moving forward.

Governance is a wicked problem which means that often efforts to solve one challenge will create negative, unintended and unanticipated consequences elsewhere. This is the nature of the complex challenges we now face. But when the crowd, affected by those challenges and the proposed solution, have a platform to start a new conversation, or alert the other members of the crowd to any unintended consequences and bring their diverse wisdom to the challenge in real time, then ongoing progress becomes possible.

Of course, the executive officers need to work transparently, and be answerable to the crowd and the crowd can – according to its own procedures – decide to fire them. Within the delegated authority and in accordance with the crowdocratic process, the executive officers are empowered to take decisions and action. This empowerment is very important: the executives need to have the space, time and means to implement policy, without being constantly harassed by the public. This harassment slows progress and yet it currently occurs in most democracies where ministers are constantly challenged by the parliamentarians trying to score political points. Crowdocracy will herald an end to this time wasting.

We foresee that over time the focus will be much more on competent execution. The crowd has no interest in constantly changing the direction of policy or shuffling those that execute around various roles they may or may not have any experience in. The crowd also has no interest in likeability contests – and so those politicians that are in politics today for the joy of holding power, will likely not be in the executive offices. Executive office means serious business.

An important role for the executive offices will be to represent the community to other communities. For example, in multilateral negotiations or discussions an executive officer would need to conduct those negotiations on behalf of the community they serve. Communities will continue to need spokespeople and negotiators to represent them, unless the communities involved are able to create their joint interactions using the crowdocratic platform as well. Over time, treaties may well be the result of multilateral crowdocratic process. After all, if Iceland can crowdsource an enlightened constitution there's no reason the crowd can't also determine treaties.

Until that point, communities will still need people to represent them. These functions could take the form of institutions that we have known for a long time, such as Mayors, Presidents, Queens and Ministers. But maybe the crowd will come up with innovative forms and more collective bodies which may include a team or delegation rather than an individual.

It is also likely that different communities will take different directions and over time they will learn from their own experience and those of other communities. Some communities will choose to utilise more privatised solutions, others will emphasise more citizen activities, while some will create larger bureaucracies. History and culture will play important roles here. We have no preference – we trust the crowds will be wise in their own way.

Finally, it's worth pointing out that such an approach would further remove the undue influence that money has in politics. Crowdocracy makes lobbying a lot harder: influencing a crowd requires a mass-media approach and *very* deep pockets. The days of dealings in back rooms and exclusive restaurants would be over. Of course, we are not naïve enough to think that those with significant interests and the requisite pocket length will not try to sway the entire crowd, but an alert crowd will be much harder to influence than individual politicians and civil servants.

The Judiciary as Guardians

In all democracies there is an independent judiciary that protects the system and has an independent role in keeping the rules of society intact and alive. Traditionally, the judiciary is the guardian of the process by way of a system of courts that interprets and applies the law in the name of the state and ultimately the people. This would also be the case with crowdocracy – the only difference is that the laws that they guard and uphold would be proposed, drafted and altered by the majority of the people and not by a handful of elected or unelected legislative representatives.

Of course, crowdocracy would also need its checks and balances so that the crowd can tap into its collective wisdom instead of degenerating into a mindless mob. It would be possible to organise these checks and balances from within the crowd (like in Wikipedia), but we believe they are so important that they require formalisation within the system. An independent judiciary as such does not participate as Shaper or participant in the legislature, or as an executive.

Next to its role in criminal and civil procedures, the judiciary assumes a new role as guardian of the crowdocratic process. While we acknowledge that in many democracies the judiciary already acts as guardian of the democratic process (protecting the constitution, and hearing cases of citizens brought against the government), in the crowdocratic process the role is far more active.

To enable the crowd to participate and to ensure a fair and smooth process, the guardians need to be active during all the phases of the process. This is contrary to most current processes, whereby the judiciary only gets involved after the fact. The guardians need to be available to explain the process, offer procedural advice, monitor the fairness and intervene when Shapers or citizens go outside the agreed procedural rules. They need to be available when Shapers ask for advice (for example, as to whether their proposal would fit within the constitutional framework or not).

We could imagine that several levels of guardians would be active – first line layperson guardians who are representatives of the crowd itself (for example, experienced and respected Shapers) and full-time guardians who oversee the larger scale process and who act as the final decision-makers on process.

Of course, the immediate question we need to address is, 'OK, but what's to stop the guardians –, at whatever level, from subverting the process in the same way that traditional politicians do or can do right now?' The answer is through a binding constitution and through targeted development of the guardians themselves. In fact, crowdocracy would need to have a very strong, crowdsourced constitution that sets up the rules of the game that would be enforced across all arms of government.

Anyone in the legislative, executive or judiciary found flouting the rules would be immediately disqualified from participation or removed from their post.

In addition, all guardians would need to go through training to ensure they are sufficiently developed to enable them to skilfully integrate multiple perspectives. They would also need to be capable of working in an integrative way. In many ways we already expect those in the current judiciary to be intellectually and ethically more developed than the general population. We look at Supreme Court judges and we expect a certain level of competence in that role. That expectation of competence would remain with crowdocracy. However, it would tend to focus around specific areas of development that increase capability and sophistication including cognitive ability, emotional management, self-regulation and ego maturity.

This development issue is nullified by the crowd in the legislative arm and diminished via meritocracy in the executive arm but it's essential in the judiciary because even with crowdocratic principles the possibility exists to exert influence on judiciary members to rule in favour or against legislation. That said, the fact that the legislation is created by the crowd makes this much less likely.

While guardians are independent in their functioning and would in principle propose other guardians to be appointed, the crowd needs to be able to balance their influence and power as well, for example through a confirmation process and feedback loops. Guardians may not develop their role into a power structure – which is partly achievable by only giving them authority over the procedural aspects of crowdocracy, but partly also by allowing the crowd a right to impeach guardians when they go beyond their authority as laid down by the constitution.

To further separate power, guardians may not be active as Shapers or participating citizens in the areas of the crowdocratic process where they act as guardians. They may however take on such roles in other areas. For example, if someone is a guardian at local level for aspects of the local constitution, they may well participate at a national level on things like education reform. In fact, we believe that active participation will help guardians become better in their roles.

Principles that Underpin Crowdocracy

To ensure the four conditions for the emergence of crowd wisdom are met and to distinguish crowdocracy from other systemic approaches, there are certain principles to be upheld. They will serve to underpin crowdocracy in order to maintain system integrity while allowing the crowd to flourish. In the end the crowd will decide what they will be. Each community and organisation will create its own version, but some principles will need to apply universally for the system to be crowdocratic. We envisage those to include:

1. *Everyone can and should be encouraged to participate in crowdocracy*

   Each individual in a community (not company, organisation or group) can and should be encouraged to participate. Crowd wisdom can only emerge if all of us have one vote. The technological platform will therefore need to be accessible to all and easy to use. Short YouTube style training videos on how to use the platform should be enough to allow widescale participation, yet the challenge of how to create access for all needs to be tackled. Although there may be regional variations to participation rules, we imagine that the age of participation in the crowdocractic process would be lower than the typical voting age of 18 years old. This would allow young people to participate in the drafting of legislation that will affect them.

   Of course, the question arises, 'What crowd will you be part of?' We will address this in more detail in Chapter 8, but for now suffice to say that everyone has a say in any proposal that they are directly affected by. In practice, this may still be challenging and the crowd will need to carefully design the specifics. Yet we realise we do not start in a vacuum: democracy has demarcated cities, states, provinces and nations and so initially we may follow those lines.

It is important to highlight that we believe only individuals should be able to participate – not legal entities. While individuals may participate from the professional roles, for example, an employee of an NGO may want to work on a proposal; this should not be done in full anonymity. Every person should always be aware that what they contribute is attributable to them.

2. *No crowd delegation*

We envisage that crowdocracy would maintain the separation of powers between the legislative, executive and judiciary, as we have described in the first part of this chapter. While variations may be created over time as the crowd engages more fully and comes up with wiser solutions than we have proposed here, the variations will still need robust checks and balances.

For the system to be crowdocratic, the legislative, decision-making authority on policy may not be delegated by the crowd. Thus the crowd will always make the legislative decisions in that community rather than allowing an elite delegation decide.

3. *Semi-anonymity*

Diversity and independence are critical if group intelligence or the wisdom of the crowd is to emerge. The integrated wisdom of the crowd requires the unadulterated opinion and input of each independent individual to ensure diversity. While we will keep our world of personal interaction where people will source their information via the media and share their views via blogs and social media, the crowdocracy platform will function on a semi-anonymous basis. As Shapers and participating citizens, we will not use our own names. This will allow for a freer and unbiased exchange of views – it takes much 'ego' out of the system.

But we will also not be able to hide behind that pseudonym or handle because the guardians will have access to our real identity – enabling them to step in when someone steps out of line. Whilst technology has often given the voiceless a voice – it has also created a platform where the normal Social Contract of decency and behaviour etiquette has broken down. People now 'talk' to each other online in a way they would never do in a face-to-face interaction. Ironically, this is now making the voiceless voiceless again because individuals are too scared to post anything online for fear of the potential backlash.[6] Whilst online communication and the anonymity it can provide can be potentially liberating in getting to what people really believe and think about a proposed policy, it is also potentially toxic. Semi-anonymity allows for the best elements of anonymity to flourish while preventing the very worst.

4. *Basic rules laid out in a constitution*

Every community and organisation needs to establish its ground rules, which govern the way the community members coordinate their actions, inside and outside the community.

This constitution needs to be agreed by the crowd and can evolve over time, with the consent and participation of the crowd. While today only nations have a constitution, we advocate that smaller communities also adopt one. It creates the basis for the community to act together. The process of enacting a constitution is an important, fundamental process to go through. It creates clarity on the purpose, the values and the process.

5. *Integrative process*

We need to learn how to integrate opposing views into our

---

[6] Ronson, J. (2015) *So You've Been Publicly Shamed*, London: Picador.

decision-making. As outlined in Chapter 4, we have to move beyond dialectic reasoning. It is not about I am right, you are wrong. Each of us, regardless of education or background or culture has something to add to the debate, we each have a different take on the issues. These differing perspectives can, if integrated, shine increasingly more light on the challenges we face which in turn facilitates a better, faster solution.

The process itself needs to facilitate integration (we will get into that soon) and the Shapers and citizens need to develop the ability to integrate multiple perspectives effectively. Guardians need to be masters at integration and need to guide the crowd in how to develop this ability. Semi-anonymity will help, because we will read comments and suggestions at face value – not through the lens of who has written them.

We will need to learn to embrace second person perspective taking: putting ourselves in the shoes of others to create a shared view. As said, in today's world we usually either operate from first person perspective (what do I think/want/feel/need/etc?) or third person perspective (what are the data/facts/circumstances?) When we become responsible for our collective governance, we have to learn to embrace the situations and perspectives of where others come from to reach a united view.

The technology platform should also help in this integration. Just like the 'git' in Linux, the technology itself should be able to weed out duplicating views or identify similar views. With the development of artificial intelligence, the technology itself may have an increasingly important role in finding and articulating the best solution.

Crowdocratic Policy Making – The Process

In this section, we will explain the process of crowdocratic policy-making and will provide a couple of examples, to demonstrate how the process may work in practice. To get to the wisest (balanced, integrative) solution available at any given time, we suggest the following six-phase process:

1. Proposing
2. Shaping
3. Public Consultation
4. Final Check
5. Vote
6. Execution

1. Proposing

In this phase, any citizen or group of citizens in the crowd decides to take action by outlining their ideas. This may be a suggestion for legislation, a change to existing legislation, or for policy decisions or suggestions. It could be anything from small changes such as alterations to traffic regulations in their town or an amendment to existing legislation. The proposal could also be more complex such as overhauling the criminal code, amending the constitution or deciding on going to war. Initiatives can be presented in various formats such as text, video or infographics and this initial proposal is meant to provoke discussion and gauge initial reactions as well as inspire potential Shapers – those people who will shape the idea into a formal proposal.

The Shaper of a proposal doesn't need to be the person who came up with the proposal, although they could be. The executive office does not have the right to initiate a proposal although we can imagine that it can request the guardians to inform the public of certain execution inefficiencies or desired policy. The guardians can take a view as to the legitimacy and urgency of this and present the views on the platform, so that members of the crowd can take action, or not.

It is essential that it is easy to make a proposal to encourage participation. Starting a proposal may be as easy as starting a project on the crowdsourcing platform Kickstarter. On Kickstarter, you click on the tab 'Start a Project', you are then asked, 'What are you going to create?' and you choose a category for the project you are seeking funding for and give it a name. A similar process could work here where anyone wishing to make a proposal simple clicks on a tab 'Start a Proposal', gives it a name and identifies a category or subject area the proposal is related to.

The crowd can then look at all the proposals or select areas of interest so that each individual only sees proposals for areas they are interested in. For example, someone might select 'education', 'environment' and 'fiscal policy' as their core interests. Whenever anyone creates a proposal within those categories the person would receive an alert so they could track that proposal or get actively involved in shaping that proposal or creating an alternative proposal.

If there are lots of competing proposals on the same topic, the crowd will decide which ones get any traction by their involvement. Remember the Princeton study in the US, when the researchers looked at what proposals became law, whether *no one* agreed with that idea or *everyone* agreed with it – there was a 30 per cent chance that it would become law.[7] That couldn't happen in crowdocracy because unless the proposal was supported by the

[7] Gilens, M. and Page, B.I. (2014) 'Testing Theories of American Politics: Elites, Interest Groups, and Average Citizens', *Perspective on Politics*, 12, no. 3, pp. 564–81, accessed 30 December 2015, http://scholar.princeton.edu/sites/default/files/mgilens/files/gilens_and_page_2014_-testing_theories_of_american_politics.doc.pdf

crowd, it would disappear into the archives.

On the basis of initial reactions, a Shaper or Shapers would move the proposal to the next phase. If investigation is needed to further the proposal, the Shapers may also apply to the crowd for funding, however this would be linked to a minimum threshold. In other words, a proposal would need a certain number of initial backers before it could apply and potentially receive procedural funding.

This first proposing phase therefore not only opens up the possibility for everyone to propose anything; it also provides the necessary filters to ensure the crowd only starts the serious work on proposals that stand a fair chance of passing. In practice it is likely that the proposals that will gain traction are those that address an existing problem that needs better resolution. The Shapers or guardians may need to provide guidance on the nature of the problem and what may already be known. This will minimise the generation of proposals that are addressing problems that have already been solved. It will also reduce the number of proposals that are based on significant misunderstandings of the problem.

2. Shaping

In the next phase, one or more Shapers take the idea and create a first formal proposal. They need to follow a template and involve one or more guardians who are assigned to the project.

Depending on the scale and complexity of the idea, procedures may vary in length. The guardians would explain to the Shapers what process to follow, and they would be available for advice (for example, whether the idea needs new legislation or simply policy instructions to the executive office). They also help determine which crowd needs to be involved, that is, who is affected by the proposal. For example, a local policy may have wider implications or need national funding.

We envisage that the proposal would be pitched clearly and

succinctly in text and video formats. It is essential that interested parties can quickly get a sense of what the proposal covers so a short YouTube style video may be the delivery channel.

3. Public Consultation

Once the proposal is shaped, it is formally presented to the relevant crowd (the community/ies affected by the proposal). At this stage, all citizens can read or see the proposal and react to it. They can show support or dissent. In addition to 'reactions', the crowd can make suggestions for alterations or ask clarifying questions. These two types of responses should be clearly differentiated. This phase is where the integrative principle becomes crucial. The Shapers continue to shape the final proposal, but they need to focus on creating the wisest possible proposal, taking account of the input from the crowd including reactions, suggestions and clarifying questions. As part of this phase, people are encouraged not to simply object to a proposal but offer a reason why they think a proposal may be unworkable. These insights may then allow the Shaper to improve what is being proposed. All dissenting views need to be integrated as much as possible. The guardians will have an important role here, and as indicated before, the technology may also help.

If it is really impossible to integrate objections this would be a reason for the triggering of a second alternate proposal. Fundamental dissenters can therefore either formulate their rationale for a 'no' vote or they may propose alternatives. Again, the guardians play an active role in making this call: when can we still work towards integration, where do we need to formulate an alternative or opposing proposal? Remember, integration is profoundly different from consensus, where ideas get watered down to become acceptable to all. Here ideas become enhanced by integrating new perspectives.

The guardians are also responsible for ensuring that everyone respects the crowdocratic process and they can step in when a debate becomes a shouting contest.

The executive office is also invited to share views on the proposal – but only regarding execution feasibility. They can also support the process by sharing data or presenting budget implications. The Shapers and guardians can also choose to let the process be informed by think tanks, academic institutions, etc., that can offer their informed opinions, but can't directly participate in the shaping.

This round ends with a refined proposal.

4. Final Check

The final check phase allows the crowd to see the full proposal(s) in its complete form. At that stage, only formal challenges can still be made (for example, the constitutionality of the proposal) and the executive office can once again share information and views with respect to the execution (not on the desirability of the policy).

The guardians take a final view on the procedural aspects and the proposal is ready for the public vote.

5. Vote

The crowd is then asked to vote on the final proposal. The Shapers present the proposal, the technicalities, the proposed way of execution and the expected implications. They are encouraged to highlight how the proposal has integrated differing views.

Opponents can either present a collective view as to why the crowd should not support the proposal or they can formulate an alternative proposal. The guardians work with opponents to guide them through this process, which needs to be a balance between due process and efficiency (counterproposals should not be the instrument for filibusters).

The crowd is asked to vote on the proposals – each citizen has a single vote. Voting happens online on the secure crowdocracy platform (The Crowd). Depending on the complexity or importance of the proposal, a minimum threshold may be applied for participation and qualified majorities may need to be applied for a vote to be passed. The constitution will need to specify these rules.

Considering that diversity is so central to the emergence of group intelligence, it is likely that the process may need to encourage participation by enough citizens to ensure a sufficiently large and diverse enough sample within the community. This may include occasional mandatory participation in areas they know nothing about.

Even in a small community setting, there could potentially be hundreds of ideas circulating at any one time. Most of us don't have thousands of free hours to trawl through all the potential legislative changes that citizens are suggesting we make. As a result, we imagine the platform would allow you to identify your topic preferences. In the same way that you can identify topics of interest on many of the social media platforms you can indicate what you want to be informed about. If, as mentioned earlier, you selected 'education', 'environment' and 'fiscal policy' as your core interests those topics, along with all other topics will have a pre-specified hashtag. When someone proposes a change to legislation, or proposes policy in the area they would make their case against at least that primary hashtag which would then automatically notify everyone who had already indicated they want to be informed about changes in that area.

Of course, the danger with this approach is that choosing topics will limit diversity of opinion, which is one of the main requirements of smart crowds. You may for example know you are interested in 'education', 'environment and 'fiscal policy' but you might be interested in the 'arts' but you've just never really spent a lot of time thinking about the arts. Often, we don't really know what we are interested in until it crosses our path. The platform might therefore initiate a monthly 'civic duty participation' topic where everyone is sent a message to participate in a random nonselected topic that the citizen has no experience or even interest in. This approach acknowledges that we all have something valuable to add to other debates. Every citizen could therefore be required to vote a number of times on areas outside their interests as a minimum participatory requirement.

6. Execution

For a proposal to pass into execution, the agreed-upon threshold of votes in favour of the proposal must be met. This can take the form of new legislation or the executive office taking executive policy steps. From here, the executive office is empowered to act as it deems fit. The crowd needs to step back and only perform its checks, not take an active guiding role along the way.

The guardians continue to follow this process and they may step in when the crowd becomes too active in its oversight. As part of the execution, feedback is also gathered and presented to the crowd – what are the implications of the decisions that have been made? The crowd needs to be informed with the insights so that it can grow its wisdom over time or be in a position to amend its earlier decisions if necessary.

Examples of Crowdocracy in Action

The following examples of crowdocracy in action are created from our imagination and seek to paint a picture of what crowdocracy could look like in reality. Again, we do not claim that our view of this process is the only right view – in fact, the crowd will undoubtedly come up with the wisest possible process. This is presented as a starting point for debate. From a small scale local example of missing streetlights, to a more involved policy of building a bridge, we are seeking to show how crowdocracy can be used to step-change the way decisions are made while also improving the quality of those decisions in highly volatile and complex times.

Missing Streetlights

Let's imagine you live in a town where austerity measures have eroded some public services. One thing that annoys you is that half the streetlights no longer work and the bulbs don't appear to get replaced with any regularity – if at all. As a result, you and your family don't feel as safe as you used to when all the streetlights were working.

In the traditional democratic system, you have very few options. You could write a stern letter to your local MP, councillor or other representative. Anyone who has ever tried this route will already know how ineffective that is. With crowdocracy, however, real solutions are possible, relatively quickly.

You decide to do something about this because you want people (including your children) to feel safe again walking home in the evening.

Proposing

You log on to the crowdocracy platform, and go through the short 'taking an initiative' tutorial. This helps you get a few basics in place, like clarifying the problem you want to address, what solution you are proposing, what regulations currently exist and why you think it's necessary to regulate this.

With some help from the site, you start recording a three-minute video message, in which you describe your view of the situation and your proposed solution – that the local executive powers, as part of their public duties, need to replace lights that are no longer working within two days of being notified. You also propose that citizens can notify that a light is broken through a dedicated system mailbox, so that everyone in the community takes responsibility for this problem. In your video, you ask your fellow citizens if anyone is interested in helping to work out the details of this proposal.

You post the video on the crowdocracy platform along with a few pertinent hashtags such as #Townname #BrokenStreetlights to ensure everyone in your town is notified about it and is able to view the short proposal video. As stated in the constitution, the video will stay active and visible on the platform for two weeks, after which time you have to take action in shaping a formal proposal.

After three days, 350 people have watched your video and you have 125 'thumbs up' for your idea, and seven people have indicated they are willing to actively support you. Only five people have given a 'thumbs down' to indicate an initial negative response and the reason they state is because they don't like bright lights. For some, this impacts their ability to sleep well and someone else is concerned about nocturnal animals. One person indicates that she does not believe this needs regulation and it is already part of the responsibilities of the executive powers. As there are 5000 people in your town, you're encouraged by these initial reactions and you reach out to the seven volunteers.

Shaping

With the seven volunteers, you agree that four of you will make an initial draft of the regulations, while two others do a check with the guardians in the judiciary to work out the current legal requirements regarding streetlights. For example, you want to find out if this currently regulated. If so, where is this currently regulated, does this indeed justify policy setting or is a conversation with the executive powers enough? The last two volunteers check in with the executive office to get their views on why streetlights are currently not being replaced at the moment. What costs are involved? Is the slow replacement of streetlights a cost issue, a time issue or a manpower issue?

The guardians come back immediately with the response that currently the regulation is broad. The executive powers need to ensure proper lighting between dusk and dawn throughout the town and a specification of replacing within two days is a legal possibility. The executive office responds that they would be happy to execute such a proposal but they have no way of checking the working of the lights throughout the town and they have no funds available to meet such ambitious timelines.

Armed with this input, those involved start drafting the formal proposal. Initially, three Shapers are instrumental but eventually all eight put their ideas on the online platform which helps to integrate opinion, identify words to be changed for greater agreement and adding clarifications and fresh input. It takes about a week to come to a proposal that all the Shapers think will work and create a new video. Again, using the simple tutorial on the crowdocracy platform, a short video along with a brief written proposal is created. You send it to the judiciary who make a few small suggestions. In the proposal, it is suggested that the executive powers have the obligation to change all lights that are reported broken within 72 hours. Citizens take it on themselves to report broken lights on a dedicated mailbox in the system.

Public Consultation

The proposal goes live and all citizens have three weeks to react and suggest amendments. In those weeks, 300 reactions from various people are received – most of them simple expressions of support. About 50 are content related. Most questions are raised by the executive office in a special section where they post their responses, although everyone can see those questions and responses. The executive states that they have no funds for the initiative. In the online discussion that follows, someone suggests some volunteers could support the executive powers a few hours per week in executing this task. This idea is welcomed and immediately four volunteers (including you) offer to take on a supporting role.

One interesting conversation takes place with one of the first-round critics regarding the brightness of the lights. Initially she is just writing negative comments, but with some questions, it becomes clear that she is not against light per se, but objects to the lights that are currently being used. They are too bright and not very high quality. The Shapers had not considered bulb quality up to this point so we flag the concern and ask the executive to comment. The executive confirms that the town uses cheaper bulbs. The downside is that these bulbs are very bright and may well disturb nocturnal animals and they don't last as long as other varieties but with cutbacks these have been considered the best option.

We check in with the executive, of a few surrounding towns and find out that other lights are on the market but they are 40 per cent more expensive – however they last twice as long.

With these insights, we redraft our proposal and post it again after a very quick check by the judiciary who have no further comments. It is about seven weeks since you first starting thinking about doing something about the missing streetlights.

Final Check

The proposal is posted again for two weeks.

During this phase, no more content changes can take place; only challenges to the legal aspects (for example, constitutionality, or process flaws) can be raised to the judiciary. Also, the executive power can raise final objections. In this case no further comments are raised and so the final proposal is put to a public vote.

Vote

On Friday afternoon, together with five other proposals for that week, your proposal is put up for a vote. This means that all citizens get a notification in their system inbox that they are asked to vote on this subject. If they choose to, they can watch the three-minute video and read the entire proposal, including all the online discussions that have taken place. Using a mobile app or button on the crowdocracy platform, citizens are asked to vote in favour or against the initiative.

For this subject, a voter turnout of at least ten per cent of the voting community and a simple majority of those people voting is required to allow the proposal to successfully pass into execution phase. The vote is open for a week, during which time interim results are not published (to ensure the independence of decision-making). As legislative Shapers, you and your fellow Shapers are only allowed to draw attention to the fact that people are asked to vote – apart from the formal proposal, you are not allowed to lobby for it.

After the week of voting, the judiciary announce the results: 1,080 people have voted (more than 20 per cent of the crowd), and 85 per cent of people have supported the proposal. It is therefore passed.

Execution

Following the vote, the regulation is officially amended. The identified volunteers are invited to the executive office to discuss the details of the arrangement. The judiciary require a formal confirmation of this arrangement. Less than three months after your initial idea, following a short safety training, you go out on a Sunday morning to replace two lights. You are also using the alternative high quality lights that have been purchased in bulk by joining forces with nearby towns so the bulbs are cheaper than if your town had bought them alone. After a while, you post the initial results of the change on the community platform, so that everyone can see what the result and impact have been from the proposal.

Imagine this type of initiative in different areas of your community. While the example may be a simple, local issue, its implications are significant. Crowdocracy gives you a voice and direct platform for action; it allows you to open discussion on issues that are important to you which are probably important to others. By getting involved, our political apathy diminishes and we move from frustrated observer to empowered citizen, which fosters an ever-increasing virtuous cycle of greater and greater involvement and more and more genuine governance.

Now, let's explore the crowdocratic process in a more complex issue.

Building a Bridge

Building a bridge is a more complex process than dealing with missing streetlights because it involves more dimensions and a wider community. It is also much more expensive. But crowdocracy could still provide a wise solution for bridge building.

Say you live in a city located on a wide river, not far from the sea. There is a sizable harbour and on either side of the river are two growing cities. You live in the one backing on to the mountains so there is no room to grow. The other city is surrounded by hinterland that is ripe for development and could easily accommodate the rising population and land is currently quite cheap.

For years, there have been discussions on the feasibility of building a bridge over the river to connect the two cities. It was clearly a major infrastructure project with significant expense and the opposing sides of the argument always seem to end in deadlock. Because of political party infighting, the politics between the two cities, national government demands from other competing projects, the lobbying efforts of the business community and the environmental NGOs, no progress had been made.

The nearest bridge is, however, 20 kilometres upstream. On a good day, with light traffic you can get from one city centre to the other in about an hour. On a bad day it can be double that. As you are stuck in traffic on one of the bad days, you start thinking about just how useful that bridge would be.

Following the successful roll out of various crowdocratic initiatives and some fine-tuning of the technology platform, it was clear this approach worked so all the legislative institutions were closed. Now you, along with the rest of the population are in charge of your own governance through the crowdocratic platform. You decide to do something about the bridge and put forward a new proposal.

Proposing

It is interesting because just as you decide to grab the bull by the horns and make the initial proposal for the new bridge yourself, you read various media pundits and local blog posts asking why no one has so far taken the initiative.

You can see the potential of the bridge and sense that both cities are ready for the financial boost it will provide to both. Besides, the pollution and the traffic drive you crazy and you would love to move across the river. With a bridge, you could still commute to your job or you may even be able to persuade your boss to move the business to the other side.

You log on to the crowdocracy platform and, using the tutorial, you make a short three-minute video outlining your proposal to build the bridge. The technology platform even converts your image to a cartoon so that you can stay anonymous while outlining why you think a bridge would benefit both communities and the surrounding areas. It takes you half a day to prepare what you want to say and make the recording – making sure to cover off a number of basic questions that you're prompted to answer. The whole process is inspiring and you're excited at what could happen as a result of your proposal but you can already see that taking charge of this whole process would be way beyond your comfort zone. In your initiative, you clearly highlight that you will be a passionate supporter, rather than a real Shaper and invite other Shapers to get involved to help move the proposal along.

The proposal also prompts you to indicate which communities are in scope for the 'new bridge' proposal. The main communities targeted would be the two cities connected by the bridge and their surrounding area. Who would be eligible to vote on this proposal would depend on a variety of factors including whether the funding is coming from local government or the bridge is to be partially funded by national government. In addition, you will need to categorise your proposal from a long list of possible topic areas. You check the online boxes next to 'infrastructure improvement', 'roads', and add a number of hashtag keywords that will immediately alert your target audience to your proposal – just like Twitter does now.

Once complete, you post your proposal video and wait. Within half an hour hundreds of people respond. In the next few days several thousand more respond and it is clear that this is a divisive topic, just like in the old political system!

Shaping

Of the thousands of responses, 80 people have indicated they want to take a role as a Shaper of this project. In addition five experienced guardians are assigned to the project and they organise an online process meeting via web forum. In that meeting, the guardians explain the process for a large infrastructural project. They start by explaining the existing legislation including relevant parts of the constitution, planning laws, environmental regulations and the crowdocratic process. On the forum, 12 people electronically step forward to indicate interest to take a very active role in shaping the proposal. Some have very direct and relevant experience building large infrastructure projects and some come from completely unrelated backgrounds.

One thing that is clarified immediately is the fact that the bridge project will need national approval as projects of this size are partly funded from a national budget. This has significant implications for the level of support needed from the community, who is eligible to vote on the proposal and the expected timelines.

One person asks whether it is a problem that she is working for a construction firm, which could later have an interest in bidding for contracts. The guardians explain that as the entire process is public, Shapers have no significant benefit over others and so there can be no advantageous position. But the guardians will closely watch whether the process in further stages is nudged in certain directions because of commercial interests.

The group of 12 start work to shape the initial proposal, adding depth and breadth of information and experience to add 'meat to the bones' of the initial proposal. This is all done online – none of the Shapers physically meet each other – using the crowdocracy platform which allows multiple inputs to be assimilated and integrated, making use of the technology that makes that easier for them.

Given the complexity of the project, there is an additional step in the process – a high level draft to gather a sense of how the public will react and to get funding for the project analysis. This is often done to avoid wasting too much time creating a full first proposal that may not generate enough interest to pursue. While there will be no formal vote, the initial high-level draft could attract so little support that the guardians may advise against a further detailed proposal – and there would be no funding. Facts are gathered, opinions circulated, and within a few weeks, the 12 Shapers agree on a first version to be presented. They have a written text explaining what a bridge could bring, but also outlining what challenges need to be overcome. One aspect they cover is the necessary height for the bridge to protect the commercial interest of the harbour. Also, the environmental impact is given full attention, citing examples from similar cities. It also outlines ideas on implementation and how the project would need to be run. The project itself needs funding now.

The guardians only need to step in once when one of the Shapers appears to raise so many obstacles that it looks like he has joined the group with an intention of derailing the process. The guardians have a conversation with the person who discloses he is an environmentalists and sceptic of the bridge project. He is presented with the choice to either participate constructively or leave the group and be active later by voting against the proposal, or in creating an alternative proposal.

The initial funding proposal goes live, with a written report, a short video and an infographic. Thousands of people download these and give an initial polling. It becomes apparent that a significant majority likes the idea of the bridge, and while there are many objections, they have mostly to do with how the bridge will impact the environment, rather than being completely opposed to the project. The guardians conclude that the funding can be made available for the creation of the proposal.

The Shapers (by now a group of 17) go back to work and create a formal project team that will provide input and information on the technical, environmental and financial aspects of the project. The executive office for infrastructural projects becomes involved although they are now tasked with informing the Shapers with neutrality rather than actively seeking to direct the outcome one way or the other.

Over a period of nearly a year, the various project groups gather facts, perform initial environmental impact analysis, make budget estimates and issue reports. All reports are made public on the platform as the proposal is shaped and refined. The crowd has already made decisions about whether Shapers are paid for their time and/or expenses on projects of this size to recognise the effort that is required.

One of the main reasons the Shapers are able to make a lot of progress is because they use two case examples of large infrastructural projects in neighbouring counties. They have asked to review the files and proposals for those projects and they serve as useful templates. This is becoming a main advantage of crowdocracy: the sharing of knowledge and experience across communities. Shapers are much more inclined to learn from other places than the bureaucrats used to in the past.

The Shapers, with the support of the various project teams, come to the formulation of a proposal. This comes in the form of a report and a presentation that concludes in favour of building a bridge. It takes into account various environmental concerns and mitigations and it has a clear path forward to the execution phase. It also contains the draft legislation that will need to be put in place, which has been drafted with support from the guardians and experts from the executive office.

Public Consultation

This proposal is posted and the crowd are given three months to give feedback, suggest improvements or alterations and share their views. The 12 Shapers and the five guardians now have the busy task of reviewing comments and applying an integrative approach. Many comments require clarification, and it is sometimes hard to manage the sheer volume of comments.

One of the strong indications from the crowd is the desire for more environmental data. Thousands of citizens, in one form or another have raised environmental concerns. Some love the idea of the bridge but are concerned about the impact it would have on the river ecosystem and surrounding landscape. Others are very much against the bridge and are clearly seeking additional ammunition to halt the process. The beauty of the integrative process is that, whatever the reason, large numbers of people share the opinion that a more rigorous environmental impact study is required.

The impact study is commissioned with a local expert institution.

While it is clear that some people are fundamentally opposed to building a bridge, they do not derail the process. They know they can position their arguments in an opposing view when the final proposal goes to vote. Attempts by some opponents to slow down or weaken the proposal in favour of a bridge, are quickly detected by the guardians and they issue warnings to those involved. In one case, they decide to exclude a participant who engages in bullying tactics from taking part in any future conversations on this subject.

After the period of three months, a full proposal is ready, including the results of the environmental impact study. Many comments have strengthened the original proposal and the Shapers feel that while the process was intense and at some points confusing, the end result represents the desire of the crowd by incorporating the best, most popular suggestions while mitigating some of the identified disadvantages. One great suggestion that received wide support was to open opinion on the design of the bridge up to the community in a 'beauty contest' so that everyone could be involved in choosing the winning bridge design and appointing the winning architect. The proposal clearly is 'the best possible at this time' and it covers many angles and perspectives.

The financial aspects of the bridge project are fairly complicated. Just like the old democratic process, policy must always consider its own affordability based on local or national budgets. Most policy implementations cost money and as a society, the crowd will need to make choices about what taxes to collect and how to spend that revenue for the benefit of the collective. Crowdocracy wouldn't change that fundamental principle. Budgeting decisions and policy decisions must still be linked and will require considerable reflection and the wisdom of a community to get right.

In this example, the budget for infrastructure projects needs to come from national and local sources. But as no one in the preparation phase has to answer to a political body, the teams on local and national level have worked out a scenario that is balanced – and this attracted very limited comments from the crowd. Some people have suggested that the costs are underestimated and so the Shapers and guardians have agreed to raise the suggested budget. A proposal that is underfunded will always run into trouble in the execution phase. It is always better to secure enough funds in the public vote upfront.

Final Check

After the extensive phase of public consultation, there is a final check. The executive office offers a final opinion on the feasibility of the project and suggests some changes in the ambitious time schedule. There are no issues with the constitutionality of the proposal. This phase is therefore concluded within the timeframe and the proposal goes to a vote.

Vote

The adjusted full proposal now goes live. It is a lengthy document, but the Shapers have created a short summary and an artist's impression of how the bridge could look, supported by a ten-minute documentary explaining the project, the impact and the investments needed. It describes the project from various angles.

Opponents to the new bridge have also been working on a video explaining why the bridge is not a good idea. They object to the environmental impact and the financial commitments – believing the money could be better spent elsewhere.

What is striking in this crowdocracy system is the fact that views are presented but no one knows who is behind the views presented. Various people also describe their views in the media, whether online, in print or on TV but organisations and individuals have already been restricted in the amount of time or money they can spend on advertising or lobbying for a certain outcome – this was the result of another crowdocratic debate and was enshrined in an amendment to the constitution. Also, individuals are not allowed to declare what contributions they make in the crowdocratic platform.

There really are two separate worlds: the crowdocratic platform on which people create policy in the semi-autonomous way and the public world where people are spectators. As politics has become an active sport, the opinion makers have become quieter since crowdocracy has taken off – there is much less to gain from commenting on politics these days; it really has become serious policy creation.

When the proposal goes live to the country, the constitution ensures that everyone has a vote. This makes sense as the entire nation needs to fund at least part of the project and the two cities involved need to vote in favour of the project. The results are overwhelming: more than two-thirds support the proposal, even more in the two cities.

Execution

The crowd have voted in favour of the bridge and the proposal moves into the execution phase. Companies are invited to tender while oversight is provided by the executive offices at national and local levels.

One important thing to note is the potential to speed up decisions and execution.

In Western Europe, the consensus driven decision-making models and legal challenges often result in significant delays to large decisions such as whether to build a bridge or not. Creating a road, expanding a village, changing the educational curriculum are all decisions that can take years to resolve. Yet the quality of decision-making does not get better with all those delays; they are often extended battles between people with entrenched beliefs. They become win-lose battles instead of integrated solutions that seek win/win outcomes. We believe crowdocracy will ease that pain and speed things up considerably.

When we tap into the wisdom of a huge crowd instead of expecting a chosen few to know everything about a project or topic we get access to much more information, ideas and insights. Those various views, ideas and opinions are also integrated rather than one side strong-arming the other or watering down a proposal to gain a barely satisfactory outcome for either side. Even with limited information available, the crowd consistently displays good collective judgement. Discussion about facts, science and the accuracy of data currently drives a lot of debate in the existing system. In crowdocracy, the crowd will be more inclined to collectively discover 'the best possible solution in this case'. That is not to say that disagreement on facts and interpretation of data will not remain but the collective has much more opportunity to identify the erroneous information presented to the crowd.

With large infrastructural projects such as the one outlined in this example there will always be limitations in information, but there is no need to design lengthy objection processes. Of course, the judiciary routes are still available, but the judiciary has been involved protecting the integrity of the process all along, so successful challenges to the legal aspects of the process are rare. Integrative decision-making, a focus on the wisest solution given the current status, the possible involvement of everyone, and an active role of the guardians in the process, will allow us to make much faster, better quality decisions.

A Glimpse of a Crowdocractic Future

The examples above hopefully make clear how different governance could look if we transform to crowdocracy. Unlike the potential of some current web platforms, the process is not an avenue towards anarchy which would simply allow the crowd to descend into an angry mob. With a strong constitution, clear procedural rules and clear roles and responsibilities, we can unlock the wisdom of the entire crowd without triggering the disadvantages.

It is clear from these examples that the principles we outlined in this chapter *can* be put into practice. We can also see that the four conditions for crowd wisdom can be met: as everyone can participate, we can ensure diversity. As the process is semi-anonymous and voting results are not published until everyone has voted, we also facilitate as much independence of thought as possible. As the proposals are raised by the people nearest to the issue, we also ensure a decentralised approach. Lastly, the process with its different steps and role definition of the Shapers and guardians, allows for genuine integration.

Granted, we still have a lot of mental and practical hurdles to overcome. Although impossible to source, it is said that German philosopher Arthur Schopenhauer once suggested, 'All truth passes through three stages. First it is ridiculed. Second, it is violently opposed. Third, it is accepted as being self-evident.'

We have little doubt that crowdocracy will be ridiculed and potentially violently opposed. As you read this chapter, you may have had your own concerns and questions for how certain aspects of crowdocracy might work. We don't suggest that we have the fine detail completely ironed out and we don't have all the answers. What we have presented is just one possibility. What we need is for you and the rest of the crowd to engage with us so that collectively we can find the very best way to make crowdocracy a reality.

Many elite stakeholders have a great deal to lose. We will undoubtedly be told that democracy is 'too fragile' to be left to the masses. We will be warned that such a change would make it easy for small groups of radicals of any political persuasion to hijack democracy for their own ends.

The truth is, crowdocracy should finally stop that. Even in progressive, free and open countries such as the US, most of Europe, UK and Australia, policy is decided by the chosen few over long lunches or on the golf course. Corporate lobbyists spend time and money getting access to the right people so that their clients can have the 'ear of the minister' and present their case – often even drafting legislation or making changes to legislation. Crowdocracy would finally ensure that no small, powerful or wealthy group could ever hijack our governance institutions again.

Chapter 7:

The Road to a
New Reality

'Our deepest fear is not that we are inadequate. Our deepest fear is that we are powerful beyond measure. It is our light, not our darkness that most frightens us.'[1]

– Marianne Williamson

The mathematics of crowdocracy are sound – under the right circumstances the crowd will nearly always make better choices than a small group – even if that small group is full of 'experts'. This may be counterintuitive but it remains one of the most robust facts in social science. Remember, such wisdom is an 'emergent' phenomenon – meaning that the intelligence that emerges from the crowd is not simply the sum of the crowd's parts. It is not just an aggregation of individual citizen's intelligence in whatever form that may take. Rather, this collective intelligence can't actually be found in the individuals themselves – it exists only in the whole.[2]

---

[1] Williamson, M. (1992) A Return to Love: Reflections on the Principles of "A Course in Miracles" Harper Collins, London.

[2] Landemore, H. (2013) *Democratic Reason: Politics, collective intelligence and the rule of the many*, New Jersey: Princeton University Press.

This truth coupled with the emergence of truly inclusive, accessible and relatively inexpensive technology means that we can, for the first time, access that crowd and integrate opinion into a smart, lucid, shared solution.

How do we get from where we are now to a new, fairer, more inclusive form of governance? How do we transition from democracy, even the more sophisticated social democracy, to crowdocracy?

The answer is – it depends.

Essentially crowdocracy transcends and includes democracy. In other words, it includes the strengths of democracy while transcending its failures. Crowdocracy is based on the principles that all citizens deserve equal rights and decisions should be based on majority rule. Back in 1973, classical scholar Moses Finley pointed out that while his contemporary intellectuals agreed with the concept of democracy, most also agreed that none of the principles of democracy actually worked in practice.[3] Crowdocracy seeks to move us forward toward genuine governance by the people and crowd-based policy development and decision-making.

However, the transition will very much depend on where 'here' is right now! In Chapter 3, we described the ever-advancing spiral of development that enables individuals or, more importantly, organisations and society to evolve the sophistication of their decision-making. With each new stage of development the decision-makers are able to handle greater degrees of complexity and solve more complicated and ultimately 'wicked' issues. But if an organisation or society has not properly consolidated its learning at one level then when it tries to leap forward to the next level it is highly likely to fail and collapse back down in a decision-

---

[3] Finley, M.I. (1973) *Democracy Ancient and Modern*, New Jersey: Rutgers University Press.

making implosion that impairs organisational and societal functioning. This is the reason why the road to crowdocracy will depend on where an organisation or society's' culture is right now.

Crowdocracy is very unlikely to succeed in places where tribal rule or autocratic leadership is still in place. We have seen the disastrous fallout from well-intentioned attempts to 'impose' sophisticated decision-making processes like democracy by 'developed nations' on tribal countries like Afghanistan. It's impossible to move from a level of tribalism to a level of democracy in one jump. It would therefore be completely impossible to introduce crowdocracy in such parts of the world. The transition needs to be gradual and honour where an organisation or societal culture is right now. As a result, crowdocracy can only land in those places where a sufficient number of people have a common understanding of the rule of law and other democratic principles.

The starting point for a crowdocractic revolution would therefore have to be countries and communities where democracy and preferably social democracy had already evolved as a form of governance or was at least on the agenda.

While writing this book, we frequently explored the idea of crowdocracy with other people and the reaction to the concept of challenging democracy was almost always positive – there appears to be a growing recognition that democracy is no longer fit for purpose. However, many still assume that the problem with democracy lies in our inability to elect the right people rather than the democratic process itself. Often embedded in such a statement is that if the person we were talking to and their friends were in charge of the country, things would be much better!

We suggest that no *other* group of representatives would do a substantially better job in a sustainable way. We certainly include ourselves in that statement and thoroughly acknowledge that we would not do a better job. The issues are too many and far too complex, the interests too diverse, the system too divisive and the media too interested in personalities for any group of representatives, however smart, experienced or connected to do anything other than drown under the weight of the wicked problems we now face.

In order to make progress we need all of us. We need to embrace or at least open ourselves up to the wisdom of the crowd and the notion of group intelligence. A true conviction in crowd wisdom will need to grow with experience, but there has to be some initial belief that crowds can be wise. Our initial gut response to this idea is often fear. To be fair, the fear of mob rule is justified. If we look back through history there are countless devastating examples of the ignorance of crowds. Humans can, under the wrong circumstances, turn into savages and we need to create a system that protects us against our own destructive nature. If that system is created by the crowd we are also much more likely to follow the rules we ourselves created within a system we had a hand in developing.

We may be wary of allowing crowds to make decisions in case they lynch someone and prefer to put our faith in a democratic majority but the latter often does no better. As Hélène Landemore points out, 'A majority put Socrates to death. A majority allegedly brought Hitler to power. All over the world, in fact, formal and informal majorities endorse irrational, xenophobic, racist, anti-Semitic and sexist ideologies.'[4]

Human beings are also capable of great wisdom, humanity and innovation but everything we have done as a species from the worst to the best is simply an expression of our individual and collective level of development.

Learning to trust our fellow human beings may be a mental hurdle we need to straddle but the transition process from here to there

---

[4] Landemore, H. (2013) *Democratic Reason: Politics, collective intelligence and the rule of the many, New* Jersey: Princeton University Press.

will help. Obviously trust is not something we can just switch on, it usually has to be earned. But there is nothing to stop us starting small, using crowdocracy in our local communities, our schools, our organisations or our businesses so we can start to see the power of the crowd in action. We don't need to go from zero to hero in one step. We can test crowdocracy out on smaller-scale decisions so we can witness its potential for ourselves.

In addition to the wisdom of crowds, we also need to trust that technology is capable of supporting us in this complex effort. We need to create a system that allows millions of us to collaborate. Not only do we need technology that is fast, efficient, reliable, and user-friendly; we also need to be convinced of its security. It has to be open source yet closed to intruders. We have to ensure that the data that will be generated by such a platform is safe, secure and non-commercialised. A technology platform, the likes of which we are proposing could potentially generate a goldmine of commercially valuable information. For crowdocracy to work, citizens would need to have 100 per cent faith that the data, information, and opinion they provide were secure and could not be sold or used by commercial companies to sell products and services. We would however envisage these issues being addressed and agreed on by the crowd. The crowd may, for example, agree that their data be anonymised, that is markers that identify them as a named individual are removed but their opinions could still be analysed using Big Data analytics to identify useful and potentially important insights.

At the heart of crowdocracy is an invitation to trust ourselves and each other. We need to choose to believe that we can contribute to the whole. That is the message that Marianne Williamson gave us with her poem. We believe that the reason that this poem resonates so strongly with so many people is because deep down we all know that we are far more capable than we dare admit to others and especially to ourselves.

Transition Models

As mentioned, how we travel from where we are now to where we need to be will depend on where we are now and the context for the transition. Can we evolve or do we need a revolution? Assuming you are reading this from a currently democratic country then we envisage a number of transition scenarios:

1. Top down transition led by enlightened politicians/leaders
2. Start big
3. Start small
4. Create a stronghold within the system

1. Top-down Transition Led by Enlightened Politicians/Leaders

While maybe not the most likely, it is possible that some more enlightened politicians take the lead for transition. Certainly since we started this project, we have both been quite surprised by just how many politicians or people already in government are acutely aware that something needs to change and are prepared to explore the options we are describing in this book.

Top-down transition would have several major advantages and one major disadvantage. It would allow for increasingly large experiments with full access to the resources of government. It would involve civil servants in the planning so as to effectively transition their roles and increase the likelihood of 'buy-in'. This approach would also allow the major transformation of the executive and judiciary to be planned. In addition, it would allow for the necessary training to facilitate a step change in individual and therefore collective development and a greater understanding of the integrative process.

In his book *The End of Power*, author Moises Naim suggests that the solution to the dysfunction that currently exists between governments and citizens lies in innovative approaches to

217

restoring the public trust. People must find it within themselves to consent to be governed and governments must in turn find a way to deserve that consent.[5] Nice idea, but it's hardly realistic. Governments have often done the exact opposite. According to the Edelman Trust Barometer, people are desperate for honesty and fair play, leading to stagnating trust levels despite a better economic outlook and, unbelievably, just 48 per cent of the UK population would trust a political leader to return £10 if they lent it to them![6]

Naím states, 'In short, disruptive innovation has not arrived in politics, government, and political participation.'[7] We are suggesting that crowdocracy is that disruptive innovation and when led by enlightened leaders (political or otherwise), it could allow for great communication and rebuilding of trust in public office.

Could crowdocracy be a platform to enable a major party in a position of power to change the game and put the electorate first? Maybe. It was telling that in his UK 'Prime Minister's Question Time', the new leader of the Labour party crowdsourced his line of attack. Normally these weekly televised theatrics involves the leader of the opposition asking the Prime Minister various questions they consider relevant considering the political environment at the time. This time was different – in a pretty radical break with tradition, Jeremy Corbyn chose a selection of questions submitted by the crowd who offered more than 40,000 suggestions. The crowd is clearly engaged and the result was

---

[5] Loofbourow, L. (2015) 'The End of Power by Moises Naím review' a study in mass alienation', *The Guardian*, 15 January 2015, accessed 1 Jamuary 2016, www.theguardian.com/books/2015/jan/15/the-end-of-power-moses-naim-review

[6] Edelman Trust Barometer 2015, both accessed 1 January 2016, www.edelman.co.uk/work/ and www.edelman.com/2015-edelman-trust-barometer-2/trust-and-innovation-edelman-trust-barometer/global-results/

[7] Naím, M. (2015) *The End of Power*, New York: Basic Books.

astonishing. The noisy disrespectful point scoring and heckling was, for a brief 30 minutes, replaced by a series of sober, worthy and slightly technical questions and their equally serious replies.[8]

There is definitely a glimmer of hope that enlightened politicians will lead the change but perhaps more likely is that leaders of organisations embrace the concept first, either because of their own convictions or because of the push by their stakeholders (including the public's pressure through platforms like Change. org). Specifically, organisations and businesses that are currently built around communities are ripe for crowdocracy. There is, for example, no reason why charities such as Amnesty International, sporting clubs such as Barcelona FC, member organisations such as Facebook, or companies such as Starbucks could not employ crowdocracy to ignite the wisdom of the crowd to make better decisions, find solutions or dream up new products or services. They could easily be the organisations which first empower their respective crowds and hand over their policy decisions to their crowds.

In Chapter 1, we touched on how FIFA might look if it were to embrace crowdocracy. World football would certainly be different. If all football clubs, national football associations and FIFA operated crowdocratically, the global football-loving crowd would participate in designing and agreeing the rules for their game (including experimenting with new rules). These rules could govern how to run and allocate tournaments, transnational competitions, salary caps, commercial dealings, TV rights, and so on. The executive teams would likely operate in a much nimbler way because there is no personal incentive to make it grand. Those involved would no longer be able to create favourable positions for themselves and their cronies. Companies sponsoring football would need to work under the crowd-controlled rules and deal

---

[8] Castle, S. (2015) 'Labour's New Leader, Jeremy Corbyn, Crowd-Sources Questions for British Premier', *New York Times*, 16 September 2015, accessed 1 January 2016, www.nytimes.com/2015/09/17/world/europe/jeremy-corbyn-labour-david-cameron.html

with the executive teams that have crowd defined mandates. Such a transformation would surely be an attractive alternative to today's dysfunction. Starting with FIFA is certainly worth a try: we see only upside from where we are today.

This sort of approach could work in a similar fashion in many organisations – large and small.

Of course, the major challenge with top-down transition, even by enlightened political leaders is that it doesn't sufficiently involve the crowd. As a result, the crowd won't necessarily feel the ownership to the new process any more than they feel ownership to the old.

2. Start Big: The Iceland Story

Iceland is probably the poster child for 'starting big'; because of its attempt to crowdsource a new constitution.

In Chapter 5, we pointed to Iceland as an example of what is possible when we harness the wisdom of the crowd and explained how Iceland sought to involve the crowd in rewriting their constitution in the wake of Iceland's banking collapse of 2008. In this chapter, we will explain in more detail the risks of starting so 'big' and how such a bold initiative can be derailed by vested interests and people keen to maintain the status quo.

Much has been written about what happened in Iceland post 2008 so to really understand what was achieved and how, one of us (AW) went to speak to a number of the individuals directly involved in the process. In order to fully comprehend exactly what happened and the lessons that we can take from this example we must understand the recent political history of Iceland.

In 2008, there were four main parties. On the right there was the Independence Party (IP) and the Progressive Party (PP). At the beginning of the millennium many of the left-wing parties merged to form the Social Democratic Alliance (SDA). Some left-wing members chose to join a new party, the Left-Green Movement.

In the 2007 election, the PP lost badly and as a result they ended their longstanding alliance with IP, despite still being able to form a majority. Instead the IP's leader, Geir Haarde, chose to form an unstable coalition with the Social Democrats. It was the IP and Social Democrats who were in power when the 2008 economic collapse hit. In the election that was triggered in 2009, the electorate rejected the IP, presumably blaming them more than the Social Democrats for the problems as they had been in power for over a decade. The IP lost 9 seats whereas the SDA gained two. This drove a deeper rift between the right leaning PP and IP. In the 2009 election, the SDA became the largest party with 20 seats (out of a total of 63) and they formed a government with the Left—Green movement. As part of the dissatisfaction with politicians post-2008, a new party, the Citizen's party, was formed and secured four seats and 7 per cent of the vote. But the Citizens Party subsequently imploded and their leader, Birgitta Jónsdóttir, went on to form the 'Pirate Party' in 2011. The Pirate Party subsequently captured the public imagination and is currently enjoying a 30 per cent popularity according to opinion polls (2015).

In the chaos following the 2008 economic collapse there was a strong public demand for change. Part of that change was writing a new constitution for the country. Since the original constitution had been written in 1944, there had been calls for a new constitution to be created and following the financial collapse those calls become so strong that parliament could no longer resist them, although the PP and IP still did what they could to block the process. Since parliament would have to live with a new constitutional framework they would need to be involved in the process, and hold new elections to ratify the outcome. As a result, parliament set up a Constitutional Committee to oversee the process in 2009. The original thinking was that a new constitution would put the country on a more solid footing for generations to come and therefore the process should be given at least four years to run. The Constitutional Committee set up to oversee the process was made up of seven individuals, all nonpoliticians, mainly academics from law, literature and science. The Constitutional Committee recognised that the whole process was driven by the will of the people and therefore a mechanism was needed to allow the people to participate. So the committee set up a Constitutional Council to allow the people to have their say. Anyone was allowed to put their name forward and to everyone's surprise, 950 citizens stepped forward with a desire to be elected to the council. This created a huge problem as the numbers had to be whittled down to a manageable 25. After several rounds of voting, eventually 25 private individuals were elected to the council.

Sadly, the right-wing parties, fearing that the council could undermine their powerbase, triggered a legal challenge before the council had even met. The judiciary was influenced to rule that whatever the council might come up with would effectively be 'illegal' and therefore 'null and void'. This decision by the judiciary is now widely seen as a politically motivated move by the right-wing parties and a pre-emptive strike to dismiss the will of the people, particularly if it generated what they considered to be the 'wrong' outcome. Effectively, the judiciary created an exit strategy before the process ever really began. As suspected, the judiciary's decision, which some believe is itself questionable, has indeed been used as a political weapon to undermine the will of the people.

You will remember that one of the key factors in crowdocracy is diversity. If the Icelandic people wanted to ensure that the crowd would create a wiser solution than the disaster the Icelandic politicians had created, they needed to ensure diversity of opinion and input. Interestingly, when selecting the council the only diversity criteria specified was that there should be at least 40 per cent women and no politicians. One might assume that such a lack of proactivity on the issue of diversity would generate a monoculture within the council, which might then be stuffed with political academics and political journalists but this was not the case. More by luck than by good planning or accurate judgement there was actually a reasonable educational, ethnic, age, gender and even sexual orientation diversity within the 25 council members. There was also a reasonable mix of representatives from both city and rural areas, which is recognised as a key issue in Iceland.

The role of the council was to rewrite the constitution. Some of the Social Democrats feared that the process would stall, particularly if it ran on for four years. Given the active resistance from the PP and IP politicians, presumably concerned about their own loss of power, a pragmatic decision was taken to try and complete the writing of the Constitution within the lifetime of the parliament, that is the timeframe was cut from four years to just eighteen months.

Despite these incredible constraints, and the fact that the Constitution was drafted from scratch, the council completed their work on time. The council split into three groups to take different parts of the Constitution forward with all the drafting and redrafting being completely transparent and socialised on the Internet. As mentioned in Chapter 5, the text was made public each week and the country was invited to offer comments and suggestions on an interactive website specifically designed for the purpose. Hundreds of citizens did, and many suggestions were included in the developing constitution.[9] All comments, contributions and amendments from the wider community were taken on board in subsequent revisions. As mentioned earlier, the resulting constitution put human rights at the heart of Icelandic democracy and recognised the rights of nature and gave citizens the right to call referendums, block legislation, table bills and present issues for consideration providing there was enough support for the issue. Having completed its work, the council submitted the new Constitution to Parliament.

[9] Gylfason, T. (2014) 'Events in Iceland show that a UK constitutional convention should involve politicians as minimally as possible', OXPOL, The Oxford University Politics Blog, 3 November 2014, accessed 30 December 2015, http://politicsinspires.org/events-iceland-show-uk-constitutional-convention-involve-politicians-minimally-possible/

Figure 7.1: Translation of article that appeared in Icelandic newspaper *Stundin (The Hour)*

Who killed the new constitution?

Stundin suggests these people killed the constitution. From left: Prime minister Sigmundur David Gunnlaugsson current prime minister for PP, President Olafur Ragnar Grímsson, Guðmundur Steingrimsson leader of the Bright Future party (spin off from the socialist alliance), Àrni Páll Árnason (middle front) current leader of the Socialist alliance, Bjarni Benediktsson current minister of finance and leader of the IP, and Asta Ragnheiður Jóhannesdóttir former president of parliament for the socialist democratic alliance in the 2009 government.

Unfortunately, it is yet to be fully adopted as politicians from various parties have done their best to block the will of the people. In an attempt to break the deadlock, the Social Democrats managed to initiate a referendum. Despite further political attempts to rig the question, a massive 67 per cent in the Icelandic population still voted in favour of the new crowdsourced constitution being adopted. Of course, those in power are still resisting. Figure 7.1

is an article printed by Icelandic newspaper *Stundin* naming and shaming those it considers responsible for killing the Constitution in Iceland.[10] This powerful political resistance, usually exerted from the top to maintain the status quo is the major problem with starting big and starting big within an existing system.

Although Iceland's crowdsourced constitution is still politically blocked, its 'failure' is not an example of the failure of this new form of democracy but simply another example of the failure of the current form. Many believe the constitution has been blocked because of powerful vested interests keen to avoid the natural resources of Iceland reverting to the people. Over the years, Iceland has tended to be run by those individuals and institutions that control the fishing and energy sector. The new constitution put these natural resources in the hands of the people. This simple fact may be at the heart of the current political resistance.

Thorvaldur Gylfason, Professor of Economics at the University of Iceland, stated, 'At present, the most democratic constitution bill ever drafted is being held hostage by self-serving politicians in the clearest possible demonstration of a fundamental principle of constitution-making – namely, that politicians should neither be tasked with drafting nor ratifying constitutions because of the risk that they will act against the public interest. The conduct of Parliament in Iceland is seen by many as a direct affront to democracy.'[11]

Starting big, at the level of a constitution of a nation – even one with relatively few citizens – is a really hard road to travel. That

---

[10] Jóhannsson, J.P. (2015) 'Who Killed the Constitution?', 13 September 2015, accessed 1 January 2016, http://stundin.is/frett/hver-drap-nyju-stjornarskrana/ (In Icelandic).

[11] Gylfason, T. (2014) 'Events in Iceland show that a UK constitutional convention should involve politicians as minimally as possible', OXPOL, The Oxford University Politics Blog, 3 November 2014, accessed 30 December 2015, http://politicsinspires.org/events-iceland-show-uk-constitutional-convention-involve-politicians-minimally-possible/

said, great progress was made in Iceland despite the lack of proactive insistence of diversity; despite the fact that there was no organised structure underpinning the initiative and despite the fact that the initiative did not also include the country's best minds from government think tanks. For now, a beautiful effort is stalled – for Iceland – although encouragingly it is starting to reappear on the political agenda.

The serious downside of stalled large-scale efforts is that it gives the sceptics ammunition to suggest that ideas such as crowdocracy will not work. There is therefore a strong argument for starting small.

3. Start Small: The B4RN Example

Laying the foundation for crowdocracy could start today, in your organisation, business or your local community.

Take Broadband for the Rural North Ltd or 'B4RN' as an example. In rural Lancashire, in the north west of England, broadband speeds were notoriously dismal. According to Ofcom, the UK communications regulator, the average broadband speed for UK residence, is around 23 megabits per second. The reality for most people, even in urban areas is significantly less but outside towns and cities, connectivity can easily plummet to a third of that or less.[12] In Lancashire, it was often as poor as 2 megabits per second. Despite repeated promises by British Telecom (BT) to deliver superfast broadband to the area – nothing happened. So the community took matters into their own hands.

B4RN was launched in December 2011 by a determined band of local volunteers led by industry expert Professor Barry Forde. As a leading UK specialist in networking, particularly wide area fibre networks, Forde was able to design a world-class network

---

[12] 'B4RN switch on at Tunstall', *BBC Breakfast*, 4 October 2015, accessed 1 January 2016, www.youtube.com/watch?v=NY0J-J9vwjQ&index=4&list= PLFPv2Aj590ZBx-Bb8WEGrMhMOQaO5lmq-

that is fast, resilient and expandable. Chris Conder and Lindsey Annison, also founding members of the team, brought experience from other local community wireless mesh and fibre networks. Monica Lee brought management skills, and a diverse group of volunteers, landowners and farmers made it happen.[13]

Today B4RN provide the world's fastest rural broadband – reaching download and upload speeds of 1000 megabits per second (1 gig). The £1.86 million project is funded entirely by public subscriptions. Most of the digging for cable ducts is being performed by an army of local volunteers, assisted by equipment provided by local farmers. Farmers and landowners have also allowed free access to their land for running the vast length of cable required.

Local volunteer Steve Melton says, 'Most of us got involved because we were desperately frustrated with the invisible BT Openreach rural programme that makes unceasing promises and never arrives despite the subsidies. We now live in a world where even farms can't operate without broadband and my kids get set homework they can only do online – never mind me being able to work from home. There is something pleasantly anarchic about getting one over the mighty BT and being able to sort out your own service. Even better that it is world-leading technology!'

As of August 2015, 1,250 customers have been connected and B4RN is active in over 41 parishes in Lancashire, North Yorkshire and in Cumbria. The cost for this awesome service is about £30 a month! From the outset, B4RN was registered as a community benefit society so the business could never be bought by a commercial operator and its profits can only be distributed to the community. Funding has been on a discretionary investment basis so nobody is priced out. The volunteers dig the cable trenches for those who are not able to dig themselves and keep digging even after their own homes have been connected to

---

[13] B4RN website http://b4rn.org.uk/about-us/

ensure everyone benefits.

And, those benefits are not just phenomenal Internet access as Steve Melton points out, 'What we have come to realise is that over many hours of campaigning to get the village on board, toiling in the fields digging trenches, laying conduit and cables, etc. we have gradually got to know our community more intimately than ever before. The sense of camaraderie and achievement has been more than a bonus – almost an end in itself. We have been fed tea and cakes galore. The local landowners have been made to feel like heroes for allowing their community to lay cables across their land and the cost has been a small fraction of what it would cost BT through ingenious routing coming from local knowledge and free labour.'

Perhaps this is the true benefit of starting small or starting local – not only can diverse groups of people come together to solve issues that we care about in our community but in doing so we enhance our relationships and nourish our individual and collective lives in the process.

Although not necessarily crowdocractic, B4RN is a wonderful example of what can be achieved when we start small or start local and the brilliant and innovative solutions that are possible when the crowd gets involved. So far B4RN has won the ISPA's 'Internet Hero' award and in 2015 both Barry Forde and Chris Conder were awarded MBEs.

There are countless ways to start small, inside your local community. A city council could ask its citizens to give binding advice on a small subject. That same city council could post a piece of new legislation online and ask its citizens to offer suggestions online. Or, to demonstrate and validate the notion of wise crowds, it could let a crowdocratic system run in parallel to the democratic system for some time. Once we have created a functioning version of the online crowdocratic platform, we can start experiments with larger scale initiatives.

Experiments are safe; they allow for testing, and refining and the on-going building of trust in the process. Think back to the missing streetlight example from Chapter 6 – this would be easy to initiate in your community. Or even a more ambitious, albeit local project like that undertaken by B4RN. Perhaps there is something in your own community that irritates you? Perhaps something in your child's school seems impractical or crying out for improvement – these issues could very well be initiatives that could benefit from crowd participation.

The potential risk of starting small is that small will never transition into big and the crowd will be limited to small, local issues rather than tapping into their wisdom to help us solve the many wicked problems we now face. Problems like global warming, poverty eradication, terrorism, education, health care, rampant capitalism, and so on.

Small starts often fail to gain scale. And scale is what we need.

4. Create a Stronghold Within the System

Working within the current system is the approach that Pia Mancini took in Argentina. As mentioned in Chapter 5, after developing DemocracyOS – an open-source web application that sought to bridge the gap between citizens and their elected representatives – Mancini enthusiastically took the software to the politicians.

DemocracyOS would give politicians the opportunity to open up debate and conversation with their constituents. But they were not interested, they were quite happy with the status quo – whereby they did what they thought their constituents wanted or worse what *they* wanted.

So, Mancini and her friends decided to infiltrate the system and see if they could affect change from inside. By founding their own political party El Partido de la Red, or the Net party, in Buenos Aires they became part of the political system and political conversation. The Net Party recognised that the only way to change the system was from *inside* the system. Once inside, they were able to open debate about DemocracyOS and educate other politicians about the value of crowd input.

So much so that in November 2014, Congress in Argentina launched a DemocracyOS technology platform to discuss key pieces of legislation with the electorate. Each new project that's introduced in Congress is immediately translated and explained in plain language and posted on the platform so that constituents know what's going on and have an opportunity to voice their opinion.

It's time for change. Little tweaks to the system are not enough. We need political revolution executed either as small evolutionary steps or bold leaps into the unknown. Although realistically, we don't see a viable revolutionary path for crowdocracy, we could foresee a very strong push from large groups of citizens – via online media pressure for instance; but for a true crowdocracy to emerge, differences of opinion need to be integrated rather than accentuated.

We advocate a path of determined evolution. This means building a solid foundation, creating and testing a system that is robust and embarking on a path that is gradual, but with a strong forward momentum. The risk of evolution is twofold: too slow or too fast. The current forces of power are likely to try to slow down the process, whereas those who want to go too fast are likely to find themselves making too many costly mistakes. This is not just a start-up that can fall in the category 'make your mistakes fast and cheap'. This is public governance and we are trying to bring wisdom to it.

Whatever transition model we choose, crowdocracy can become a governance reality for many of us. As Mancini says in her TED talk, 'We are twenty-first-century citizens, doing our very, very best to interact with nineteenth-century-designed institutions that are based on an information technology of the fifteenth century.'

We see most value in Mancini's model of working from within the system: it is both radical (it immediately creates a crowdocratic model) and it is evolutionary. People can start participating in creating policy and legislation and it is a democratic way to transition. Only through the next elections will the crowdocracy movement grow. Therefore, a small crowd needs to convince the rest of the crowd that this can work. In every democratic country it is feasible to start a local political party embracing crowdocracy.

Crowdocracy offers us a way to upgrade to twenty-first-century institutions using twenty-first-century technology. We believe there is enough momentum and a wise enough crowd to conceptualise a new way forward that transcends and includes all the previous ways forward. We are now capable of creating a much more sophisticated answer to the wicked challenge of governance.

Chapter 8:

A Crowdocratic Future

'The Empires of the future are the empires of the mind.'

– Sir Winston Churchill [1]

In embarking on this project we asked ourselves, 'What system could enable us to govern our communities, societies and organisations fairly and more wisely?' During the course of this book, we have sought to outline why such a governance system upgrade is so desperately needed. We've explored what such a system may look like and how crowdocracy could actually work in practice.

As crowdocracy does not yet exist anywhere in the world, at least not in the format we are suggesting, this chapter offers a glimpse into our potential future across many areas where crowdocracy could improve and invigorate decision-making and governance. We believe that this new design, or some improved crowdsourced version of it is worth developing and bringing to life.

What follows is, therefore, what we believe could be the contours of a world that is governed through crowdocracy. Of course, this is speculative and the future is uncertain but there is little

---

[1] Speech made at Harvard on 6 September 1943 by Winson Churchill.

doubt that if our communities, societies and organisations were predominantly run in a crowdocratic way, the world would be very, very different. A shift from democracy, with its elected leaders, to a world run by all of us using cutting edge, constantly evolving and improving technology to unlock our collective decision-making power, would fundamentally shift the balance of power from the few to the many. It would fundamentally change the way we relate and interact with each other.

Multi-Dimensionality of Crowdocracy

All problems, including wicked ones, are multidimensional. In fact, every aspect of human experience and every second of that experience exists or is occurring in one of three fundamental dimensions, namely the objective world or what is 'IT' that we need to do to solve this problem. This world of 'IT' is where virtually all those in power, be they politicians or business leaders, focus their attention. But we are not human doings we are human beings so in addition to the objective world of 'IT' there is a subjective interior world of 'I' or being. Thirdly there is also an interpersonal world of 'WE' or relating.

Crowdocracy impacts all three dimensions of 'I', 'WE' and 'IT' or 'being', 'relating', and 'doing'. Therefore, to embrace crowdocracy fully we must understand how it impacts all three dimensions.

In the 'IT' dimension, through the changing role of the media and civil servants, the erosion of the power of the lobby, and the disappearance of policy-making politicians, crowdocracy will create vastly different outcomes in how we organise our societies, communities and organisations.

In the 'I' dimension, crowdocracy will transform how each of us thinks and feels about power. We will no longer be able to blame 'the government' or some other outside entity for governance failings because each of us will contribute to shaping our community and each of us would be accountable for bringing about the change we wish to see in the world. Each of us would become as much of a leader as everyone else. This participation will change who we are as human beings; it is truly empowering and will help facilitate vertical adult development.[2]

In the 'WE' dimension, crowdocracy would fundamentally change the way we all relate to each other. Where politics today is framed as 'us and them', crowdocracy will shift this to 'we'. When we can appreciate that the problems we face are our collective problems – they are not 'my' problems or 'your' problems but fundamentally 'ours' and impact all of us. We may watch the evening news and be momentarily grateful that the long list of overwhelming problems are being faced by people thousands of miles away and are therefore not 'our' problems – but they are our problems. We are all connected; the pace of change and the escalating complexity of the issues we face mean that sooner or later almost all the problems we witness on national news reports come knocking on our door. Crowdocracy affords us an opportunity to embrace our humanity rather than our nationality so we can unleash our collective brilliance and find answers to the world's toughest problems.[3]

Potential Changes in the 'IT' Dimension

Below is a glimpse into how the world may look in the 'IT' dimensions from the perspective of:

- Politicians
- Civil Servants

---

[2] Watkins, A. (2015) *4D Leadership*, London: Kogan Page.

[3] Watkins, A. and Wilber, K. (2015) *Wicked & Wise: How to Solve the World's Toughest Problems*, London: Urbane Publishing.

- The Media
- The Lobby
- Business
- Countries
- The Monarchy

Politicians

The subtitle of this book is 'the end of politics'. It would be more accurate – but less appealing according to our publisher – if it read 'the end of politics as we know it'. Just as Wikipedia did not put an end to encyclopedias but it did change the role of the expert encyclopedia editor, so crowdocracy will change the profession of politician as a legislative representative of the people. We will no longer need individuals who spend much of their time and energy trying to get re-elected, or currying favour with the media, vested interest, the electorate or a party whip so they can stay in a job.

It is important to reiterate that crowdocracy is explicitly different from all the models and proposals for participatory democracy, in which politicians get better informed about what their constituencies want. All these initiatives may be a step forward from democratic models in which politicians get elected and then freely use their own or party intelligence to come to decisions, policy and compromise. We advocate, however, that the way to unlock the real wisdom of the crowd is to go further and hand the full legislative powers directly to the public. Leaving the politicians in place would simply pollute the dialogue as politicians would always add their own bias in an effort to influence the crowd. The crowd would also remain on the outside – spectators in their own policy.

There is also no way that politicians could deal with the sheer quantity of ideas and proposals that the public could come up with. They would literally drag the system down. Imagine that Wikipedia had been set up as an online encyclopedia in which we could all inform the expert editors but they would still make the ultimate decisions and have the final say in what was posted – there would have been little chance Wikipedia would be the success it is today, let alone have the scale it now enjoys. It's worth pointing out as a side bar that several highly educated people have suggested to us that Wikipedia is not a success and therefore referring to it as a potential model for crowdocracy casts doubt on the whole idea. Certainly Wikipedia is not perfect and it still struggles with funding, regularly seeking donations from users. Still, the English version contains nearly 5 million entries, which translates into about 2,206 volumes of the *Encyclopaedia Britannica*; it adds 750 articles per day, and it is free to use for anyone with access to the Internet – without advertising. It is used by 475 million unique visitors every month and some academic studies have estimated Wikipedia's accuracy ratio above 95 per cent. We call that a success.

The jobs in the executive office will remain, but these jobs can no longer be called 'political' – because the people in those jobs have no primary role in coming up with policy. They can share their views on the policy that is being developed by the crowd, but their primary role is to execute policy. They could still be elected officials, which may mean that some element of the political popularity contest will remain but the focus of the public will shift to an assessment of competency.

It is, however, more likely that the crowd will come up with new models of appointing the executive office – blends between civil servants, private enterprise and volunteer workers. In the example of the missing streetlights in Chapter 6, we painted such a picture. Execution was laid in the hands of civil servants, with the help of community volunteers and private companies supplying the materials.

Crowdocracy takes away the incentive for anyone striving for a position of individual power to find that role in public governance. After the rule by kings, dictators, oligarchy, and career politicians, we believe this will create a major shift in a positive direction

– but one that will take time to adjust to, particularly for those people with political careers and ambitions.

Civil Servants

Civil servants today hold much power. They often design policy. They inform politicians, generally run the executive arm of government, and through politicians they wield wide influence over the legislative power as well.

The relationship between civil servants and the politicians differs from one country or regional location to the next. Some countries have a high proportion of public roles directly appointed by politicians. In the US, for instance, ambassadors are politically appointed; they change when a new president takes office. In continental Europe, this is very different: most civil servants are appointed without any involvement from politicians. In the Netherlands, for instance, it is very unusual and legally almost impossible for a minister to change any of the civil servants, even the ones in the most senior roles. Thus, senior civil servants may serve ministers of very different political opinion.

In crowdocracy, the role of civil servants transforms. They no longer have a primary role in the design of policy. They no longer write the new laws, they no longer inform politicians. They no longer serve politicians. They now serve the public. We argue that finally civil servants would truly become civil servants.

Civil servants could also have a crucial role in informing the crowd of data, for example by analysing the results of implemented policy, or by running scenarios about the possible outcomes of policies. The crowd needs to be able to gather data before it forms its own assessments of the policy direction. This is a core role that civil servants could play. The role for civil servants in the creation of policy therefore shifts from creating it to serving those who create it. Of course, it could be argued that those people could manipulate the information to present a bias one way or another but this is much more likely to be uncovered by the crowd than it currently is.

We expect that the lines between 'public' and 'private' execution will blur. It could well be that the crowd creates implementation strategies that does not allow for competition, and limits a profit-making purpose, yet does create incentives for those in the execution role to be professional and efficient. For instance, we could imagine that for railway services, the concept of competition is abandoned because it's unrealistic but still executed by enterprises that resemble corporate entities. In such ways, we could imagine that many roles become a blend of private enterprise and public service. Remember: crowdocracy will transcend and include.

Civil service is therefore in for a major transformation.

The Media

If politics has become a spectator sport, it is the media that is both a major cause and the primary beneficiary. While writing this book, Donald Trump put himself forward as candidate for the US Presidency. He has an exceptional ability to play the media by fully embracing the notion that politics is entertainment. His interview with Jimmy Fallon, in which Fallon disguised as Trump speaks to the image in the mirror, played by the real Donald Trump, is the best example we have seen so far.[4] Trump creates a new level of entertainment in politics by becoming an actor in his own world.

The commercial media needs this entertainment for its ratings and advertising income. Politics sells only if it has a high entertainment value – the merits and the content are seen as too complex, and boring. Apart from really large crises (call them CNN moments), the mainstream media spend little time on the issues and challenges of our time. They blame the public and vice versa.

---

[4] Jimmy Fallon sketch (2015) 'Donald Trump interviews himself in the mirror', accessed 27 December 2015, www.youtube.com/watch?v=c2DgwPG7mAA

In a crowdocratic system, politics is no longer a personality-based spectator sport – because there are no more individuals or parties trying to convince the public to support their election. As the crowdocracy platform is semi-autonomous, the media can only follow the content and the process, not the actors. Power in crowdocracy is dissolved among the participants.

The executive office will maintain a certain attraction for the media, but as the executives have little policy-making powers, these offices are likely to become more 'technocratic' and therefore much less a source of celebrity and a lead story.

Away from the 'participatory' world on the crowdocratic platform, people will debate, write blogs, hold conferences and engage in all other activities to discuss their views on how the world is organised and run. This 'observer' world will continue to be very attractive for media to host and to comment on, but the shift will be seismic – simply because we will now be able to do something about the observations we make. We can no longer play the 'blame the politician game'.

We believe the media will become an important force in crowdocracy. Commentators will be able to highlight to the public what interesting subjects are being discussed; they will give certain proposals or discussions the attention they need and the media will need to become excellent synthesisers of ongoing debates. In fact, this is exactly what has happened in Iceland, when frustrated by the lack of implementation of the crowdsourced Constitution, the national newspaper ran a story entitled 'Who killed our Constitution?' with photos of various politicians (see Figure 7.1 in Chapter 7).[5]

Potentially, political journalism could once again return to focusing on the issues rather than the personalities. They could focus on deeply analysing the issues and providing commentary,

---

[5] Jóhannsson, J.P. (2015) 'Who Killed the Constitution?', 13 September 2015, accessed 1 January 2016,   http://stundin.is/frett/hver-drap-nyju-stjornarskrana/ (In Icelandic).

in order to guide the public through the vastness and complexity of policy-making.

The Lobby

Crowdocracy aims to tap into the collective wisdom of the crowd and place power into the hands of the crowd. The lobby of today exists for the sake of influencing those in power for special interests – from well-meaning NGOs to regulation-evading corporations.

Special interests will continue to want to control the system. Some people that we have spoken with in writing this book have cautioned us that the real risk comes from the lobby flooding the crowdocracy system to manipulate it. We should have no doubts they will try. They do it today through their intricate system of influencing politicians, civil servants and the media. Governance is often about power and, as we have set out, few people are at developmental levels whereby they genuinely appreciate how a more integral approach benefits everyone, including the individual power brokers. Certainly, such an approach is significantly superior, in every way, to the inequitable system we currently have. Until that particular penny drops however, those individuals and organisations that are obsessed with power and wealth will try to game the system – there is no doubt about that. But as they currently game the system we have now, we will be no worse off.

Having put the power in the hands of the many, the many will be better able to neutralise the few still clinging on to the old power paradigms. The size of the vote will make it much, much harder for any special interest group to have their way. If a corporation nowadays needs to influence policy, legally or otherwise, it can map out which individuals it needs to get to and influence. In a crowdocratic system, there are no key individuals to get to – the lobby needs to secure the votes of many and that is significantly harder and much more costly to achieve. That is not to say that mass marketing campaigns and media barons may not seek to manipulate mainstream opinion. That too will probably still happen but it will be more difficult than ever before. Many of the younger generations no longer read newspapers or mainstream media and gain their information from other online sources so this influence is also likely to diminish over time.

We predict that in the early stages of crowdocracy, special interests will have a relatively high degree of power. Large corporations and rich individuals may be the first to organise themselves to be fully capable participants in the crowdocratic system. But with some experience, people will learn to participate and are more likely to take a little time and energy to ensure their voices are heard. Once people know their voice matters, they will show up.

This will be greatly facilitated by a clean and simple platform that is easy to use. The system needs tutorials that guide people through the steps. People need to be able to get training in the crowdocratic system and we envisage this training will start early in schools so that new generations get used to participatory politics from an early age. Just as we now see three-year-olds happily swiping through pages on their iPads, while granny struggles – crowdocracy will take time to become 'normal'.

The lobby will also be greatly hindered by the guardians who will need to detect manipulation and interference in the system. They need to be able to spot it – with the help of technological power and Big Data – and then act. The way guardians act within the system will be crucial in making crowdocracy work. It is important that they are dedicated to a fair process, unattached to the outcomes and seen to be so by the crowd.

Business

Having laid out a bleak picture for the lobby and special interests, can we conclude that crowdocracy is bad for business? Absolutely not, we believe the exact opposite: we believe business will flourish in a crowdocratic world. A more involved community that directly takes ownership over its own economic policy will likely come up with a balanced and long-term view. Crowdocracy eliminates the uncertainty of elections and shifting policy that occurs when a new political party comes to power. This instability is notoriously bad for business, with policy changes instigated by successive governments often representing a major shift in direction, which can have knock-on effects for business. With crowdocracy, the crowd can debate an economic philosophy and build a model that lasts for that community. No doubt this debate will be strong, but we envisage that the crowd will balance the various economic policies with a view of economic wealth creation and social distribution.

It is also worth pointing out that if businesses themselves operate crowdocratically, they are likely to have a more engaged workforce. Employees who feel listened to and who are encouraged to share insights and participate are much more likely to engage their discretionary effort and increase productivity. If they believe others are genuinely listening, they are also much more likely to come up with more competitively advantageous ideas.

We believe the crowd will create a more level playing field for businesses – eliminating the advantages very large players have. Institutions that are 'too big to fail' are more likely to be dealt with, as the crowd will not accept the risk. Subsidies and tax incentives that benefit a few but not the greater good, are likely to be eliminated. The drive for shareholder value may be the way the game of business is currently constructed but there is no reason that can't change. Indeed, there are many in business itself that believe this singular focus on profit *must* change. Before the 1970s, when Milton Friedman suggested the sole purpose of business was to make money for its shareholders[6] and finance Professor Michael Jensen and Dean William Meckling of the Simon School of Business at the University of Rochester published a paper that

---

[6] Friedman, M. (1970) 'The Social Responsibility of Business is to Increase its Profits', *The New York Times Magazine*, 13 September 1970, accessed 1 January 2016, www.colorado.edu/studentgroups/libertarians/issues/friedman-soc-resp-business.html

provided an 'action plan' to that thinking,[7] business was viewed as more than simply a vehicle to make money. Business had a social function to look after its stakeholders, community and make a positive contribution to society through the creation of jobs, products and services. The social purpose for business is back on the agenda.[8]

Crowdocracy would help us return to a more inclusive role for business so that corporations can once again become a force for good and promote desirable 'social' ends, while delivering a reasonable (not ridiculous) return for shareholders. When everyone benefits, through better wages and everyone pays a fair rate of tax then everyone benefits. There is more money in the system, which means more people will buy the businesses' products and services anyway – it's a genuine win/win/win. Business does have a social responsibility to its employees, suppliers, customers, community and the environment in which it operates. The belief, triggered by Friedman, and taken to heart by the business community as licence to inflate top-end salaries has distorted business and led to many toxic side effects – not least the global financial crisis.

Crowdocracy will mean a major shift for business – and a huge benefit for economic life. We believe that it could well be the business community, particularly small business owners, that could be the first to experiment with crowdocracy and may therefore be the main promoters for the full roll-out of the new governance system.

Countries

While the concept of a 'country' as a cultural and ethnic unit of people has been around for a long time (Japan is the oldest

[7] Jensen, M.C. and Meckling, W.H. (1976) 'Theory of the Firm: Managerial Behaviour, Agency Costs and Ownership Structure', *Journal of Financial Economics*, 3, no. 4, pp. 305–60.

[8] A Blueprint for Better Business, accessed 1 January 2016, www.blueprintforbusiness.org/principles-and-framework/

existing nation, founded in 660 BC), the average age of the countries in the world today is only 160 years. In some countries, people can relate to one another through cultural and ethnic heritage (again, Japan is a good example). In other countries, such as the US, there is wide diversity; in countries such as Spain, a combination of a few ethnic/cultural groups make up the population. Technological advances including the Internet, cheaper travel and open borders, international commerce, and immigration, challenge the very concept of governance as a nation. An example: 1 in 5 people with Portuguese nationality live outside Portugal, and 1 in 4 people in Luxembourg have Portuguese nationality. What does this say about the concept of the 'Portuguese people' and the nation state of Luxembourg?

In the increasing complexity of this world, the push is often to further centralise. The EU institutions take over more and more legislative power from the countries – while creating more and more disenfranchisement among the public. Within countries progress is often blocked because of the tension between the central government and different population groups. Remember the Belgian example: in 2010–2011 the country went for 589 days without any government at all – largely the result of endless tensions between the politicians representing the Flemish- and French-speaking populations. (This is also pretty telling about the necessity of government!)

Centralising power is often driven by the conviction of politicians that this will create clarity and efficiency although much of the evidence would suggest the outcome is the exact opposite. More likely, the drive toward centralising power is little more than a power grab and an effort to limit control to an elite minority. It may be true that in a more globalised world, central coordination can be very useful but centralisation often creates institutions that are simply too big to govern effectively or efficiently.

Switzerland is probably the best example of a country that has created many limitations in its constitution to centralise. The cantons all have their own full body of legislation, including separate tax regimes. It may come across as 'inefficient', but Switzerland is still a politically stable and wealthy country. Politicians are relatively unknown figures in Switzerland – while we have no substantial evidence for this, it would appear that because there is limited power available in Swiss politics, it does not attract power-hungry pseudo-celebrity types to the political life.

We foresee that crowdocracy will drive localisation – policy being developed at the lowest possible level. Communities like autonomy. Once people have the opportunity to organise things at a local level, they will. This was evidenced by the example we shared in the previous chapter about B4RN that successfully brought world-beating Internet connectivity to rural North Yorkshire in England.

There will be little drive to 'rule' – as the individual drive for power is neutralised. At the same time, many things will need coordination and collaboration: infrastructure, tax rates, and economic policy, to name a few. The crowd will want to brainstorm and regulate all these elements at a higher level and so a logical starting place is countries. That said, it may turn out that there is more coordination between large cities and between various rural areas than between cities and their rural neighbours – simply because they have more in common. The crowds in Vienna and Munich have more to share on how to effectively govern their cities than they do on how the rural areas outside of these cities are governed.

We believe there will be a lot of sharing between various communities. In a large-scale transition to crowdocracy, much will need to be redesigned from scratch – and the upside of learning from others and sharing ideas across communities is therefore significant. The fact that governance will move online also makes sharing easier and more accessible. It will for instance be easy for the crowd in Seattle to amend and adopt environmental legislation from the Copenhagen crowd.

We predict the nation state will significantly reduce in importance over time, maybe even disappear, to be replaced by communities of more manageable scale with coordination mechanisms among them. We will be members of our village crowd, or our city crowd and, beyond that, larger regional crowds. In our case, one of us would be part of the Romsey (UK) crowd, the small towns of Southern UK, the UK and Ireland crowd and the EU crowd. The other would be part of the Colares (Portugal) crowd, the Greater Lisbon area crowd, the Iberia crowd and the EU crowd.

Being part of crowds at different levels creates checks and balances. Being part of the EU crowd for instance, particularly through the constitution, provides boundaries for what its constituent crowds can decide. We envisage that these frameworks will be more principle-based than rule-based, so that local crowds have far more autonomy in their governance than nations now have inside the EU.

This transformation may take time and will not be easy. Communities that have long-held wishes of independence, such as the Scots, the Flemish, the Catalan and the Basque people, could well drive it, at least initially.

The Monarchy

Will the monarchy survive in crowdocracy?

While we do not think the question is very important in terms of governance because most monarchs in democratic countries have limited actual power, we believe the question will have high emotional value.

The answer is fairly simple: if the crowd wants a king or queen, or grand duchess, or any other regal head of state, it can decide to. The crowd can decide whom it wants as its representatives, and how they get appointed or elected. Given the popularity of monarchs in some countries such as the Netherlands, we think it is likely that we will see a future in which a monarch or royal family is endorsed directly by the people.

Potential Changes in the 'I' Dimension

Crowdocracy will transform each of us individually from a spectator to an actor in the governance of the communities we are part of. In the new world created by crowdocracy we become much more engaged, empowered, individually responsible and accountable within the crowds we live. This is very different to our level of accountability in the current democratic process where our only moment of active participation and accountability is the day we vote. In crowdocracy that accountability is permanent and it's shared as we are equally accountable as everyone else.

That shifts our individual perspective. If we are actors, we have a choice. We can participate; we can share ideas and take the initiative. We can play a role in everything that we see happening that has a relation to how we govern our community. We can take the lead and make or shape a proposal or we can simple endorse the proposals of others.

Of course, when we participate as individual citizens in the crowd, will we vote according to our own self-interest or will we take a wider collective view? As the whole of the crowd has the chance to vote, we will need to consider finding a balance between what we want to achieve and what is likely to get support. The proposal phase will allow us to gauge initial support which will further help us get the balance right. The guardians are also available to advise if our thinking fits within the constitutional boundaries that we have all agreed to. We are likely to come up with ideas we are very passionate about individually, but to frame them in such a way that they will be convincing for enough people.

What excites us is that we can now participate in policy-making on subjects that are not our areas of expertise from a work perspective, but they are areas of interest and passion. For instance, you may have had ideas about how the roads should be designed around your city to improve traffic flow. Until crowdocracy, there was no place for you to contribute your ideas and you probably felt ignored. Even if you told your local councillor it's unlikely that your idea would go anywhere. Now, you can create a proposal and put it to the crowd.

That leads to a risk we would like to signal. While most people we have spoken to raise concern about the lack of engagement, we would like to highlight the opposite risk: high participation. With the possible involvement of all, some communities could initially be flooded by initiatives. They could be inclined to create rules and regulations for many things. Just as Wikipedia has become much larger than any traditional encyclopaedia, some crowdocracies could see a huge increase in the number of policies and rules – until the community realises that it needs more integrated policy, not necessarily more policies and rules per se. The steering by guardians will be crucial in this regard.

The reverse could also happen. Some communities that have historically had a distrust of government – for example, in parts of the US where the Tea Party movement is strong – may initially see crowdocracy as the way to drop even more rules and regulations. We are convinced this will be short-lived and these communities will start to put some structure into place as well. But as this will be their structure, the distrust may dissipate.

Whatever the direction, it is the opportunity to participate that is so important because it means we are more likely than ever to support the policies that are created by the crowd. Even if we did not participate in a particular piece of policy we know we could have and that makes a huge difference to ownership. If we have participated and the majority held a different view, we are still much more likely to adopt the chosen policy as evidenced by the Swiss garbage bag example from Chapter 4. We realise that despite our disagreement, we were part of the process and embrace the change as the majority choice. Remember behavioural science has robustly proven that human beings tend to believe in what they create or have a part in creating.

Potential Changes in the 'WE' Dimension

The transformation of the 'I' perspective towards policy-making, translates even more strongly in the 'WE' perspective. Politics today eliminates the 'WE' perspective in the domain of public governance. You and the two of us can discuss the 'IT' of politics (what 'they' are deciding 'for us') but as we have elected representatives, how we collectively relate to one another in this domain is irrelevant. We are simply the objects of policy and need to abide by the laws that have been created for us, albeit with our delegated authority.

In crowdocracy, we are all actors in this domain. There is still plenty of reason to sit down for a coffee with our neighbourhood friends to discuss the state of current affairs, but no longer reason to agree what a mess other people are making of it. The whole nature and tone of those conversations change as we move from despondent blame to discussing what we are doing about the issues. How are we getting organised, what arguments should we use, how likely is it that our proposal will pass?

There is a major upside when the crowd gets involved in governance: just as the two of us now have a place where we can contribute our ideas, we now benefit from you contributing your ideas. If all of us dedicated just an hour a month to the policy-making process, this would be an enormous increase in idea generation. We could well see an explosion of creativity in how we govern our world and how we can finally solve some of the most intractable problems we face. There is little doubt such input would massively increase both the quantity and the quality of potential solutions.

And while some people may still fear that the crowd could 'go wild', it is interesting to note that we feel perfectly comfortable interacting with the crowd in everyday life (on the road, in the subway, on Facebook, Wikipedia, in stores, concerts and parks), but many of us do not intuitively trust all of us to deal with the responsibility of governing ourselves. Implicitly, we also say that we do not trust ourselves with this authority. We believe this is because we have become so used to the fact that we have outsourced our power to govern. We may be nervous to consider how we will deal with power once the politicians step back into the crowd but we are also perfectly capable of successfully crossing that bridge when we come to it.

Crowdocracy redefines how we all relate to each other; it redefines our Social Contract. This redefinition is urgently needed. A 2015 Pew Research study shows that the US hasn't been as politically polarised as it is now for 150 years. But far from being a problem, Integral author Jeff Salzman suggests that the tension and friction that arises out of the ideological rifts between the left and right could actually be a tremendously creative force that wants to give birth to something new.[9] We agree and it's not just happening in the US, it's happening in the UK, Europe, Australia and beyond. Perhaps that something new will be crowdocracy.

When we set out on this journey, we did not want to just write a book and make a noise. We genuinely believe that the tough and wicked problems every nation faces requires more than just words. It requires action. So, we have taken action beyond just writing this book. We have established a not-for-profit organisation – the Crowd Foundation – that can serve all of us and move the debate forward. Hopefully it can also create some real momentum around the idea of crowdocracy. In support of the Foundation we have set up a website – **www.crowd.ngo** – where we have laid out the basic ideas; where people can get more involved and donate to the cause if they want. The money will be used solely to finance wider engagement globally and encourage views from those that are often excluded or aren't able to participate which will be vital for increasing the diversity of opinion and therefore the wisdom of the crowd. Such interventions should help us all to evolve our system of governance and government along the lines

---

[9] Walker, B. (2015) 'The Hidden Power of Political Polarization', *Integral Life*, 26 October 2015, accessed 1 January 2016, https://www.integrallife.com/daily-evolver/hidden-power-political-polarization

we have outlined. We hope you will participate on www.crowd.ngo in moving these ideas forward.

To start the dialogue we have also organised a series of conversations of different aspects of crowdocracy that will be filmed and shared on the website. These conversations will take place at the UK House of Lords from January 2016 onwards very kindly hosted by Lord Andrew Stone. We have invited a diverse range of interested parties to these initial conversations. We aim to explore different aspects of the wicked problems we face including government and governance to see if, when we follow crowdocratic principles, we can generate wiser solutions that will allow us to move forward more successfully together. If you care about what happens in your world, we would encourage you to participate in these conversations, certainly online and maybe in person. Please disagree with us; support us; comment on what we and others share; sign up for the newsletter or share your own ideas with the crowd so we can collectively progress together and build something that serves all of us and not just some of us.

You may wonder what the end result might be. Will this new system of governance live up to the challenge of creating fair and wise decision-making? The answer is in the hands of all of us – ultimately whether the potential of this idea is achieved or not is up the crowd.

However, if we get this right we will facilitate the best of all worlds – the best of the individual and the best of the collective. The best of East and the best of West. The best of right-wing politics and the best of left-wing politics. We will no longer be looking at a government that we do not feel intrinsically part of. And this may well be the ultimate reason to embrace crowdocracy as the next form of governance for our world.

In crowdocracy, all of us can truly say: 'L'état, c'est nous' (We are the State).

Chapter 9:

Crowdocracy: Wicked and Wise Context

'The adventure of awakening is among the most universal of human dramas.'

– Ken Wilber[1]

As we have mentioned, the challenge of governments and governance is a wicked problem. But it is not the only one we face. This final chapter is an addendum within that context. In other words, it is not essential reading to understand crowdocracy but seeks to put this particular challenge into a wider context and illustrate why governments and governance is a wicked problem and how crowdocracy may be an equally wicked, albeit, wise solution. We hope you stay with us for a little longer.

As we have alluded to throughout this book, it is increasingly impossible to observe the world around us and not come to the conclusion that something is wrong. There are, of course,

---

[1] Wilbe, K., Patten, T., Leonard, A. and Morelli, M. (2008) *Integral Life Practice: A 21st-Century Blueprint for Physical Health, Emotional Balance, Mental Clarity, and Spiritual Awakening*, Boston: Integral Books.

many wonderful things happening in the world too, but watch the nightly news and we are left with the inevitable feeling that we have some *serious* problems. Many of these problems seem intractable or so complicated that it is impossible to know what our response should be. These challenges are called 'wicked problems' because they are beyond complicated. Governance and who decides our future at a national level definitely falls into this category.

The term 'wicked problem' was first coined by Professor Horst W.J. Rittel, who discussed the idea in seminars as early as 1967. He would talk of the difference between a 'tame', solvable problem and a 'wicked' intractable problem that was difficult or impossible to solve. The term 'wicked' was used not to suggest that the problem was somehow evil, although those affected by these issues could be forgiven for thinking they were, but rather that the problem is wickedly complex, that our knowledge and appreciation of the problem is incomplete; the nature of the problem appears contradictory and is constantly changing.

In 1973, while Professor of Science of Design at the University of California, Berkley, Rittel and colleague Melvin M. Webber formalised the concept and definition of wicked problems in their seminal paper.[2] Rittel and Webber noted, 'As distinguishable from problems in the natural sciences, which are definable and separable and may have solutions that are findable, the problems of governmental planning – especially those of social or policy planning – are ill-defined; and they rely upon elusive political judgement for resolution.'

In this book, we have explored the wicked problem of politics and governance and have sought to present a wise way forward which, if properly executed, could step-change the quality of

---

[2] Rittel, H.W.J. and Webber, M.M. (1973) 'Dilemmas in General Theory of Planning', *Policy Sciences*, 4, pp. 155–69, accessed 1 January 2016, www.uctc.net/mwebber/Rittel+Webber+Dilemmas+General_Theory_of_Planning.pdf

political decision-making. What we are proposing is the end of politics as we know it. Crowdocracy is a radical new form of governance that transcends and includes democracy to ensure that the power is handed to the people and the wisdom of the crowd is unlocked for all of our benefit.

But before we enthusiastically rally behind change, it is vital for us to understand the depth and dimensions of the challenges we face as we move toward that change.

The Definition of a Wicked Problem for the Twenty-first Century

If we want to solve any problem, especially a wicked one, we must first be able to define that problem. A thorough definition of the challenge we face ensures we have a complete understanding and appreciation of exactly what we are up against. When elements or perspectives of the problem are unknown, underestimated, unappreciated, ignored or just a little fuzzy then we always run the risk of being blindsided in our attempts to find a workable solution. It is therefore useful to look at the wicked problem of governance and political decision-making through the lens of the six key properties of wicked problems (Figure 9.1). As mentioned in the preface, if we stand any chance of solving wicked problems we must first appreciate that a wicked problem:

1. Is multi-dimensional
2. Has multiple stakeholders
3. Has multiple causes
4. Has multiple symptoms
5. Has multiple solutions
6. Is constantly evolving

Figure 9.1: Definition of Wicked Problems

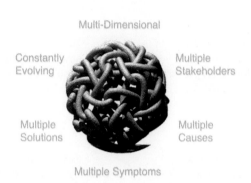

Multi-Dimensional

Constantly
Evolving

Multiple
Stakeholders

Multiple
Solutions

Multiple
Causes

Multiple Symptoms

Multi-dimensional

All problems, including wicked ones are multi-dimensional. It is therefore not a definitive characteristic of just wicked problems but it is included because we almost never consider the multi-dimensional nature of our existence. As a result, these crucial vantage points are ignored along with the significant insights an awareness of dimensionality can bring.

As mentioned in Chapter 8, every aspect of human experience and every second of that experience exists or is occurring in one or more of three or four critical dimensions. Although we've simplified into 'being' ('I'), 'doing' ('IT') and 'relating' ('WE'), these dimensions were first identified by Ken Wilber as individual interior ('I'), collective interior ('WE'), Individual exterior ('IT') and collective exterior ('ITS') (see Figure 9.2).

Right now as you read the words on this page or screen you are having an individual interior experience. Additional thoughts may bubble up as the words on the page trigger your own thoughts.

Figure 9.2 Ken Wilber's All Quadrants All Lines (AQAL) Model

I	IT
(individual interior) Self and consciousness – invisible (i.e. thinking, feeling, emotions & awareness)	(individual exterior) Action and System (visible behaviour)
WE	ITS
(collective interior) Culture and worldview	(collective exterior) Social system and environment

For example, you might be thinking, 'Are these guys mad – are they seriously considering handing power over to the many?' You may find yourself having an emotional reaction to the book – perhaps you have been irritated at some of the things we've said, excited by others or confused occasionally. Whatever your thoughts and feelings are, they are a purely individual, interior experience. No one else is privy to what's happening inside you. As such, you are experiencing this moment from the subjective interior dimension of 'I' or 'being'.

Say you are reading the book on the train to work, as you approach your stop you will put the book or e-reader away and do something like line up to disembark the train. You may still be having an individual interior experience as you think about the day ahead but you are also having an individual exterior experience as you get up from the seat and walk to the doors. It is exterior because other people can witness you standing up and making your way to the exit. In that moment, your experience is both individual interior 'I' and individual exterior 'IT'. The 'IT' dimension is the dimension of 'doing'.

As you wait at the train doors to exit on to the platform, you may meet two of your colleagues from work and you engage the 'WE' dimension of 'relating'. You may talk to your colleagues about a meeting you are due to have when you arrive at the office and as such you are relating to your colleagues. The 'WE' experience is, like the individual experience, occurring in two dimensions inside and out. Your conversation with your colleagues is observable by a third party as an exterior reality – 'there is a bunch of people chatting over there' (the systems or 'ITS' the group create). But there is also an inner dimension to the group of colleagues chatting (the cultural 'WE', shared values). The inner 'WE' experience is different for each of your colleagues; but you all know exactly who your colleagues are and who is not a colleague; you know who belongs and who doesn't belong. You can't see this 'WE' connection 'out there' in the exterior world; just as your interior 'I' experience can't be seen 'out there' in the objective world. But none of your colleagues doubt the existence of this shared knowledge. No one doubts the existence of the shared dimension that makes up the relationship. Each 'I' in the 'WE' group feels connected, strongly or weakly to every other 'I' in the group, this is the 'relating' dimension.

Therefore, every single moment of our lives is occurring simultaneously in all dimensions: 'I', 'WE', 'IT', and 'ITS' only we just don't realise it. Or if we do, we certainly don't see the relevance or importance of this insight. This deceptively simple frame allows us to understand a good deal of the complexity of the modern world, and allows us to see why some of the most intractable wicked problems have become so intractable.

All problems, wicked or otherwise, can be viewed from these dimensions – 'doing', 'being', 'subjectively relating', or 'objectively interacting'. When it comes to wicked problems, the common tendency is to almost exclusively focus on the exterior objective dimensions. In other words, we exclusively look at behaviours ('IT') or systems, processes ('ITS') in the world of 'doing'. What are people doing about the problem? What systems and structures do we need to put in place?

Just look at our efforts to improve democracy, so far. There are two main schools of thought – get better representatives who will behave better ('IT') or push through electoral reform to change the voting system ('ITS').

We completely ignore the interior subjective 'being' and 'relating' dimensions and any changes that will be required in those dimensions. This is despite the fact that we already know that human relationships and social transactions are almost always at the epicentre of all wicked problems. Wicked problems are social problems. Everything from escalating terrorism to global warming to corruption to poverty to the dysfunction of the world's governance systems requires individuals to change what they are 'doing' in significant numbers. But this won't happen unless our inner beliefs and values change and how we show up matures so we can much more effectively connect with others whether they are like-minded or have diverse opinions from ours. In the end, it is individuals who start to 'relate' differently that push through the change that alters what we all end up 'doing' in the world. Crowdocracy has the potential to transform how we show up and how we relate to each other as we decide our own futures. It redefines our Social Contract.

The more we connect to one another, share opinion and engage with the issues, the more it will change our Social Contract and the way we relate to each other. In Vermont, USA, local communities have been holding 'town meetings' for more than three centuries. These meetings, open to all residents, decide the budget, what it's then spent on and reserve the right to make local laws for themselves. Chaired by a moderator, these meetings follow state law and Robert's Rules of Order. This guidebook, written in 1876 to manage these meetings, includes rules such as, 'No citizen may speak twice on an issue until everyone else who wants to speak has had a chance to.'

Depending on the topic and the emotion, these meetings can

become heated and are often emotional and tense – but they work. The wisdom of the crowd prevails and perhaps more importantly they build the community together. This exchange of views is not always easy or comfortable but it changes the Social Contract. For example, when the town of Brattleboro, Vermont, issued the first same-sex marriage licence in the USA, not everyone was happy about it. Town meeting debates all over Vermont were intense and threatened to tear some communities apart. Anti-gay slogans were painted on roadsides and some hateful things were said. People would state they didn't want 'those people' in their community and a movement called 'Take Back Vermont' was initiated to prevent same-sex marriage. But the town meetings provided a platform for people to talk. It wasn't always pretty but people started to realise that there were already 'those people' in the community and they liked and respected them. The opportunity to talk to people that they didn't even know were gay before changed opinion and today if you ask Vermonters about same-sex couples it is simply not an issue and many admit to feeling ashamed of how they initially acted.[3]

We can't solve what we don't appreciate

A lack of awareness of the multi-dimensional nature of the challenges we face from the very start means that our attempts to solve them continue to fail because they are always only partial solutions.

Take the Ukraine, for example. The country is deeply divided with the west of the country leaning towards the European Union and the east of the country leaning towards Russia. The current instability and safety issues in the east could be addressed by flooding the eastern Ukrainian cities with pro-European security forces from the west. But a dramatic increase in gates, guards and guns will do very little to address the feelings of insecurity and fear of the people in those cities. Viewing security and

---

[3] Miller, P. (2010) *Smart Swarm: Using Animal Behaviour to Organise Our World*, Collins.

safety as a purely external problem without addressing the multi-dimensional nature of security and safety means that it may not actually matter how many gates, guards and guns are employed – the people will still not *feel* safe and secure. You cannot solve an interior problem (feeling unsafe and insecure) by only employing an exterior solution (gates, guards and guns). Conversely, you cannot solve an exterior problem by employing an interior solution. If the entire population of Ukraine decided to just ignore the problem and hope it goes away, then nothing gets done and the problem becomes more deeply entrenched.

In Greece, the people are understandably angry at on-going austerity measures imposed by their creditors to keep the country afloat and in the eurozone. The bail-out negotiations were brutal but they are almost entirely focused on the 'IT' and 'ITS' dimensions – what needs to be done, what systems need to be put in place to keep Greece on track to pay off its debts and get the economy back on its feet. What is not being discussed is the 'I' and 'WE' dimensions of the Greek people. In a little over ten years during a period of low interest rates, high spending and a direct line to European wealth some commentators have suggested, and many people in Northern Europe agree, that Greece experienced a moral and ethical shift.[4] Morality is an 'I' phenomenon. If the majority of Greek people were indeed to share the belief that tax evasion is totally legitimate and everyone is engaged in it and believe there are no adverse personal, social or national consequences then that is almost certainly going to cause problems particularly when the country is in a relationship with other EU nations that do have a robust taxation system. When all those 'I's come together to form the collective 'WE' of Greek society – a society that believes that fraud, waste and bribery are simply 'business as usual' then, it really doesn't matter what external 'IT' solutions are imposed. But we don't really know what is going on in the collective Greek 'I' and 'WE' because no one has seriously investigated it. Unless the solutions to the Greek

4   Lewis, M. (2012) *Boomerang*, London: Penguin.

debt crisis involves all four dimensions and the interior 'I' and 'WE' are rehabilitated to the strong, innovative and proud culture of old, then any and all solutions are almost guaranteed to fail. We could not imagine that a significant proportion of the Greeks are dishonest, but it is what many people in Northern Europe have come to believe. We could also just as easily question the ethics of those who cooked the books to allow Greece to enter the European Union in the first place, those that didn't conduct sufficient due diligence on those accounts because it suited the European narrative or those that are now profiteering from Greece's financial problems. But, the point we are seeking to make is the multi-dimensional nature of the problem. There are 'I' and 'WE' challenges that must also be addressed for any real progress to be made.

The crux, of course, is that we cannot deal with the dimensionality of a problem if we do not even realise the problem has a number of different dimensions to begin with. To make matters more complex, each one of these four dimensions is affected by global megatrends often described using the PESTLE acronym (Political, Economic, Social, Technical, Legal and Environmental).

Taking a multi-dimensional approach can profoundly affect our ability to solve wicked problems. For example, this approach is used by Foundation Paraguay – consistently voted as one of the top two or three organisations in the world for effectively ending poverty.[5] Founder Martin Burt, former Chief of Staff to the President of Paraguay, started looking at poverty; and the first thing he noticed in all of the existing programmes around the world was how narrowly they defined poverty. Again, most of them were focused almost exclusively on the 'ITS' quadrant in some version of the PESTLE framework. Instead, Burt gathered evidence of what poverty looks like *in all four quadrants*. This gave him, not just the standard half-dozen or so PESTLE type items, but 50 elements, each explored from all four dimensions.

---

[5] Fundación Paraguaya, accessed 1 January 2016, www.
    fundacionparaguaya.org.py/?lang=en

The result was 200 'characteristics' of poverty. He then searched extensively for programmes and systems that showed some capacity to handle all 200 characteristics to create a total interwoven integral approach. Foundation Paraguay's success in tackling poverty and their recognition in the field is a direct result of employing this more inclusive and comprehensive methodology.

Multiple Stakeholders

Not only are wicked problems multi-dimensional, but they also involve multiple stakeholders – each of which is multi-dimensional in their own right.

Wicked problems are wicked mainly because they involve people – usually a lot of people. Unfortunately, people are notoriously difficult to manage or change. Everyone is different. Each person sees the world in their own unique way based on where they were brought up, who brought them up, what culture they live in, what language they speak, their religious and political convictions, and so forth. People have different values; they have different cognitive capabilities, different levels of emotional intelligence, and different levels of maturity, different belief systems and therefore different ideas about the problems we face and how to tackle them.

Each stakeholder group views the problem differently; they have different motives, opinions and objectives and will invariably stand behind a version of 'the truth' that suits their purpose, while simultaneously dismissing all others. There are definitely multiple stakeholders in the wicked problem of political decision-making. There are the politicians of various political parties, the civil servants, business, the media, lobby groups and of course all of us. It would be safe to say that none of those stakeholder groups see the challenges the same way and certainly don't all agree on how to manage them.

Making real headway in tackling wicked problems such as governance is especially thorny because the responsibility for finding a workable solution almost always cuts across many groups of people who will not all be aligned on the problem, the cause or the solution.

The solutions therefore come down to a matter of judgement about what is 'better', 'worse', 'good enough' or 'not good enough'. If we can't define the problem or the definition varies depending on the stakeholder we ask, then there can't be an accepted objective determination of the problem or the quality of the solution.

Take climate change as a political and policy issue for example. Each political party has a different official party line on climate change – from whether it exists at all to what's causing it and what government could and should be doing about it. Even within each political party, individual politicians will hold wildly different opinions about climate change. Of course, these opinions will invariably influence how these individuals vote around proposed legislation and how enthusiastic they are for proposed solutions or interventions. Finding solutions when there are so many stakeholders with such different views is almost impossible and more often than not negotiations or discussions end in deadlock.

Perspective Taking – Who's on First?

At the heart of this deadlock is the fact that most stakeholders get stuck in a singular perspective and will often defend their view to 'the death'. Most people are totally immersed in their own perspective and believe themselves to be 'right' and therefore all others must be 'wrong'. They are wedded to their 'I' perspective with unshakable certainty. Such a binary right/wrong duality combined with the lack of awareness of which perspective they are taking is actually the real problem we need to address. In other words, the problem is not that we have different views, it is that we are unyieldingly stuck in our one view with no awareness that we are stuck. Involving as many different views as possible is essential for a high quality solution but this lack of awareness of perspective taking is seriously holding us back – especially in the current political system.

Most people, when arguing about anything – a tame or a wicked problem – take one of three perspectives. These, as we mentioned briefly in Chapter 5 are called first, second or third person perspective.

First person perspective is the personal subjective perspective. Stakeholders operating from the first person are focused on 'Me, My, I'. They enter discussions about how to grapple with and solve the problem believing they are right and everyone else is wrong. Their priority is to deliver on their own agenda and protect their own interests. When stakeholders communicate in the first person perspective, they are putting a stake in the ground about what they want, think or believe. As a result, they tend to be very attached to what they communicate in the first person. The first person perspective is very passionate, it is powerful and engaging, but it can also be dogmatic and unyielding. It is based on personal experiences in the world, things the stakeholder has witnessed and 'knows' to be true because they have seen them with their own eyes. In the run up to the 2016 presidential election in the US, Donald Trump communicates almost exclusively from the first perspective. Although overly-simplistic and demonstrating a profound lack of appreciation for the complexity of the issues we all face, his direct, black and white, emotive message clearly resonates with large parts of US society. This is often the approach of religion or faith, as well as certain die-hard political positions.

If the stakeholders do not get stuck in first person perspective, then they are most likely stuck in the third person rational, objective perspective. Stakeholders operating from the third person will helicopter up above the issue and present facts, figures and data to support their case. They believe the 'evidence' reveals 'the truth' and the answer must be evidence-based. This is the approach of science. These stakeholders will say things like, 'the evidence states' or 'the data doesn't lie'. This perspective is very common in business. It is often claimed that the answer is 'nothing personal'. As such people taking the third person perspective can inadvertently abdicate any personal responsibility for the outcome – a sort of 'it is not my fault...I was simply doing what the evidence suggested I should do' approach.

If stakeholders are not stuck in first or third then they may flip between the two. At times they will hold firm to the direct, passionate first person perspective, stating their case and hanging on to that position come hell or high water. If such passionate advocacy doesn't work they may then flip into an objective rational third person perspective in an attempt to win the argument through 'meritocracy'.

To add to the complexity, these two perspectives (first and third) are often deeply intertwined. For example, stakeholders will often use the objective data to validate their own first person perspective while disguising themselves as dispassionate, rational observers. Alternatively, they may delude themselves that they are taking an evidence-based approach when they are selectively choosing only those pieces of evidence that they happen to believe are correct based on their first person values.[6]

The great irony is that progress only ever tends to be made when stakeholders can access the gap between first and third and get into genuine, broad-based second person perspective taking – this is why integration is so essential for the wisdom of the crowd.

Of course, a narrow-view second person perspective is still not helpful. For example, a fundamentalist believer in a particular religion is extremely wedded to their religion and their religion alone is true and real, and all others are false or even demonic. They may expand their identity from a narrow first person

---

[6] Wilber, K. (1998) *The Marriage of Sense and Soul: Integrating Science and Religion*, New York: Random House.

'me' to a wider 'us', which technically includes second person perspective but that 'us' is a specifically chosen 'us' selected by God to rule the world rather than the collective 'us' as a global population. It is this type of narrow second person perspective taking that celebrates the execution of French cartoonists and inspires young men to shoot random people enjoying a rock concert at the Bataclan or a meal in a restaurant on a normal Parisian evening.

But the more mature version of second person is the perspective where a person can drop or expand their own narrow first person viewpoints and collaborate with others in making a larger 'WE' or 'us'. Real collaboration occurs in the second person perspective. Unfortunately very few people operate from this perspective, or have any real world experience of the difference it can make to successful collaboration; so they stop at a narrow, fundamentalist or extremely limited version of it.

Most problems, even complex problems have a few stakeholders and usually they all have different opinions about the nature of the problem and how to solve it. But the limited number of stakeholders involved in complex problems means that resolution is often likely – eventually – especially if those stakeholders can move into the shared space of the second person perspective. In contrast, wicked problems always have multiple stakeholders. Often they are all pulling in opposite directions and so no real headway is ever really made. It is often this endless bickering and infighting that fuels the sense of futility around wicked problems, which makes them feel inevitable and un-solvable. But when stakeholders learn about the second person perspective – and actually take it to heart – the endless rounds of futile positioning can be transcended and some real connection and progress can be made. Crowdocracy creates the opportunity for this to occur, plus it is decentralised and diverse opinion is integrated with the help of technology, which means we can finally tap into the cognitive diversity that multiple stakeholders provide while mitigating the minefield that can occur in unmanaged collectives.

Multiple Causes

Not only are wicked problems multi-dimensional and involve multiple stakeholders, but they have multiple causes. Of course, the multiple stakeholders almost never agree about the multiple causes!

When there are multiple causes, it becomes very difficult to separate them and identify which are having the biggest impact. They are often so intertwined and interdependent it's impossible to know for certain what is causing the wicked problem.

If we look at poverty, the political inclination to tackle poverty and the solutions that those political parties will propose depends on what those parties believe is causing the poverty in the first place. Right-wing, republican or conservative politicians tend to believe that each individual is responsible for themselves and if they don't have enough money then the individual needs to work harder, be more innovative, and so on. Conversely, democratic or labour politicians tend to believe more in the collective and will point to the unwillingness of big business to pay taxes while driving down costs in the form of wages which is escalating poverty for many. Of course, whether you believe that it's up to the individual or you believe that society needs to do more to alleviate poverty will radically influence your proposed solutions.

Unfortunately, it's only when we have spent a great deal of time and money implementing a solution that we more fully appreciate the causes. Sometimes nothing changes. Sometimes the situation is made worse. Sometimes it improves. Ironically, we only really start to understand the *real* causes of a wicked problem, the degree of multi-dimensionality and stakeholder interdependency, once we've failed to solve it. However, this necessary failure runs contrary to the way we've been taught to solve problems.

Traditionally, we've been told that in order to solve a problem we need to gather all the relevant information, analyse that information and decide on the best course of action to solve it. Such an approach doesn't work with wicked problems because we can't understand the problem without knowing its context and we can't meaningfully search for all the information we need without first having some idea about what we think the cause is and therefore what we think the solution might be. In other words, for wicked problems, everything is back to front. Only when we have implemented solutions based on judgement and assumption around cause do we work out if we are correct or not. It is often through the implementation of these so-called solutions that we more fully appreciate the far-reaching interdependent complexity of the problem in the first place.

We are also encouraged to avoid failure at all costs from an early age. When it comes to solving wicked problems with improving democracy, we must learn how to be comfortable with failure so that we can get closer to success. This is why of all the transition models proposed in Chapter 7, starting small may be the best way forward because it allows us to test, learn, adapt and test again. It will allow us to evolve and build on our failures when those failures are not too important.

Paradoxically when it comes to wicked problems, it's failure that often facilitates success, which may be one of the reasons we can't seem to solve them. We are so obsessed with success that the very notion of failure has become so unpalatable that we have simply stopped trying.

It is however only through our repeated attempts to understand the causes and interdependencies between those causes that we begin to appreciate how inadequate our approach is, or how our proposed solution may have knock-on effects elsewhere that were not previously considered. These new insights require on-going adjustment to the definition of the problem *and* the proposed solution. Ultimately, when we can't identify what is really causing the problem, we can't fully appreciate the interdependencies of these causes and that certainly amplifies the wickedness.

If we stand any real chance of solving wicked problems we need a framework to systematically identify all the deeply significant causal factors, many of which are currently simply ignored. Opening that information gathering up to the crowd allows for a much faster and potentially more accurate understanding of the problems we face and the possible causes. Those affected by the issues are almost always the best suited to identifying the causes or possible causes because they are often at the 'coal face' of the problem.

Multiple Symptoms

Not only are wicked problems multi-dimensional, involve multiple stakeholders, and have multiple causes that no one can agree on, but they also have multiple symptoms. It is often these multiple symptoms that muddy the water when it comes to the various causes of the problem. Many of the symptoms of one wicked problem are also wicked problems in their own right.

If you think about poverty and poor education, for example, both are wicked problems and each is a symptom of the other. Poverty can be a symptom of poor education because unless an individual can gain at least a basic education where they can read, write and count, then it becomes much harder to secure a well-paying job.

Conversely, poor education can also be a symptom of poverty because if a child is continuously sent to school without food because the parents can't afford breakfast, then that child will probably not have the concentration necessary to attain a good education that could help lift them out of poverty. In many developing countries there may not be a school nearby, or the children may be removed from school and sent out to work to supplement the family income because the family is so poor. Of course, those children then never get the education that could help them to break the poverty cycle.

Wicked problems are incredibly challenging to handle because of the interdependencies between causes, symptoms and potential solutions. If your overall approach, from the beginning, is geared to multiple dimensions and interdependencies in virtually all realms, then you are much more likely to be able to spot – and address – these multiple complexities from the start. Crowdocracy facilitates a significantly faster and potentially more accurate feedback loop between the people and the impact of a particular policy.

We are profoundly linked to each other and our actions impact on others whether we intend that impact or not. In one study, for example, researchers looked at 43,060 transnational corporations and suggested that there were, in reality, only 147 companies that actually determine, global outcomes across the planet.[7] Due to their shared ownership, these companies, many of which are banks or financial institutions, control what happens in most of the other companies. For example, a few pension funds, insurance companies, mutual funds and sovereign wealth funds hold \$65 trillion, or 35 per cent of all the world's financial assets.[8] In effect, this means that 500 individuals, mainly men, pull the ownership strings of 147 companies which indirectly control the other 43,060 companies which in turn drive the global economy and determine the destiny of over 7 billion people.[9]

This interdependence is increasing. Of course, when we don't understand the phenomena of interdependency, it is either your fault and your problem or my fault and my problem. We either ignore it or wash our hands of the situation because it has nothing to do with us, or we storm in believing ours is the only right definition or solution. Either way, the problem persists because

[7] Vitali, S. Glattfelder, J.B. and Battiston, S. (2011) 'The network of global corporate control', PLoS One, 6 no. 10, Epub 26 October 2011, accessed 2 January 2016, www.ncbi.nlm.nih.gov/pubmed/?term=The+network+of+global+corporate+control

[8] Barton, D. (2011) 'Capitalism for the long term', Harvard Business Review, March 2011.

[9] Rothkopf, D. (2009) Superclass: The Global Power Elite and the World They Are Making, New York: Farrar, Straus and Giroux.

we don't fully appreciate these interconnections between causes, symptoms and how the proposed solutions will have a knock-on effect and create unintended consequences in areas far removed from the original problem.

Take the European Refugee Crisis of 2015 as a classic example. For years, we have watched the nightly news with horror as the fighting in Syria has escalated. Although terrible, many of us probably felt it was not our problem. It was happening thousands of miles away and yet that fighting had the knock-on effect of contributing to the creation of the extremist group known as Islamic State. In 2015, millions of people are fleeing from Syria, Iraq and many other countries in Northern and Central Africa currently in the grip of extreme violence. People are literally running for their lives, risking death in perilous journeys with their families as they desperately try to reach Europe and safety. Opinion about what to do with these refugees is deeply divided. At a time when many European countries are still recovering from the global financial crisis, the cost is challenging as is the cultural assimilation and increased pressure on infrastructure. Our lives may seem completely different, we may originate from countries thousands of miles apart but we are all connected and what happens in one place always has a knock-on effect somewhere else. Right now, many Europeans are appreciating that interdependency very strongly.

We may want to believe that we can turn our back, on wicked problems, ignore the causes and pretend the symptoms do not exist, but the escalating interdependencies inherent in these issues mean that they are not your problems or my problems – they are universally *our* problems, and pretending otherwise is utterly futile. We simply can't afford to stick our heads in the sand indefinitely – we need to find a collective, workable solution.

Multiple Solutions

Clearly if a wicked problem is multi-dimensional, involves multiple stakeholders, has multiple causes that no one can agree on, and displays multiple symptoms, then there will inevitably be multiple potential solutions.

If, for example, a stakeholder group believes that poverty is caused by low educational attainment, then their conviction in that cause will influence their choice of potential solution. When sourcing a solution, they will only look at education and how they can 'fix' education from their perspective. Many different stakeholders have proposed many different solutions for fixing education. For example, school league tables were introduced in the UK to rank all schools against each other based on student results. The idea was that if performance was measured and ranked it would improve education, but it is fraught with problems. School league tables don't improve student performance in the same way that health care waiting lists don't improve the performance of the health care professional. What waiting lists and league tables really do is allow those within the various systems to take their eye off the real objective so as to effectively manipulate the outward appearance of performance. This drift towards the 'gamification' of any metric has become a huge, time-consuming activity in its own right. But just because we can manipulate the data to look like performance is improving, either by refusing to add people to waiting lists until the very last minute or by lowering the level at which an exam or assessment pass is granted, does not mean that performance is *actually* improving. It just means it looks like it is improving.

Another stakeholder group determined to reduce poverty may believe that the solution lies in increasing the income that enters a household. Pretty logical – poverty is after all a lack of money. In an effort to alleviate child poverty, for example, many countries pay child benefit and ensure additional support is available to families with children. The unintended consequence of this well-intentioned initiative is that there is now a financial and social incentive to have children. As well as receiving government money per child, social housing is prioritised to parents, especially single parents. This seems logical in order to protect the children, but it also means that people game the system.

Instead of using the money as it was intended, people are simply having more children than they really want, so they receive an income and have a place to live. Of course, if someone's primary purpose for having children is to get extra money and have their rent paid, the money paid out to prevent child poverty is almost certainly not being spent on the children.

There are a myriad of possible solutions to every wicked problem; which one is decided upon will depend on the stakeholders, their level of development, their agenda, their conviction in the root causes of the problem, and which symptoms they are seeking to alleviate first. There are also possible solutions that are never even considered.

Ultimately whether a solution is 'good enough' or not will largely depend on the social context and who is making the assessment and the stakeholder's interdependent values and objectives. The interconnected nature of the causes and symptoms also means that binary 'right' and 'wrong' assessments are impossible. When it comes to wicked problems, 'most workable for now' is often the best we can hope for. But with crowdocracy that may not be good enough. The sheer numbers in the crowd will allow us to potentially solve a great deal more than we can currently solve. People will, over time, begin to appreciate that they do have a voice and engage in the political arena, proposing, shaping and voting on policy, which can then be implemented. The results of that policy will be known much quicker and the policy can then be tweaked or altered accordingly.

Constantly Evolving

Of course, all this means that wicked problems are constantly evolving. The stakeholders involved in solving the wicked problem are constantly changing. Politicians themselves come and go, elections lead to regime change, and cabinets are simply reshuffled. The stakeholders themselves are also personally evolving as their understanding, views and opinions morph over time. The causes are also constantly evolving: new causes are identified and new symptoms manifest.

Each solution usually highlights a new, different and often conflicting aspect of the nature of the problem, so there is no end point. We will never reach a point where we can, for example, tick off 'poverty' as a task that has been completed and a wicked problem that has been eradicated. The problem-solving process as well as the problem itself is constantly shifting and evolving. It only ends when we run out of resources, be that time, money or the desire to solve it. Successive governments, for example, may shift their focus from one area to another because of their political persuasion, but the problems themselves are still there.

Trying to solve a wicked problem is often like trying to hit a moving target. Paradoxically, solving wicked problems requires us to appreciate that we probably can't definitively solve them but try anyway. We are only able to get a handle on a challenge at a given point in time. Any solution therefore will probably be out of date or even obsolete by the time it's evaluated and implemented. Instead of attempting, failing and turning away from the problem, we need to attempt, fail and turn back to the problem armed with fresh insights and a new, better understanding of what we face.

There is no end, or as Rittel and Webber called it, 'no stopping rule,' because the landscape is evolving so quickly that it is impossible to know when we have 'finished' or been successful. The fact that there is no end is itself not a bad thing. Evolution has no end and we still consider that to be positive and powerful phenomena.

Even if we reach a point where we think we've nailed it because the symptoms of the wicked problem have abated and we hubristically think we've solved it, all that's usually happened is the problem has become dormant or simply shifted elsewhere – popping up somewhere else in a different form. But with crowdocracy we will know about it sooner and have enough collective wisdom to hopefully find alternative solutions. In most cases there is no definitive test to determine if the solution has been successful anyway because the consequences of each implemented solution can be far-reaching. These solutions, whether successful or not, can't easily be undone, so trial and error is not often possible with wicked problems. It may however be possible with crowdocracy if we start small. The move from democracy to crowdocracy doesn't have to be revolutionary; we can implement this new form of governance in our local community groups, school, sports clubs or regional councils. Such small experiments could potentially allow us to benefit from trial and error and gain faith in the wisdom of the crowd.

For most wicked problems however trial and error is not an option. Again this is due to the complex, known and unknown interdependencies that are the hallmark of wicked problems. Tackling wicked problems is like playing that 'whack a mole' game at a funfair. As soon as you whack one mole, another two pop up somewhere else!

How can we ever really nail anything if the environment in which we are implementing the solution is changing all the time? We will only ever be able to solve and re-solve them over and over again. This constant evolution is part of the very fabric of life. We don't need to be scared of it; we just need to embrace it with a wider understanding. Crowdocracy allows us to do that.

Wicked Problems Require Wicked Solutions

If we are serious about solving and re-solving wicked problems, we must recognise that the solution needs to be every bit as wicked as the problem it is designed to solve.

It has been suggested that there is no obvious answer to wicked problems but there is an obvious answer – the solution must match the nature of the problem. If we are facing a wicked problem that is multi-dimensional, then the solution must be multi-dimensional and address all dimensions. If the wicked problem involves multiple stakeholders, then the solution must involve and collaborate with all those multiple stakeholders. If the wicked problem has multiple causes, then the solution must take those multiple causes into account and expect and seek to anticipate multiple far-reaching repercussions. If the wicked problem has multiple symptoms, then the solution must address all those symptoms so as to ensure that at the very least the solution doesn't exacerbate those symptoms or create new, potentially worse symptoms! If the wicked problem has multiple potential solutions, then we must accept that we will need to implement multiple solutions before we can make any real progress. Finally, if the wicked problem is constantly evolving, then the solutions we implement must also constantly evolve.

Let's look at crowdocracy from that context…

Crowdocracy may manage or at least account for all the dimensions. The crowdocracy platform will address the 'ITS' dimension and encourage everyone to get involved ('I'), the sharing of views may over time improve the way we engage with each other and strengthen our Social Contract ('WE') – all of which may, in time, change our behaviour ('IT'). Like the Vermonters who came to embrace same-sex marriage, we may all foster more compassion and cross-cultural understanding. Crowdocracy will by definition involve multiple stakeholders. Everyone will be able to contribute and vote on the issues that are important to them. Due to the connection to multiple stakeholders, we will more quickly be able to create a picture of the challenges we face and the multiple causes that have or may have created them. There will never just be one solution – the crowd will most likely create multiple solutions to the challenges which will each be designed to address the various multiple causes and address the multiple symptoms. The close proximity and direct lines of communication between the interventions and the crowd also mean we can fail faster and get to real long-term sustainable solutions quicker. As the crowd is constantly evolving so too will the proposed solutions.

The real beauty of crowdocracy is that is it greater than the sum of its parts. It won't actually matter how smart, developed or mature the individuals in the crowd are because the mathematics of crowd wisdom will still deliver the best outcome. It will however matter for the executors and the judiciary.

Executors and Judiciary Development

In the first book in the series, the authors Alan Watkins and Ken Wilber unpacked Integral Coherence in great detail. Integral Coherence is a combination of the Integral Frame and an appreciation that human beings need to be personally coherent to effectively unlock their 'I' capability to implement the Integral Frame effectively. In addition, this implementation needs to be implemented coherently, that is, the emphasis on the different dimensions needs to be balanced including the emphasis on the different aspects of the wickedness of the problem. Finally, the various stakeholders need to be able to interact in a coherent way to make real progress. If there is no real coherent connection between these different dimensions – both internally and externally – then it is likely that little will get solved because even if we manage to bring together a range of smart, enlightened and highly-trained executors and guardians, if they can't 'play nice' together to get stuff done then little will actually change. In effect, there needs to be 'I', 'WE' and 'IT' coherence in the application of the Integral Frame.

Knowing how we can behave in the various quadrants or what perspectives we can view the problem from is incredibly helpful in finding genuine solutions to the problems we face. Although in crowdocracy the crowd determines those variables, which should cancel out individual bias and vested interest, individual human beings will still be involved in moving the process along from policy formation to execution and guarding the process. If those executors or judiciary guardians are stuck in one dimension or are operating from a particular evolutionary developmental level, and that level is not sufficiently sophisticated, or is significantly out of step with their progress in another dimension, then they may slow progress. This is extremely important for the guardians in the judiciary arm and somewhat less crucial for the executive arm.

The wicked problems we face are *shared problems.* We need to appreciate that we *are* all in this together and solving them and re-solving them will need all of us, individually and collectively. We will need to coherently integrate all aspects of who we are and work together in this crucial endeavour, otherwise we will continue to have partial, incomplete, ineffective answers. And we will all continue to suffer.

Crowdocracy may be our salvation. Not only does crowdocracy offer us a direction for a wise solution to the wicked problem of governance itself, it may also provide the frame for allowing all of us to generate wise solutions to the many other wicked problems we desperately need to solve.

Biographies

Alan Watkins

Alan Watkins is recognized as an international expert on leadership and human performance. Over the past 18 years he has been a coach to many of Europe's top business leaders. Alan is currently the CEO of a leadership consultancy, Complete Coherence, that works to develop enlightened leaders in all walks of life. His company is particularly focused on working with leaders and executive teams in large multinational organisations and helping them to make a more positive impact on all our lives. He is an inspiring and entertaining keynote and TEDx speaker and was the sole 'expert' in a BBC1 series, Temper your Temper, where he coached ten people with anger issues live on TV. As well as his work with global business leaders Alan advised the GB Olympic squad, coaches and athletes prior to London 2012. He continues to work with them in the run-up to Rio in 2016.

Alan originally trained as a physician at Imperial College in London and worked for 11 years in the UK's National Health Service. He also worked for a year as a physician in Australia and a year in academic medical research in the USA. An integrationist at heart, he ended up in neuroscience research before leaving medicine to work on a more global stage. In addition to his medical degree Alan has a first class degree in Psychology from the University of London and a PhD in Immunology from Southampton University, UK. He has written numerous scientific papers in peer reviewed journals on a wide variety of subjects and many book chapters. So far (2016), he is the author or co-author of four books, this one being the fifth.

He lives with his wife and their four boys in Hampshire, England

Iman Stratenus

Iman Stratenus devotes his professional life to system transformations. He works as an advisor and coach to organisational leaders assisting with their personal and organisational transformations. For the past 2 years he has been working on unravelling and redesigning the governance system, which led him to write Crowdocracy with Dr Alan Watkins. He has also launched the Crowd Foundation, which aims to bring crowdocracy to life.

Before his work on governance, Iman worked as a lawyer, management consultant and business leader across many countries. He wrote his first book in 2011 about the transformation of the company he led in China in a book called 'In China, We Trust'. Iman lives with his wife and their crowd of five children in Portugal.

Index

Wicked and Wise: How to Solve the World's Toughest Problems is the first compelling title in a brand new series launched with Urbane Publications. Devised by leading consultant Dr Alan Watkins, the Wicked and Wise series explores a number of hotly debated and wicked issues facing the planet and its people, and offers some intelligent, challenging and wise ways forward that may be able to break through the current intractable position. Each book in the series is co-authored by Alan and a hand-picked expert in each subject field. The first book in the series looks at some of the most pressing and topical issues affecting the world today, from the clash of religions and cultures in a globalised world to the growing dominance of technology. Co-written with renowned social thinker and philosopher Ken Wilber the book sets the scene for debating the key challenges facing current and future generations, and sets possible agendas for how leaders, and potential leaders, can solve challenges through the wise application of multi-tiered multi-channel, multi-organisational intervention and lead in a highly developed, enlightened and selfless way.

Urbane Publications Limited, 320pp, £12.99   ISBN 9781909273641

Urbane Publications is dedicated to
developing new author voices, and publishing
fiction and non-fiction that challenges, thrills and
fascinates. From page-turning novels to innovative
reference books, our goal is to publish what
YOU want to read.

Find out more at

urbanepublications.com